# BEST OF REGIONAL
# AFRICAN COOKING

*Hippocrene is NUMBER ONE in*

# *International Cookbooks*

***Africa and Oceania***

Best of Regional African Cooking
Good Food from Australia
Traditional South African Cookery

***Asia and Near East***

Best of Goan Cooking
The Joy of Chinese Cooking
The Art of South Indian Cooking
The Art of Persian Cooking
The Art of Israeli Cooking
The Art of Turkish Cooking

***Mediterranean***

Best of Greek Cuisine
Taste of Malta
A Spanish Family Cookbook

***Western Europe***

Art of Dutch Cooking
Best of Austrian Cuisine
A Belgian Cookbook
Celtic Cookbook
Traditional Recipes from Old England
The Art of Irish Cooking
Traditional Food from Scotland
Traditional Food from Wales

***Scandinavia***

Best of Scandinavian Cooking
The Best of Finnish Cooking
The Best of Smorgasbord Cooking
Good Food from Sweden

***Central Europe***

All Along the Danube
Bavarian Cooking
Bulgarian Cookbook
The Best of Czech Cooking
The Art of Hungarian Cooking
Polish Heritage Cookery
The Best of Polish Cooking
Old Warsaw Cookbook
Old Polish Traditions
Taste of Romania

***Eastern Europe***

The Cuisine of Armenia
The Best of Russian Cooking
The Best of Ukrainian Cuisine

***Americas***

Mayan Cooking
The Honey Cookbook
The Art of Brazilian Cookery
The Art of South American Cookery

# BEST OF REGIONAL AFRICAN COOKING

*Harva Hachten*

HIPPOCRENE BOOKS
New York

Originally published by Atheneum.

Hippocrene paperback edition, 1998.



For information, address:
HIPPOCRENE BOOKS, INC.
171 Madison Avenue
New York, NY 1006

ISBN 0-7818-0598-8

Printed in the United States of America.

Book design by Kathleen Carey.

*For my mother, Evelyn Sprager,*
*who always wanted me to write a book,*

AND

*For Bill,*
*who made sure I did*

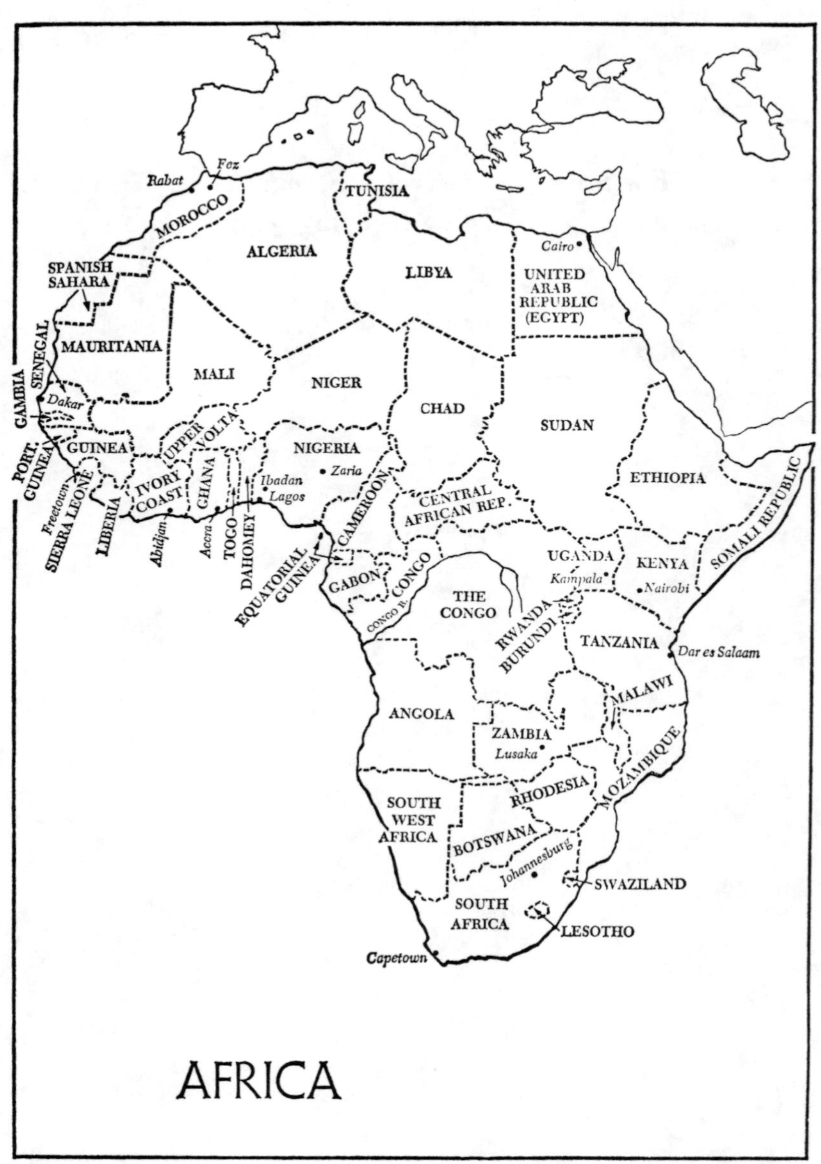

Fez
Rabat
MOROCCO
TUNISIA
ALGERIA
LIBYA
Cairo
UNITED
ARAB
REPUBLIC
(EGYPT)
SPANISH
SAHARA
SENEGAL
MAURITANIA
MALI
NIGER
CHAD
SUDAN
GAMBIA
Dakar
UPPER
VOLTA
GUINEA
PORT.
GUINEA
NIGERIA
Zaria
Ibadan
Lagos
IVORY
COAST
GHANA
CAMEROON
CENTRAL
AFRICAN REP.
ETHIOPIA
SOMALI REPUBLIC
Freetown
SIERRA LEONE
LIBERIA
Abidjan
Accra
TOGO
DAHOMEY
EQUATORIAL
GUINEA
GABON
CONGO
CONGO B.
THE
CONGO
UGANDA
Kampala
KENYA
Nairobi
RWANDA
BURUNDI
TANZANIA
Dar es Salaam
MALAWI
ANGOLA
ZAMBIA
Lusaka
MOZAMBIQUE
RHODESIA
SOUTH
WEST
AFRICA
BOTSWANA
Johannesburg
SWAZILAND
SOUTH
AFRICA
LESOTHO
Capetown
AFRICA

# PREFACE

WHEN I FIRST WENT TO AFRICA in 1965, an air of optimism swirled around most of the countries south of the Sahara. Decolonization was underway, and the conventional wisdom among African specialists—in academe, government circles, and among the African leaders themselves—was that once the heavy lid on the pot of colonialism was lifted, a great surge of prosperity, creativity, and economic and political development would be released. All that was needed was an infusion of Western capital and Western expertise.

And they got it. The United States and most countries of Europe provided loans and grants of money and established aid programs of all varieties. Flocks of experts in virtually all fields of endeavor were dispatched to show how things were done in the developed West. The Soviet bloc joined in, since the continent became a pawn in the Cold War.

Things, however, did not turn out as envisioned, as anyone who follows the news knows. Perhaps we were all naive to think Africa could be transformed in short order. I know I certainly was as you will see when you read the Introduction to the first edition of this book which was published in 1971. Tourism, which I expected would help bring understanding and progress, hasn't made much of a dent.

Not that things haven't changed. Africa is no longer a remote or exotic destination on tourist itineraries (though since wild game safaris are still the main attraction, increased understanding of the peoples and the culture that I predicted is minimal). If those tourists are gastronomically adventurous, they now can sample traditional foods in hotel dining rooms and popular restaurants.

In addition, travellers have access to lots of African guide books, none of which were available when I and my family first visited. Nor were there any continent-wide African cook books to whet the appetite; mine was the first.

Some of the countries I mention in the book have taken new names. Upper Volta is now Burkino Faso; Dahomey, Benin; South West Africa, Namibia; Congo, Zaire; Rhodesia, Zimbabwe. Furthermore, many of the unfamiliar ingredients for these dishes no longer need be mail ordered from specialty shops but can be picked up in local supermarkets, gourmet shops, and ethnic groceries in larger cities and university towns. What has remained constant are the recipes themselves. The dishes described here are still the mainstay of the peoples of that vast and varied continent. Enjoy.

— Harva Hachten
Madison, Wisconsin
April 1997

# INTRODUCTION

SOMEONE ONCE CALLED AFRICA "the continent God held in reserve." It has been within only the last 100 years that the rest of the world has started to draw on that reserve to any extent. Beginning in the middle years of the last century, Africa attracted increasing attention from Westerners who explored, exploited, colonized, and, in some places, settled. Then in the 1950s the sparks of nationalism danced and flamed and the map of Africa changed from the great blotches of colonial pinks, blues, and greens to a multicolored patchwork of new nations as riotously bright as cloth in a West African market.

It wouldn't be accurate to say, however, that Africa is now a known quantity. Even though independence has brought a great deal of coming and going of businessmen, diplomats, teachers, geologists, mining engineers, Peace Corps volunteers, and even tourists, Africa is still very unfamiliar and greatly misunderstood. And as often happens in dealing with the unknown, we tend to think in stereotypes.

Africa! When we see that word, most of us think of wild animals and safaris, or rain forests, or heat and humidity, or Tarzan. Indeed, there are marvelous safaris and magnificent wild animals; here and there you'll find rain forests; some areas have a hot and humid season; but there wasn't ever any Tarzan.

These stereotypes, thankfully, are gradually giving way under the weight of the increasing contacts between Africa and the rest of the world.

I've long had a theory that peace and understanding in the world won't be wrought by diplomats with attaché cases, but by tourists with cameras. It is the tourists (and their needed hard currencies) who have cut what significant chinks there are in the Iron Curtain. And it will be tourists, I think, who will finally and completely bring Africa into clear focus.

Tourists are starting to set out in increasing numbers—to a half-dozen or so well-known attractions. Morocco, touristically, is like Spain in the mid-1950s—a bit off the beaten path but accessible and cheap. On the other side of the Sahara, the great game parks of East Africa probably lure the greatest number of Americans. A three-week photo-safari out of Nairobi looks mighty attractive to lovers of wild animals and those who have already "done" Europe. With the expansion of air routes and availability of hotels, such a trip is now well within the vacation time limits and the budgets of many.

So far, this flow of visitors is just a narrow little stream slowly starting to flow through previously uncharted tourist terrain. It will be some time before it even approaches the flood of tourists that inundates Europe each year. Besides, there are all sorts of little dams across that stream. One is visa formalities and another, frequently whimsical customs inspections. But the biggest is the lack of tourist literature about the continent, with the possible exception of the East

African game parks. There isn't really one up-to-date guidebook to Africa as a whole to spur the embarking tourist or to set the armchair traveler to dreaming. Moreover, there is no comprehensive African cookbook for those who like to explore the culinary byways without even leaving home. In an occasional cookbook that purports to be a world-wide collection, you just might find an African recipe or two, but you really have to dig for that. A huge cookbook anthology with "world" in the title, published in 1968, didn't include one recipe from south of the Sahara.

There hasn't been any African cookbook for the whole continent—until now, that is.

I once mentioned this lack of an African cookbook to a food expert who sniffed: "Of course not. The Africans have no cuisine." Using the highly developed art of the French chef as a criterion, that's true. After all, the term "cuisine" implies a variety of foodstuffs, the leisure to develop different and delicious ways of preparing them, and the affluence to afford the finished product. Cuisine, in other words, is just another by-product of a high-rising society with lots of hard cash as the yeast.

This is a state of affairs that does not yet prevail in Africa. But to imply there is nothing worth eating and enjoying there is entirely false. All areas of Africa—both north and south of the Sahara—have food specialties that can perk up sagging menus and enhance a cook's reputation.

Not that African dishes (and their recipes) are easy to come by—even in Africa. The average tourist in Africa has a hard time sampling true African dishes, unless he is fortunate enough to be invited into someone's home.

There are many reasons for this. The overriding one is the state of Africa itself. Fascinating though it is to visit, it *is* part of the developing world, with all the problems that involves, including those of sanitation and health. Consequently, Western tourists are pretty much limited in their choice of hotels and restaurants—limited to those designed to keep a visitor's stomach in proper working order. The antibodies in the blood of Westerners reared on indoor plumbing and hygienic food-handling can't cope with African experimentation. Therefore you cannot enjoy the pleasure of discovering a quaint "native" café tucked away on a side street of Lagos or Dar es Salaam. Nor dare you sample a *kenkey* (a ball of fermented corn dough, steam-cooked, and then rubbed in black leaf for its charcoal color) sold by a tall, willowy Ghanaian girl on the noisy streets of Accra. It's safer to look and not buy one of those shiny (from the deep-fry oil and a heavy honey syrup) doughnuts being hawked by an Arab street urchin in the *souk* of Tangiers.

So most tourists take their meals at the big, modern, new hotels or the several restaurants certified safe by the airline office or the local national tourist bureau. The cuisine of these hotels and "safe" restaurants is influenced, not by the country itself, but by the culinary traditions of the former colonial power. That means that in former French territories the cuisine is French (and while terribly expensive, usually tasty) and in former English areas the cuisine is English (down to Brussels sprouts and slathers of custard sauce on the puddings and cakes). The food markets in the capitals of the French-speaking countries still bear a remarkable resemblance to the weekly street market of almost any French provincial city, with artistically arrayed displays of artichokes, eggplants, salad greens, and even bouquets of flowers.

This tradition persists because the preferences of the former colonial masters have become the standards of excellence and status to which the Africans themselves aspire. Consequently, in the hotels that do include a local dish or two—usually as one of the specials at lunch—it is the expatriates and visitors who order them; the Africans choose the roast beef and roasted potato or the *coq au vin.*

Admittedly, I'm generalizing—a risky practice at any time and particularly so when discussing Africa. After all, the continent is enormous—5,000 miles from the Pillars of Hercules to the Cape of Good Hope and 4,700 from Cape Verde in the west to the Horn of East Africa—and the diversity of peoples and customs matches the physical proportions. There are over 800 languages spoken by the roughly 300,000,000 people who inhabit Africa (and usually language means tribe). There is, in fact, far greater diversity among the peoples of Africa than there is between the peoples of Europe. A Finn and an Italian, for example, have more in common than a Sudanese and a Bushman. When you come right down to it, the term *Africa* is in itself a vague generalization.

So what holds true in one section of Africa may not in another, even if that section is right next door. There are places where local dishes are readily available to the tourist. In Morocco, for instance, the succulent specialties of the Arab world are prepared in nearly all hotels and many of the restaurants. In South Africa, on the other hand, you find French restaurants and Portuguese restaurants and pizza-spaghetti parlors, but not one establishment that serves any of the fabulous dishes first developed by the Malays brought to Cape Town as slaves in the seventeenth century. In West African hotels one or two regional specialties are regularly available at noon, but in East Africa they're virtually impossible to come by.

Since most of Africa is part of the developing world, few visitors would want to go "completely native" when it comes to food. Almost everywhere they'd find it dull. As is true in poorer regions all over the world, the backbone of the diet is a starch served with stew. Depending on what grows where, the starch could be semolina for the *couscous* of North Africa, yams and cassava root in the west, cornmeal in the south and central regions, and bananas and plantain in the wet areas. The stews go by many names—*tajin* in North

Africa; soups, stews, or sauces (depending on the amount of liquid) in West Africa; *bredie* in the south. Whatever the name, their purpose is the same—to stretch the meager food supply as far as possible. And since within each area the stews are seasoned from a fairly limited spice shelf (North Africa is an exception), there is a certain sameness to all the stews, no matter what goes into the pot, which adds to the monotony of the diet. Comparing one region with another, though, they are entirely different.

I've had the opportunity to compare the differences, and collect the recipes in this book, on two trips to Africa—three trips, really, if you count a four-day weekend in Tangier during a tour of Europe in 1954. But my first extensive trip was in 1965. I went with my husband, a University of Wisconsin journalism professor who had a research grant to study the mass media in the developing nations of Africa. We started in Cairo, then went to Kenya and Tanzania in East Africa, briefly to South Africa and South West Africa to visit a college friend, and up the west coast of Africa to Nigeria, Ivory Coast, Sierra Leone, and Senegal.

In 1968 my husband received another grant—a Fulbright—to update and expand his project. This time we took our two subteen daughters along and reversed the direction. We started on the northwestern side of the continent and transcribed a great, wobbly V to the south and then the east—Morocco, Ghana, Nigeria, South Africa, Zambia, Kenya, and Uganda.

It was second nature for me to turn my attention to the foods of these countries. From 1961 to 1968 I was the women's editor of Madison's morning newspaper, *The Wisconsin State Journal*, and food stories and recipes were among my responsibilities. After the first trip, when I wanted to make the few dishes tourists could get in 1965, I discovered this lack of African cookbooks—though there seems to be a cookbook for every other cuisine under the sun. On the second trip I set out to sample and collect recipes of every dish I possibly could.

Please note the use of the personal pronoun singular. I'm one of those people who is game to taste anything different —at least once!—no matter how strange to Western palates it may be. At a dining table away from home, my husband isn't at all adventurous. I can't recall him trying any local dish south of the Sahara. In all fairness, though, I should add that never during either trip did he suffer from a stomach ailment of any kind, a record I cannot match.

Elizabeth, our older daughter, shares my eclectic palate to some extent, but Marianne staunchly supports and practices her father's conservative gustatory philosophy. In fact, in the first six days of her African trip Marianne subsisted almost entirely on *bifteck* and *pommes frites* (steak and French-fried potatoes) in the French restaurants in Rabat, Morocco. She was persuaded to try Pepper Chicken in Nigeria, however, and became addicted to the dish, as has the whole family since.

As you can see from our itineraries, I've had the chance to sample foods at many spots on the perimeter of Africa. What exactly they eat in Chad or the Central African Republic or Upper Volta, I don't know first hand. However, the places we did visit are quite representative of their contiguous areas, and, allowing for the differences in crops and tastes, the eating habits of the peoples there are not, I gather, too different from those in the rest of their general region.

To present dramatically the flavor of each area, I've arranged this book regionally rather than by categories of dishes. I begin this gastronomic safari in North Africa, an area most familiar and accessible to tourists. Except for Egypt and Libya, the influences on this region have been largely French, aside from a few Spanish enclaves scattered here and there.

That is to say, there is a French overlay on top of the long-established and highly developed Arabic culture implanted across North Africa a thousand years ago. The food of the region is essentially Arabic and Near Eastern with a few European touches, mostly in the vegetable department.

The Sahara desert is a formidable geographic barrier. Though it was regularly crossed by camel caravans and traders, the food cultures of North Africa and West Africa intermixed very little, as the West African chapter clearly shows. In colonial times, the British and French played a sort of empire hopscotch down the coast, so English-speaking nations are now neighbors of French-speaking nations. However, although there is little interchange between the French and English speakers in Africa, the traditional tribal societies have ignored borders. The food of this entire area is quite similar, again allowing for differences in growing conditions and regional tastes. The former French territories in West Africa represented in this book include Senegal, Mali, Upper Volta, Dahomey, Ivory Coast, Guinea, Niger, Cameroon, and Togo. The new nations which were formerly British are The Gambia, Sierra Leone, Ghana, Nigeria, and the former West Cameroons, now partly in Nigeria and partly in Cameroon.

Central Africa is a designation I've applied to countries central in a north-south orientation as well as an east-west one—the two Congos, Gabon, Zambia, Chad, Malawi. The western part of this area is made up of French-oriented nations that were formerly French and Belgian colonies. The rest is largely formerly British.

The chapter on southern Africa includes everything south of the Zambezi River, while East Africa comprises Tanzania, Uganda, and Kenya—all once under Britain and still in the Commonwealth.

To some extent, I used practicality as a guide to what to include and what to leave out. Many foods and ingredients required are just not available in this country; there's not even a substitute that could give the right idea. That's the sort of thing I left out. Usually, that is. I have included several recipes for their curiosity value—like the Moroccan confection that calls for (in addition to some easily obtainable ingredients) an aphrodisiac, hashish, and acorns. Also, you'll be able to make such exotica as *samp* (dried corn), sun-dried fish, and *biltong* (dried, salted meat similar to the jerky of the old American West)—though I am not sure how many of you will ever want to.

As with American dishes, there are many ways to prepare most of the recipes included here. I've no doubt many an African could look at this book and remark that's not the way *she* makes a *tajin* or Pepper Chicken or *Matoke* or *Bobotie* or whatever. She'd be right; but that doesn't mean that I'm wrong. I've opted for the version that worked the best for me or that I feel produced the best-tasting result or was the best considering American materials and utensils. When I've had to adjust ingredient amounts (particularly pepper and oil) I've tried not to alter the overall authenticity of the final taste; when a recipe is an out-and-out adaptation, I'll tell you so. Authenticity is what I was after—not how to "cook English" or "cook French" if you happen to be living in Africa.

The spelling of these dishes (as with African place names) frequently comes in several versions, too. I've arbitrarily chosen the one that seems the easiest. Rendering Arabic names into English script is something even the experts don't do consistently. In some places in North Africa, for instance, the "k" sound is indicated by a "q" (without the "u"), some places by "ch," sometimes by "c," and still other places by "k." I've generally used "k" except for *couscous*, which seems to be the standard spelling in the Western world.

Finally, before getting out the pots and pans, I would like

to thank all those who gave me a hand with this project. All over Africa, U.S. Information Service officers and their wives, colleagues of my husband who live in Africa or who have lived there, friends and acquaintances, newspaper people—all directed me to food experts or places to get recipes or to restaurants where we could eat traditional dishes.

Among the USIS or U.S. government people who were particularly helpful were Mrs. Lee Fairley in Morocco; Mr. Irwin Teven and his wife, Lynn, in Ghana; Mrs. T. D. C. Sodeinde, assistant to the cultural affairs officer in Nigeria as well as a tribal chief in her own right and a devoted contributor to the cause of equality for women in Nigeria; Mrs. Roger Ross and the ambassador's wife, Mrs. Robert C. Good, in Zambia.

"Nongovernmental" friends and acquaintances to whom I'm most indebted include Michigan sociology Professor and Mrs. Horace Miner in Fez; Mr. Eldon Green of the *Cape Argus*, Cape Town; Mrs. Elsie Pitman, who writes as Ann Wise, women's editor of the *Sunday Times* of Johannesburg; Professor and Mrs. Robert Tabachnick, fellow Wisconsonites whom we visited in Zaria, Northern Nigeria, on our first trip; Miss Barbara Baeta of the YWCA in Accra, Ghana; Gus and Nerissa Williams, of Freetown, Sierra Leone; Mrs. Leslie Faull of the Silwood Kitchens in Cape Town, and long-time friends Burt and Helen Wyss in Windhoek, South West Africa.

Back home in Madison, I received valuable assists from Mary Ellen Hughes, Mrs. Edwin Traisman, and Charlotte Dunn.

And, of course, a special thanks to my daughters and my husband, who dined on my testings (the successes and the failures) without complaint. Usually.

# CONTENTS

# KITCHEN SAFARI

# NORTH AFRICA

THE ARABIC COUNTRIES north of the Sahara are included here because they do lie on the vast African continent. But culturally, economically, and gastronomically they are really more a part of the Mediterranean and the Near East.

Because of centuries of social interchange with Europe, plus the fact that North Africa is richer agriculturally than most places below the Sahara, the North African cuisine tends to be more elaborate and multi-coursed. Furthermore, in this region, unlike many other places on the continent, visitors have no trouble finding occasions to partake of its specialties.

You can dine in all sorts of settings: in the special North African rooms (done up in arabesque style) of the big tourist hotels in the modern, shiny cities situated here and there in the green, fertile strip that outlines the coastal lands from Morocco to Egypt; or you may favor a converted palace deep inside the maze of narrow streets that twist through the crowded *medinas*—native quarters—of the big cities; or on a Nile houseboat, where dinner is followed by a performance of that ancient folk-art form, belly dancing.

Hokey-tourist or authentic ambiance, the food you'll be served can best be described as lush. The dishes are velvety and smooth to match the silky plush of the bolsters and pillows padding the low couches and benches you sit upon. The menus may be lacking in green vegetables and salads, but in very little else.

Dining in North Africa is designed to be an experience that sates all the senses, not just the one of taste. The sense of sight is feasted in many ways—the rich colors of the velvet cushions and the shiny intricacy of the brocade hangings (these opulent settings are not a tourist gimmick; Arabs provide these things for themselves to the limit they can afford); the spotless white cloths on the low round tables; the gleam of the heavily chased brass or silver trays, pots, and serving dishes; the orderly geometric designs on the pottery serving pieces.

For the sense of smell, there's first of all the redolent food itself. Then there is the incense that is lighted near the end of the meal and the rose and orange water that's sprinkled over the table and on the diners, too, about the time tea is served. The North African considers pleasant fragrances necessary to satisfying dining, both as a sensual experience and to promote a feeling of luxury.

Since Arabs eat with their fingers, the sense of touch and feel is also catered to. The smoothness of the thick sauces and the tenderness of the meat can be fully savored and appreciated even before they're popped into the mouth.

North African meals are sensual, the food is lush and the courses are seemingly endless. They are not limited to a beginning, a middle, and an end—there are all sorts of embellishments and cadenzas between each stage. This is true whether you are a guest in a hotel or at someone's home; a meal is always a feast. There is no such thing as sharing a family meal or taking pot luck with an Arab. If you're invited to a North African's home, it is an occasion for considerable ceremony and as much abundance as the host can afford. When a North African dines *en famille,* the diet tends to be simple, even frugal—generally *couscous* (a starch and a stew) and, if he can afford it, possibly a soup to start with and fruit and nuts for dessert. But when company comes —mere acquaintance or long-time friend—the menu expands like rice in boiling water and in about the same proportion.

I well remember my first experience with North African hospitality. It was in Cairo in 1965. We were there near the end of Ramadan, one of Islam's most important observances, marking Mohammed's wanderings in the desert to escape persecution. For one month, from sun-up to sun-down Moslems neither eat nor drink anything. (The Moslem calendar has thirteen months, which means Ramadan doesn't always come at the same season each year. Sometimes it falls in the winter when the days are not too long. If it comes during the long, hot days of summer, the fasting can be extremely difficult.) Breakfast then becomes a meal of some importance. We were invited to breakfast one evening at the home of one of my husband's former students, an Egyptian who lived with his wife in a modern apartment in Heliopolis, a Cairo suburb. We chatted in the living room for a while with the radio going almost full blast so the host would be sure to hear the broadcast of the firing of the cannon precisely at sunset. Though our hosts obviously preferred European household accoutrements, there was one very evident concession to the old ways—a "parlor" reserved for high ceremonial and important occasions. It was an almost room-size alcove separated from the living room by a gauze curtain and chock-full of brocaded, gilded furniture in the Louis XV manner—a highly expensive spatial status symbol in a small apartment.

When the cannon boomed, we filed into the dining room for breakfast, a meal which combined traditional and modern dishes. First came a fairly thick soup called *Harira*, a year-round favorite all across North Africa but traditionally the fast-breaker at Ramadan. Then, a dish of rice and one of bread were passed for soaking up any last drops of soup left in the bowl. Next came platters of cold chicken and cold French-fried potatoes. This was followed by another cold dish —*El Belehat*, a meat loaf made with hard-cooked eggs in the center. At that point, the hot dishes started again. There was a macaroni-cheese-meat casserole and then meat and vegetable *tajin*. While all these courses were coming and going, platters of lettuce and tomato, sliced beets and potatoes in vinaigrette sauce, green salt olives, and bread were periodically circulated. Orange juice (for the faithful) and beer (for the infidels) were also served throughout the meal. Dessert was the ubiquitous *crème caramel*, followed by a heaping bowl of in-season fruit, followed by *Konafa* (a widely popular confection of nuts, sugar, spices, and wheat), candy, and coffee or tea.

The hostess, I hardly need add, spent all day preparing that meal. How long it took her to do the dishes, I wasn't permitted to observe.

Restaurants and hotels practice this gargantuan-abundance-for-company custom plus some traditional rituals and ceremonies our Egyptian friends felt they had outgrown. Our most memorable meal in a public place was appropriately enough in Fez, Morocco. Fez is a sort of holy city of the culinary arts for that part of the world—at least that's what the *Fassis* tell you.

This restaurant was deep in the ancient Fez *medina* in an old palace. The dining rooms were on the second floor and done in the traditional mode—low, wide banquettes along the walls, padded with brocaded cushions with lots of matching bolsters and loose cushions for reclining. And recline the Arabs do, not lean forward with elbows propped on knees as Westerners automatically, inevitably sit. The round tables were equally low and were provided with generous, squishy poufs for the diners whom the banquettes couldn't accommodate.

We were first given outsized, white damask napkins. These were to be opened out fully and draped to cover as much of our clothing as possible. Their purpose is to protect your wearing apparel—it is considered bad form to use them to wipe your fingers. You're not supposed to lick your fingers during the meal, either. Since, of course, there are no knives and forks provided, it takes an old North African hand indeed to refrain from wiping or licking. The Moroccan compromise is to use the coarse Moroccan bread for cleaning off your fingers. That way, you can swallow all evidence of your drippy fingers while observing the Arab amenities.

Our first course was artichokes. They had been boiled, well doused in a hot vinaigrette sauce, and then allowed to cool to lukewarm. There were about four or five for each person and everyone ate from the commodious, shallow earthenware serving dish set in the middle of the table. (Artichokes are not really traditional North African. This is a manifestation of the French influences that have become integrated into the Moroccan way of life. Most of Morocco was a French protectorate from 1912 to 1956.)

Next came a whole loin of lamb which had been delicately spiced and roasted over charcoal. This was followed by a *tajin* of chickens—three whole chickens—with almonds. Plenty of bread was provided to soak up the sauces and drippings. Traditionally, we should then have had *couscous*, too, but the generous portions up to that point compelled us to eliminate that specialty. Dessert started with the passing of round wicker trays heaped with shelled nuts, giant dates, and fresh fruit—tangerines, bananas, and oranges. Moroccan oranges are the largest, juiciest, and sweetest that I, a Californian born and bred, have ever enjoyed anywhere. The fruit and nuts were eventually replaced with a platter of *Kab el Ghzal* —gazelle horns. These are a crescent cooky of almond paste encased in a firm pastry dough. Like most North African confections, they are extremely sweet. It is bad form, though, to refuse *Kab el Ghzal* when offered. If you are too full to eat one on the spot, you're supposed to take it away with you. Finally, there was mint tea, made with much ceremony by the waiter.

Before getting down to the recipes themselves, I should explain a bit about spices and flavorings.

The North African housewife can choose from up to 200 different spices and herbs when she stops to replenish her supplies at a spice stall in the *souks* of the *medinas*. There are no neatly labeled tins or boxes. These spices and flavorings from China, India, Java, Egypt, tropical Africa, Spain, and elsewhere in North Africa are offered whole and in bulk, displayed in large and small baskets and in 100-pound sacks. There are various leaves, seeds, bark chips, and stalks—and ground red peppers.

Naturally, many spices from this enormous array are used only rarely in special dishes. The North African cook relies mostly on cumin, caraway, garlic, coriander, saffron, wild ginger, white pepper, cinnamon, and the red peppers, which range in strength from hot to hotter to hottest. And there's mint, for the mint tea.

Many recipes from Morocco call for a pre-mixed spice and herb blend, something like Indian curry. It is called *Ras el Hanout*, literally "head of the shop." Each spice stall mixes up its own, using between 25 and 30 different flavorings—and aphrodisiacs—many completely unknown to American cooks, even the gourmet ones.

Some of the familiar spices in *Ras el Hanout* are cardamon, caraway, mace, nutmeg, cinnamon, cloves, ginger, orrisroot, black pepper, lavender, rosebuds, and fennel. Those out of the American ken (at least as cooking spices) include ash and belladonna berries, galingale (stalk of the ginger tree), cantharides (a preparation of dried beetles colloquially known as "Spanish fly"), iris leaves, cyparacée (a strong-smelling stalk grown in Mali and Upper Volta), curcuma (the yellow root of the Indian ginger tree), and cubeb (a gray pepper with a heavy perfume).

Other stalls in the *souks* sell preserved lemons and another important flavoring ingredient, olives. The choice is not limited to black and green olives; they vary in color and degree of curing. Particularly favored are ripe black olives which have been cured in salt for several months and then dried, or pale gray-green ones that taste as if they've been only partially cured in oil and a little salt. The latter are frequently teamed in chicken dishes with the lemons which have been preserved in salt for several months.

Strangely, all these spices notwithstanding, North African cooking doesn't taste particularly spicy. In fact, much of it is almost bland—particularly compared with tropical African dishes or even a good, zippy chili con carne. With some dishes, the diner is permitted to add "heat" as he desires. (Food otherwise is not seasoned at the table.) Kebabs and other charcoal-roasted meats are usually served with a small dish of fresh-ground cumin and one of ground red peppers mixed with a little oil. The procedure is to dip the meat in the cumin first, then in the red pepper sauce. Beginners should proceed with caution: the cumin isn't too bad, but too much of the red pepper is guaranteed to clear your sinuses immediately and could deaden your palate for several days. A hot pepper sauce is also served with *couscous*.

*Ras el Hanout,* olives, and preserved lemons are often available in foreign or gourmet specialty food shops around the United States. If *Ras el Hanout* is unavailable, a good, hot curry powder can be substituted (add, if you wish for greater authenticity, two or three freshly crushed spices like allspice, cloves, etc.). Black or stuffed green olives will pass for the North African varieties. Salted lemon slices steeped for a while in boiling water may be used as a last resort for preserved lemons.

Actually, the lemons are easily made at home.

## PRESERVED LEMONS

Soak lemons (as many as you wish—4 to 12 pounds) in cold water for five days, changing the water daily. Then cut each lemon in quarters, but take care not to sever the skin entirely. Put a pinch of salt in the middle of each lemon and press the lemon back into shape. Place in a clean jar or crock and weight with a heavy platter or a clean stone placed on top of the fruit. Keep in a fairly cool place. A thick, salty juice will ooze out as the lemons stand. Do not discard. This juice may be used to keep the lemons indefinitely or in place of vinegar in salad dressings. The lemons will be usable after a month.

Specialty food stores also carry distilled rose and orange flower water, ingredients often required. These are highly distinctive flavorings, and I know of no substitutes. If you cannot get them, leave them out—it will alter the taste and aroma only slightly since they are used in small amounts and their effect is exceedingly subtle.

## SOUPS

North African soups are nothing if not hearty. Often with just the addition of bread, they serve as an entire meal.

*Harira,* as I've said, is served all during the year and is usually the first food taken after the sun goes down during Ramadan. The many "*harira* bars" in the *medinas,* well patronized at all times of the day, best illustrate its popularity.

### HARIRA

*1 cup dry chick peas (or 1 can chick peas, drained)*
*Neck, gizzard, and wings of three chickens*
*1 pound lamb or beef, cut in small pieces*
*1 large onion, finely chopped*
*¼ to ½ teaspoon ginger*
*Pinch saffron, powdered with a little salt*
*Pinch pepper*
*4 teaspoons salt (about)*
*½ cup chopped parsley*
*8 tablespoons butter*
*1 cup rice*
*1 teaspoon pepper*
*1 cake yeast*
*4 large tomatoes, peeled and coarsely chopped*
*1 tablespoon dried coriander or 1 teaspoon ground coriander*

12 to 15 servings

Soak the chick peas overnight. Drain.

In a large, heavy saucepan, place chicken parts, meat, and three pints water. Bring to a boil and skim. Add chopped onions, soaked chick peas (if using canned peas, add to stock after 1½ hours of cooking), ginger, saffron, generous pinch of pepper, 1 teaspoon salt, and parsley. Bring to a boil again. Add 4 tablespoons butter. Cover and simmer about 2 hours.

One half hour before stock is ready, cook rice in boiling salted water, using 1 cup more water than package directs and adding 4 tablespoons butter and the 1 teaspoon pepper to the water.

Meanwhile, dissolve yeast in ¼ cup lukewarm water. Combine 5 cups cold water, tomatoes, coriander, 2 teaspoons salt, and dissolved yeast. Mix well. Bring to a boil over a hot fire, stirring often, and boil 10 minutes. Combine with the rice and its cooking liquid.

To serve, combine rice mixture with the stock, including vegetables and meat.

Another filling soup is called *Cheurba.* You may have trouble getting the required lamb tail. (As the third butcher I tried said: "That's the weirdest request I've ever had.") Since then, I've substituted ½ pound lamb bones for the tail as the tail has hardly any meat on it. Also you can use one (16 oz.)can each of lima beans and chick peas instead of the dry ones.

## CHERUBA

*½ cup each dried lima beans and dried chick peas*
*½ cup oil*
*1 lamb tail or ½ pound lamb bones*
*1 ½ pounds boned leg or shoulder of lamb, cut in small pieces*
*1 large onion, coarsely chopped*
*1 pound tomatoes, peeled and coarsely chopped or canned tomatoes*
*8 ½ cups hot water*
*1 clove garlic, chopped*
*1 tablespoon chopped parsley*
*Pinch of cayenne or to taste*
*¼ teaspoon pepper*

*1/8 teaspoon saffron*
*1 teaspoon salt*
*Pinch of thyme*
*1 bay leaf*
*1/2 large zucchini, cubed*
*1 cup elbow macroni or vermicelli*

12 to 15 servings

Soak lima beans and chick peas at least 12 hours. Drain.

Heat oil in dutch oven. Sauté onion until soft; add tomatoes and sauté slightly. Add bones and meat and brown lightly. Add water, bring to a boil, and skim. Add garlic, parsley, cayenne, pepper, saffron, salt, thyme, and bay leaf. Add hot water, beans and peas. Boil, reduce heat, cover, and simmer 2 hours. (If using canned beans and peas, add when meat is almost done.) Add cubed zucchini 10 minutes before the soup is ready.

Cook macaroni and drain; add 5 minutes before serving.

## BEGINNING COURSES

The visitor to North Africa is easily left with the impression that at any given moment one-half of the population is engaged in selling something to the other half. Only a highly trained expert could possibly explain the economics of the countless little stalls, one after another, that line the *souks* and market areas of the *medinas,* the cloth sellers on one street, spice shops on another, hammered brass and silver artisans on another. All along the walks and streets in front of the shops are the street hawkers who are still too poor to have accumulated enough merchandise or cash to afford a proper shop.

Many of these street merchants sell food of one kind or another. Your nose will draw you to the brochette purveyor. He squats in front of a long iron brazier, cooking six or seven brochettes at a time over glowing charcoal. If he's far from his source of meat supply, he'll probably have a rectangular glass box beside him for the extra meat. He'll keep the long rolls (they look like hot-dog buns) in the glass box, too; when he makes a sale, he opens a roll and slides off the savory, piping-hot meat.

In hotels and restaurants, brochettes are served as an appetizer or one of the first courses in an elaborate *diffa*—an Arabic word for meal.

Generally, there's a choice of two types of brochette—one of ground meat, *Kefta,* and one of tender cubes, *Kebab.* Though both are spicy, the *Kefta* is more so. Much more so, as a matter of fact. The *Kebabs* are always served with the small dishes of ground cumin and red pepper in a little oil.

Both *Kefta* and *Kebabs* would translate nicely to a summer cookout. Charcoal-broiling would give the most authentic flavor. However, they also may be cooked under an oven broiler.

## KEBAB

*1½ pounds marbled beef or leg of lamb, cut in 1½-inch cubes*
*2 medium onions, minced*
*1 tablespoon chopped parsley*
*1 teaspoon salt*
*½ teaspoon pepper*

4 servings as main dish
8 to 10 as appetizer

Mix all ingredients well. Allow to stand 2 or 3 hours.

To cook, string meat on skewers and grill over glowing coals, turning often. Any pieces of onion or parsley that cling to the meat should be left for flavor; discard remainder.

## KEFTA

*1 pound ground chuck (finely ground as possible)*
*½ teaspoon coriander*
*1 teaspoon chopped parsley*
*1 teaspoon salt*
*¼ teaspoon marjoram*
*½ teaspoon pepper*
*¼ teaspoon cayenne*
*1 teaspoon* Ras el Hanout *or curry powder*
*1 teaspoon cumin*
*1 onion, finely chopped*

4 servings as main dish
8 as appetizer

Combine all ingredients and let stand at least 1 hour; 2 would be better.

To cook, take enough meat to make a ball about the size of an egg. Pack on a skewer in a sausage shape. Two or three should fit onto one skewer. Grill quickly over glowing coals, turning often.

*Kefta* may also be made like hamburger patties. And, of course, they may be made less spicy.

## KEFTA PATTIES

*1 pound ground beef or lamb*
*1 teaspoon cumin*
*1 clove garlic, chopped*
*1 teaspoon salt*
*¼ teaspoon pepper*

4 servings

Combine all ingredients and let stand 1 to 2 hours.

Fashion meat into patties and broil over glowing charcoal. Serve with a hot pepper sauce made by diluting 1 tablespoon cayenne with a little olive oil and lemon juice.

In an Egyptian version of *Kefta,* the seasoned meat is cooked in a pan rather than directly over coals.

## FRIED KEFTA BALLS

*1¼ pounds ground lamb*
*2 eggs*
*1 cup dry bread crumbs*
*1 large onion, finely chopped*
*1 clove garlic, finely chopped*
*1 tablespoon chopped parsley*
*½ teaspoon dried mint, crumbled*
*Salt and pepper to taste*
*½ teaspoon coriander*
*½ teaspoon cumin*
*Oil*

6 servings

Combine lamb, eggs, bread crumbs, onion, garlic, parsley, and mint. Season with salt, pepper, coriander, and cumin. Form mixture into small balls, about 1 to 1½ inches in diameter, then flatten slightly. Heat enough oil in a frying pan to cover the bottom and fry *Keftas* until golden, about 5 minutes on each side.

May be served unadorned or with a tomato sauce.

*Bstila* (pronounced "pastilla") is the ultimate dish in Moroccan culinary arts.

To call it a pigeon pie, which technically it is, is hardly to do it justice. What pigeon pie you ever heard of calls for 3 pounds butter, 30 eggs (true, Moroccan eggs are quite small), 4 pounds flour, 6 pigeons, 2 cups sugar, 1 pound almonds, 4 tablespoons ginger, 4 tablespoons cinnamon, 1 tablespoon allspice, ½ pound onions, pinch of saffron, and ¼ teaspoon coriander? This aggregate of ingredients will make a *Bstila* for 12, the smallest anyone would bother preparing. Obviously, this is party fare if only in view of the time and investment required to produce this succulent offering.

Perhaps more than anything else, the *Bstila* illustrates the Moroccan's approach to entertaining. After all, this dish is not the main course; it is merely the first or second course.

To make a proper *Bstila,* you must first of all be born a Moroccan and serve a long apprenticeship at your mother's elbow. Even that is no guarantee of perfection. Many Moroccan women today do not know how to make this specialty. Many who do, however, hire out to prepare this dish for someone else's special occasion. And it takes a *Bstila* maker all day to produce her masterpiece.

Most of the time and skill is invested in producing the pastry that all those good things are layered in. And quite a production it is when you consider a *Bstila* has between 95 and 110 layers of transparent, flaky dough.

This dough is prepared on a special utensil called a *tobsil dail louarka,* a shallow tray with a copper bottom, which is placed over a charcoal cooker. It requires years of practice to learn the technique of mixing the dough to the proper consistency and then how to throw and immediately withdraw the small pieces of dough so they form a thin transparent circle about 16 inches in diameter on the *tobsil.*

I have worked out an adaptation of this recipe using frozen phyllo dough (also spelled filo or fillo), a product available in most grocery stores. (It is similar to strudel dough). It is used in Greek cookery for, among other things, baklava. Phyllo is made of the same ingredients as *Bstila* dough—just water, flour, and salt. Another substitution I've made is chicken instead of pigeon; you could use Cornish game hens instead.

This is not the true, absolutely authentic *Bstila*, but it is a mighty good imitation.

## BSTILA

*1 chicken, cut up, including gizzard and liver*
*2 cups water*
*¾ pound butter (about)*
*1 teaspoon salt*
*2 onions, minced*
*2 tablespoons ginger*
*Pinch cinnamon*
*1 teaspoon* Ras el Hanout *or curry powder*
*Pinch allspice*
*Pinch saffron*
*⅛ teaspoon coriander*
*1 tablespoon chopped parsley*
*6 large eggs*
*1 cup sugar*
*1½ cups almonds, browned in butter and coarsely chopped*
*1¼ tablespoons cinnamon*
*1½ pounds frozen phyllo dough, thawed*

18 to 20 servings

Combine chicken and water and bring to a boil; skim. Add ¼ pound butter, salt, onions, ginger, pinch of cinnamon, *Ras el Hanout*, allspice, saffron, coriander, and parsley.

Bring to a boil, then simmer gently, uncovered, until meat comes off the bones easily. Drain chicken well, reserving broth. Bone chicken and cut meat, including gizzard and liver, into pieces. Set aside.

Beat eggs lightly. Heat one-half of broth in a pan until it is almost boiling. Remove from heat and beat in eggs; return to a low heat, beating constantly, until mixture is as thick as scrambled eggs. Set aside.

Reduce remaining broth over high heat until smooth and thick. Set aside. As broth cools it will thicken.

Combine sugar, almonds, and 1¼ tablespoons cinnamon.

Divide phyllo dough into three equal parts. Keep the portions wrapped in a clean kitchen towel wrung out of cold water until needed; this will keep dough from drying out.

In a greased 13 by 9-inch pan, lay sheets of dough so they cover the bottom and extend over the sides of the pan, overlapping as necessary. Use one portion of dough this way, brushing every three or four layers with melted butter. Brush top layer well with melted butter. Spread almond mixture over the dough, then top with one-half of the scrambled egg mixture. Moisten with some of the jellied gravy.

Cover with sheets of second portion of dough, brushing as before with butter. Fold each sheet in half since this series of layers need only cover the mixture and not extend over the sides. Brush top layer well with melted butter. Distribute chicken and remaining scrambled egg over dough. Moisten with remaining jellied gravy.

Cover with all but five sheets of remaining dough, again brushing every three or four sheets with melted butter. Fold edges of bottom layers of dough up over top. Layer last five sheets of dough over all, brushing each lightly with butter, and tuck in around the sides. Brush all over well with melted butter. For all the brushings with melted butter you should use up about one-half pound.

*Bstila* may be prepared early in the day to this point. If it is to stand before baking, wrap pan in a towel wrung out of cold water, then cover with a dry towel. Redampen the towel every 3 hours.

Cover top of pan with foil and bake in a slow to moderate oven (325° to 350° F.) 30 minutes. Remove foil and continue baking until heated through and crust is golden and crisp, but not too dry, about 30 to 40 minutes more.

This is a very rich concoction and portions should be modest if it is served as an appetizer or first course.

## TOUAJEN

The *tajin* (the plural is *touajen*) is basic to North African cookery. The word is actually the name of the covered earthenware dish the recipe is sometimes cooked in and usually served in. The dish is comparatively shallow and the top is cone-shaped and pierced with a hole near the top. (See page 29 for a homemade adaptation.) This contrivance keeps the food properly hot for serving, but permits some steam to escape through the hole so the meat won't get saggingly moist before it's eaten.

Just about anything can be cooked as a *tajin*—chickens, pigeons, mutton, beef, goat, camel, vegetables, fruit. Pork is the exception, naturally, because of the Moslem religious taboos. Poultry or game is usually left whole; meat is generally cubed.

The cooking liquid is the secret of a *tajin's* tastiness. This is usually a combination of water and butter or oil (characteristically, olive oil) and seasonings to suit what's being cooked. Depending on the region, the ingredients are either sautéed in the oil or butter before water is added or are stewed in a combination of the two. In Egypt, for instance, everything is usually browned in fat before the water is stirred in; in Fez, it's the other way around.

But whichever comes first, the liquid is reduced during the long cooking to form a soft, velvety, and undeniably rich sauce. And with the long cooking, the meats, vegetables, or fruits are meltingly tender so they may be easily "cut" and eaten with the fingers—an obvious necessity in a culture that eschews tableware. (Long cooking is also necessary in an area where meat and fowl don't get the scientific feeding the American equivalents do and consequently are much tougher to begin with.)

In poultry and meat *tajin* recipes, I've cut the cooking time—so our lamb or chicken will not be turned into mush. If the sauce has not had time to reduce enough, I suggest removing the ingredients and cooking the liquid over a high heat until most of the water is evaporated and only the juices and oil remain.

This boiling down very likely will be necessary with most of these dishes, largely because our cooking equipment is more efficient than what the North Africans have at their disposal. Our pot lids usually fit tightly so steam can't escape during cooking. Our stoves are quicker cooking since the heat is directed and confined; most North African housewives use a charcoal or wood-burning brazier for their cooking. For me, these recipes work best in an electric frying pan with the vent in the cover left open.

You'll notice some of the *tajin* recipes call for olive oil and some for butter. Whichever is specified is traditional for that particular recipe. The butter the North Africans would use usually is *smen*, a strong, slightly rancid butter (also called *ghee*) used in Indian cooking, too. Ordinary butter works as well and is more acceptable to American tastes.

The *touajen* I've included here illustrate the wide range of ingredients and seasonings to be found in these dishes.

Though the cooking method may be similar in all of them, the results are deliciously different.

First is the ground-meat dish served us at that Ramadan breakfast in Egypt.

## EL BELEHAT (MEAT LOAF AND EGG)

*1½ pounds ground beef*
*1 teaspoon cumin*
*1 teaspoon salt*
*½ teaspoon pepper*
*2 cloves garlic, crushed*
*4 eggs*
*3 tablespoons flour*
*1 cup fresh bread crumbs*
*¼ cup olive oil*
*⅓ cup hot water*
*½ cup tomato juice* 6 to 8 servings

Combine ground beef with cumin, salt, pepper, and garlic; mix well. Hard-cook 2 of the eggs; peel but leave whole.

Sprinkle flour over a clean dish towel spread on a table. Flatten the meat out on the towel into a rectangle. Place the 2 hard-cooked eggs side-by-side near one edge and roll up the meat, jelly-roll fashion, so it looks like a large sausage. Press ends and edges together. Beat remaining eggs. Dip meat roll in the eggs, then roll in the bread crumbs.

Heat oil in a large frying pan. Brown the meat roll on all sides in the hot oil. Add hot water and tomato juice, cover, and simmer about 30 minutes or until done.

Serve hot or cold.

Poached lamb *kefta* balls plus a spiced tomato-y sauce is a Moroccan dish.

## LAMB KEFTA WITH TOMATOES

*2 pounds ground lamb*
*1 onion, finely chopped*
*3 mint leaves, chopped*
*¼ teaspoon marjoram*
*1 teaspoon chopped parsley*
*1 teaspoon* Ras el Hanout *or curry powder*
*⅛ teaspoon allspice*
*1½ teaspoons salt*
*1 teaspoon cumin*
*Cayenne to taste (at least ¼ teaspoon)*
*⅓ cup olive oil*
*1½ pounds tomatoes, peeled and cut up*
*2 onions, sliced*
*1 clove garlic, chopped*
*1 pimiento, diced*

8 servings

Combine well-ground lamb, chopped onion, chopped mint, marjoram, ½ teaspoon parsley, *Ras el Hanout*, allspice, 1 teaspoon salt, cumin, and cayenne. Form into egg-size balls.

Bring about a quart of water to a fast boil in a deep saucepan. Poach the meat balls in the boiling water about 15 minutes, turning gently to cook on all sides. Drain and let cool completely to firm up. Refrigerate until ready to use.

Heat oil in a pan or casserole. Add tomatoes, onions, garlic, remaining parsley and salt, and pimiento. Sauté briefly, then add 1 cup water. Bring slowly to a boil, then simmer, covered, 1 hour. Add *kefta* balls and continue simmering, uncovered, until they are heated through. By then, all the water should have evaporated from the sauce. If it has not, bring to a lively boil until it does, taking care not to scorch the vegetables.

Dining on a chicken *tajin* is a particularly delightful experience. The chicken is transformed in taste and texture, retaining a smoothness and a buttery quality most methods familiar to us fail to produce. I've found it easier to cut up the chicken before cooking (unless it is to be stuffed, of course), even though that's not, strictly speaking, authentic.

## CHICKEN TAJIN WITH ALMONDS AND CHICK PEAS

*2 fryer chickens, cut up*
*Pinch saffron*
*1 teaspoon salt*
*1 teaspoon pepper*
*1½-inch cinnamon stick*
*2½ pounds onions, finely chopped*
*¾ cup butter*
*2 cups blanched almonds*
*2 1-pound cans chick peas, drained*
*1 cup chopped parsley*
*2 to 3 tablespoons lemon juice*

8 servings

Into stewing pan or electric fry pan, put chicken, saffron, salt, pepper, cinnamon stick, about 1 cup chopped onion, and butter. Cover all with water, cover, and simmer 30 minutes. Add almonds and chick peas and continue simmering another 30 minutes or until chicken is tender. Remove almonds, chick peas, and chicken and keep warm. Add remaining onion and parsley. Cook uncovered until the onions are very soft, almost puréed, and the liquid is reduced. If onions cook before liquid is reduced, raise heat and boil until sauce is smooth. Return almonds, chick peas, and chicken to sauce and heat. Just before serving, add lemon juice.

VARIATION: This same *tajin* may be made with lamb. Substitute 4 to 4½ pounds lamb, cut in large pieces, for the chicken. All other ingredients remain the same. Combine lamb, saffron, salt, pepper, cinnamon, 1 cup chopped onion, and butter in pan. Cover with water, cover, and simmer 1 to 1½ hours or until meat is almost done. Add almonds and chick peas and continue cooking 30 minutes or until meat is tender. Remove almonds, chick peas, and lamb and proceed with remaining ingredients as above.

## CHICKEN TAJIN WITH OLIVES AND LEMON

*1 7-ounce jar pimiento-stuffed green olives, drained*
*Salt to taste*
*1 lemon, sliced*
*1 onion, finely chopped*
*1 clove garlic, chopped*
*1 tablespoon dried coriander or 1 teaspoon ground coriander*
*½ cup chopped parsley*
*Pinch saffron, pounded with a little salt*
*½ teaspoon pepper*
*1 broiler-fryer chicken (about 2½ pounds), cut up*
*1 teaspoon salt*
*5 tablespoons butter or oil*

4 servings

In a small saucepan, heat olives in water to cover until boiling. Drain and keep hot until needed. Sprinkle a little salt on lemon slices, pour boiling water over them, and let them steep a few minutes. Drain and keep warm.

Combine onion, garlic, coriander, parsley, saffron, and pepper. Spread in bottom of heavy pot or electric fry pan. Place chicken pieces on top. Half cover with water; add 1 teaspoon salt. Cover and bring to a boil. Add butter or oil, reduce heat, and simmer, covered, until chicken is tender, about 45 minutes. Remove chicken, increase heat, and boil uncovered until the water has completely evaporated and the sauce is reduced. Return chicken and simmer for a few minutes until chicken is very hot. Garnish with olives and lemon slices.

VARIATION: 2 to 3 pounds lamb shoulder, cut up, may be substituted for the chicken. All ingredients and procedure would remain the same.

My children are particularly fond of the following *tajin.*

## CHICKEN TAJIN WITH ALMONDS

*¼ teaspoon ginger*
*Pinch saffron, crushed with a little salt*
*1 clove garlic, crushed*
*4 tablespoons olive or peanut oil*
*4 tablespoons melted butter*
*1 broiler-fryer chicken (2 to 2½ pounds), cut up*
*1 tablespoon dried coriander or 1 teaspoon ground coriander*
*½ pound almonds, browned in butter*

4 servings

Combine ginger, saffron, crushed garlic, oil, and melted butter in a stewing pan or electric fry pan. Slowly mix in ½ cup water. Add chicken pieces and coat well. Add enough water to almost cover the chicken. Add coriander and simmer, covered (keep vent on lid open if using electric fry pan), until chicken is tender, about 45 minutes. Remove chicken and boil sauce rapidly until it is thick and fairly oily. Place chicken on serving dish and pour reduced sauce over. Garnish with browned almonds. Pass French or Italian bread for sopping up that good gravy.

You can cook a whole stuffed chicken as a *tajin*, too. Turkey may also be prepared this way (if you have a heavy, top-of-the-stove pot big enough); just triple the amount of stuffing for a 10- to 16-pound turkey.

## CHICKEN STUFFED WITH ALMONDS, SEMOLINA, AND RAISINS

*3½ ounces* couscous (*semolina*)
*7 tablespoons butter*
*½ cup coarsely chopped almonds*
*1 cup chopped raisins*
*½ teaspoon* Ras el Hanout *or curry powder*
*2 teaspoons salt*
*1 large roasting chicken or capon*
*Pinch ginger*
*1 onion, chopped*
*Pinch saffron, pounded with a little salt*

about 10 servings

Steam semolina until cooked. Toss with 1 tablespoon butter. Combine semolina with chopped almonds, raisins, *Ras el Hanout*, and 1 teaspoon salt. Stuff this mixture into chicken cavity, truss, and sew up opening tightly.

In a stewing pan combine ginger, onion, saffron, and remaining salt. Place chicken in the pan and cover halfway with water. Place on a high fire and bring to a boil. Add remaining butter. Simmer, covered, over medium heat until chicken is tender, about 2 hours, uncovering the pot after the first hour.

When chicken is tender, all the water should be evaporated, leaving only the butter and pan juices at the bottom. Increase heat a bit and brown chicken in the butter in the pan, turning carefully.

This recipe may also be used for a stuffed shoulder of lamb.

Throughout the whole Mediterranean world, lamb is the most favored meat. In North Africa, beef is generally what one eats when he cannot afford or obtain lamb. It's not surprising, once you've seen the cattle. Driving through the Moroccan countryside and glimpsing the straggly herds of pitifully bony beasts being driven by ragtag herdsmen, I became convinced those cattle were being raised for their hides. It couldn't be for the meat; there was hardly any there.

The sheep, however, always looked plump (though I never got close enough to determine how much of that was fleece). In the eating, the lamb was always of a fine texture, the beef often stringy.

The following *touajen* traditionally require lamb. Beef, of course, may be substituted in most of them.

*Bamia* is a lamb and okra dish. Note the ingredients are sautéed before liquid is added, in the Egyptian manner.

### BAMIA (LAMB TAJIN WITH OKRA)

*3 or 4 tablespoons oil*
*2 10-ounce packages frozen okra, thawed and drained*
*2 cloves garlic, chopped*
*¾ pound tomatoes, peeled and cut in pieces*
*1 pound breast of lamb, cubed (with bones) in 2-inch pieces*
*Salt and pepper to taste*
*1 cup water*

4 servings

Heat oil in a stewing pan. Brown the okra in the oil. Add garlic, tomatoes, and meat. Season with salt and pepper to taste. Add water, cover, and simmer until meat is tender, about 1½ hours.

## LAMB TAJIN WITH ONIONS AND HONEY

*2 pounds lamb, in 2-inch cubes*
*1½-inch stick cinnamon*
*¼ teaspoon ginger*
*Pinch ground saffron*
*½ pound honey*
*¼ teaspoon salt*
*1 pound small onions*

4 to 6 servings

Combine lamb, cinnamon, ginger, saffron, 2 tablespoons of the honey, salt, and enough water to half cover the meat in a heavy saucepan. Simmer, covered, 30 minutes. Uncover and continue simmering until meat is half-cooked and liquid reduced by three-fourths. Place meat in a casserole. Heap onions over meat. Fashion a cone-shaped foil cover, molding around your finger so there's a chimney-like opening at the peak. Place over casserole, sealing well along sides. Now you have a homemade *tajin* (though this dish could also be made in an electric fry pan). Bake in a hot oven (375° to 400° F.) until onions are well browned and water is evaporated, about 1 hour. Heat remaining honey and pour over meat and onions. Return uncovered to oven for 20 minutes.

The combination of honey, onions, and lamb may be curious to American tastes, but it well illustrates the Arab's love of anything sweet. I'd suggest using a light, mildly flavored honey—orange or clover. The first time I made this dish I used a dark, buckwheat honey which proved too strong. (For what it's worth, my girls don't like this one at all!) I don't recommend substituting beef for lamb in this (or the next) recipe; the flavor of beef doesn't blend well with sweetenings.

## LAMB TAJIN WITH FRUIT AND HONEY

*2 pounds lamb, in 2-inch cubes*
*Pinch each ginger, saffron, and salt*
*3 tablespoons olive oil*
*1 tablespoon dried coriander or 1 teaspoon ground coriander*
*1½-inch stick cinnamon*
*Pepper to taste*
*1 small onion, chopped*
*1 pound prune plums, pears, or apples*
*¼ cup honey*
*1 teaspoon distilled orange flower water (optional)*
*1 tablespoon sesame seeds, toasted in the oven*

4 to 6 servings

Combine meat, ginger, saffron, salt, oil, coriander, cinnamon stick, pepper, and onion. Cover with water and simmer until meat is well cooked and liquid reduced to a thick sauce. (Simmer covered half the time, then uncovered.) Remove cinnamon stick.

Prepare fruit. If using plums, pit but leave whole; core and quarter pears or apples, but do not peel. Add fruit and simmer slowly about 15 minutes. Add honey and cook another 15 minutes. Add orange flower water and bring to a boil. Sprinkle with toasted sesame seeds and serve immediately.

## LAMB TAJIN WITH LEMON

*2 pounds lamb, in 2-inch cubes*
*⅛ teaspoon cayenne*
*¼ teaspoon cumin*
*⅛ teaspoon ginger*
*Pinch saffron*

*1 clove garlic, chopped*
*½ tablespoon dried coriander or ½ teaspoon ground coriander*
*3 tablespoons lemon juice*
*1 pound onions, chopped*

4 to 6 servings

Combine meat, cayenne, cumin, ginger, saffron, garlic, coriander, 1 tablespoon lemon juice, and 1 cup chopped onion. Half cover with water and simmer until meat is tender. Remove meat. Add remaining chopped onion, cover, and simmer until onions are very soft. Arrange meat in oven-proof dish, cover with onions and any pan juices left, pour remaining lemon juice over, and brown in a hot oven (425° F.).

A cut-up chicken may be used instead of the lamb.

## LAMB TAJIN WITH VEGETABLES

*¼ cup oil*
*2 pounds lamb, in 2-inch cubes (do not use leg for this one; choose a fatter cut)*
*Salt to taste*
*½ teaspoon each paprika and cayenne*
*½ pound carrots, cut in strips*
*¼ pound turnips, cut in strips*
*1 large onion, cut in pieces*
*1 tomato, peeled and cut in pieces*
*¼ pound zucchini, cut in pieces*
*1 cup raisins*

6 servings

Heat oil in a heavy stewing pan. Add meat and brown slowly. Season with salt, paprika, and cayenne. Add carrots and turnips. Cover and simmer 1 hour. Add onion, tomato, zucchini, and raisins. Cover and simmer ½ hour more. Spoon off fat.

Note: Water is not called for in this recipe. This is not a mistake. The meat and vegetables are supposed to cook in the oil and their own juices. A heavy stewing pan and a very low fire are essential for this dish.

## LAMB TAJIN WITH TOMATOES

*2 pounds lamb, in 2-inch cubes*
*3 tablespoons olive oil*
*Pinch each cumin, ginger, and pepper*
*¼ teaspoon each paprika and cayenne*
*Salt to taste*
*2 cloves garlic, chopped*
*¾ pound onions, chopped*
*½ cup chopped parsley*
*2 pounds tomatoes, peeled, seeded, and cut in pieces*
*½ tablespoon dried coriander or ½ teaspoon ground coriander*

4 to 6 servings

Combine meat, oil, cumin, ginger, pepper, paprika, cayenne, salt, garlic, and ⅔ cup chopped onion in a stewing pan. Half cover with water. Simmer, covered, until meat is half-cooked. Add parsley, tomatoes, remaining onion, and coriander. Simmer, uncovered, until meat is tender and sauce reduced.

## LAMB TAJIN WITH OLIVES AND LEMONS

*½ cup olive oil*
*Pinch ginger*
*Pinch saffron, crushed with a little salt*
*Salt to taste*

*2 pounds shoulder of lamb, cut in pieces*
*1 large onion, finely chopped*
*½ tablespoon dried coriander or ½ teaspoon ground coriander*
*1 clove garlic, crushed*
*½ cup pimiento-stuffed green olives*
*3 preserved lemons, quartered, or 3 lemons, quartered, lightly salted, and steeped for a few minutes in boiling water*

4 to 6 servings

Combine oil, ginger, saffron, and salt in a stewing pan. Add ½ cup water slowly, stirring constantly. Roll meat in this mixture, then add enough water to almost cover the meat. Add onion, coriander, and garlic. Simmer, covered, over a moderate fire until meat is tender. Remove meat. Increase heat and cook until sauce is thick and oily. Return meat, add olives and lemon quarters, and simmer until all is heated.

Both chicken and turkey may be prepared this way.

The cooking method for this *tajin* is a little different. It's richer than most, too.

## BROWNED LAMB TAJIN

*⅛ teaspoon saffron*
*2 pounds shoulder of lamb, cut in large pieces*
*¼ cup olive oil*
*½ pound butter*
*Salt to taste*
*⅛ teaspoon each ginger and paprika*
*¼ teaspoon cumin*
*2 cloves garlic, crushed*
*1 large onion, chopped*

4 servings

Dilute the saffron with a few tablespoons water. Sprinkle over meat.

In a heavy stewing pan, combine meat, 1 tablespoon oil, 4 tablespoons butter, salt, ginger, paprika, cumin, garlic, and chopped onion. Half cover with water. Simmer, covered, until meat is well cooked. Remove meat, drain, and cool. Increase heat under pan and boil rapidly until sauce is reduced.

Heat remaining butter and oil in a frying pan. Brown cooled meat well on both sides. Serve with reduced sauce poured over.

In this recipe, too, chicken or turkey may be substituted for the lamb.

## MARINATED LAMB TAJIN

*2 cloves garlic, minced*
*Pinch saffron, crushed with a little salt*
*1/8 teaspoon each paprika, cumin, and ginger*
*1/4 teaspoon pepper*
*2 to 2 1/2 pounds shoulder of lamb, cut in large pieces*
*1/2-inch stick cinnamon*
*1/4 to 1/2 cup olive oil*
*1/2 pound onions, chopped*
*1/2 cup chopped parsley*
*1/2 tablespoon dried coriander or 1/2 teaspoon ground coriander*
*2 tablespoons lemon juice*
*2 preserved lemons, or 2 fresh lemons quartered, sprinkled lightly with salt, and steeped in boiling water (optional)*
*1/2 cup pimiento-stuffed olives (optional)*

4 to 6 servings

Combine garlic, saffron, paprika, cumin, ginger, and pepper. Rub the meat well with this mixture and let stand at least 2 hours.

Place meat in a heavy stewing pan; half cover with water. Add cinnamon stick and bring to a boil. Add oil. Simmer until meat is cooked, 1 to 1½ hours. Remove meat and set aside.

To the cooking liquid, add onions, parsley, and coriander. Simmer, uncovered, until onions are very soft and sauce is reduced and is thick and creamy. Return meat to pan and simmer about 15 minutes. Just before serving, drizzle with lemon juice and decorate with lemons and olives which have been heated in water and drained.

Goat is widely eaten in the countryside. Stringier, tougher, and a bit stronger in taste than lamb, it's well suited to the spiciness and long cooking of the *tajin*. A young, well-fed kid, however, can easily be mistaken for lamb. Though I did not eat kid in North Africa, I was served it several times in West Africa and found it delicious.

This is how goat is cooked in some parts of North Africa. The recipe works just as well with lamb.

## MERMEZ (TAJIN OF GOAT)

*2 pounds young goat meat, cut in pieces*
*1 teaspoon salt*
*2 teaspoons crushed chili peppers mixed with 1 teaspoon oil*
*1 teaspoon pepper*
*2 teaspoons cayenne*
*1 cup oil*
*½ pound onions, sliced*
*1 pound tomatoes, peeled and mashed*
*¾ pound green peppers, seeded and cut in rings*

6 servings

Season meat with salt and the spices. Heat oil in a heavy stewing pan and brown meat and onions until golden. Add tomatoes and green pepper rings. Cover and simmer slowly until done, 1½ to 2 hours. If the sauce reduces too much, add a little water as needed.

Eggs are not as much a part of the North African cuisine as they are in this country. They are used in some recipes, but as an entree their use is largely confined to family dining. Vendors sell them, hard-cooked, on the streets of the *medinas* for a quick snack—they're served with salt and powdered cumin for seasoning.

Here are several egg recipes which involve *tajin* cooking.

## TAJIN OF TOMATO AND EGGS

*1 clove garlic*
*2 tablespoons oil*
*1¼ pounds tomatoes, peeled, seeded, and cut in pieces*
*¼ cup finely chopped onions*
*Salt and pepper to taste*
*10 eggs, medium size*

6 servings

Rub a saucepan with garlic. Add oil and heat. Add tomatoes and onions and season with salt and pepper. Simmer, covered, over a low fire until the tomatoes are very soft, 20 to 25 minutes. Increase heat and boil off remaining liquid.

Meanwhile, hard-cook 2 of the eggs. Beat remaining eggs well and season with salt and pepper. Add beaten eggs to tomatoes in saucepan, cover, and cook over a low fire until eggs are well set. Garnish with sliced hard-cooked eggs.

*Tajin with Mint* is a combination lamb and egg dish with a custard texture. In North Africa, when a woman must bake a dish like this one and has no oven, she places a sheet of tin piled with burning coals on the lid of the casserole on the stove so the dish is cooked from both top and bottom at the same time.

## TAJIN WITH MINT

*½ pound boneless lamb fillet, in 1-inch cubes*
*¼ teaspoon each cloves and cinnamon*
*¼ cup oil*
*1 large onion, sliced*
*2 medium tomatoes, peeled*
*1 cup canned kidney beans, drained*
*⅓ cup grated Swiss cheese*
*½ cup dried bread crumbs*
*7 or 8 dried mint leaves, crushed to powder*
*6 eggs, beaten*
*Salt to taste*

6 servings

Dampen meat with a little water and season with cloves and cinnamon. Heat oil in a heavy stewing pan; add seasoned meat and onions and sauté until golden. Add the tomatoes which have been crushed with a little water. Simmer over a low fire until meat is tender, adding the beans in the last 30 minutes.

Combine grated cheese, bread crumbs, and mint and add to beaten eggs. Season with salt. Mix egg mixture into stewing pan, and bake in a moderate oven (350° F.) until eggs are very well set and look like a custard. Run under the broiler for a few minutes until nicely browned on top. Turn out onto a warm serving dish.

This omelet with chicken, called *Milina,* is served cold.

## MILINA (CHICKEN OMELET)

*1½ dozen small eggs*
*2 cups cooked chicken, finely minced*
*Salt and pepper to taste*
*Oil or butter*

6 to 8 servings

Hard-cook 4 of the eggs. Beat remaining eggs well. Beat in minced chicken and season with salt and pepper. Grease a 2-quart, oven-proof dish. Pour in egg mixture. Place the 4 peeled, whole, hard-cooked eggs in the mixture. Bake in a moderate oven (350° F.) 45 minutes or until completely set. Cool.

To serve, turn out of dish and cut in wedge-shaped pieces.

## COUSCOUS

*Couscous,* as I've noted, is the staple in the diet of much of North Africa's population. It *is* the whole day-in-day-out family meal; it is included as the culminating meat dish in an elaborate *diffa.*

Literally, *couscous* refers to the starch of this dish—semolina, which is wheat, millet, or rice (or a combination of all three) coarsely milled so the grains are crushed into granules. It comes in various grades from coarse to fine.

According to one food expert quoted in *Larousse Gastronomique,* the name is an onomatopoeic word emulating the sound the steam makes as the semolina cooks. In the preparation of this dish, the semolina is always steamed, usually on top of the pot in which the *tajin* is cooking. The North

African housewife has a special utensil—a *couscousier*—for this process. It consists of a deep stew pot plus a commodious steamer with holes in the bottom that sits on top of the stew pot. Stores carrying gourmet cookware have these *couscousiers* imported from France.

The *tajin* served with the *couscous* is a true stew in the sense that it contains anything and everything the family has on hand or can afford—just vegetables, one meat or many. In restaurants or for guests in the home, it usually includes chicken, lamb, *and* beef.

The cooking of the *couscous* is time-consuming and a bit complicated. It is of the utmost importance that the semolina never be permitted to come in contact with the boiling liquid itself.

There is on the market "instant" *couscous*—all you do is add boiling water, toss with butter, and serve. I recommend this convenience product—it certainly cuts the preparation time without sacrificing the proper flavor. However, for those who like to cook from scratch, I'm including the method from the beginning.

Eating *couscous* with the fingers is an art the North African learns from childhood—and he has to start that early in order to perfect it! With three fingers of the right hand (always the right) the North African takes a pinch of the *couscous* and deftly rolls it into a compact ball. He then passes it through the dish with the *tajin*, picking up some of the vegetables and meat on the way, and pops it into his mouth. Sounds simple, but just try it once before picking up your spoon.

Plan on inviting several couples in to dinner when serving this. It's almost easier to prepare *couscous* in bulk than in family-sized portions.

This particular version is taken from an Algerian recipe.

## ALGERIAN COUSCOUS

*2 pounds shoulder of lamb, cubed*
*1 large fryer chicken, including gizzard, cut into pieces*
*Olive oil*
*Salt and pepper to taste*
*2½ pounds onions (preferably Spanish onions)*
*1 pound carrots, cut in pieces*
*1 pound leeks, cut in pieces*
*2 pounds medium or fine semolina* (couscous)
*Butter*
*1½ cups raisins*
*1½ pounds ground beef*
*1 clove garlic, chopped*
*1 egg*
*Flour*
*1 pound turnips, cut in pieces*
*1½ pounds zucchini, cut in pieces*
*1 pound green peppers, seeded and cut in pieces*
*1½ pounds tomatoes, peeled and cut in pieces*
*½ head cabbage, cut in pieces*
*2 1-pound cans chick peas, drained*
*1 or 2 chili peppers, ground*
*½ teaspoon each cumin, coriander, and chopped parsley*
*Pinch saffron*
*1 tablespoon lemon juice*

10 to 12 servings

Lacking a *couscous* cooker, you will need a heavy stewing pan or dutch oven deep enough to hold the meats and vegetables, plus a colander or steamer on top for steaming the semolina.

Brown the lamb and chicken pieces in a little olive oil; season with salt and pepper.

Put browned meats (with any remaining oil) into stewing pan with 1 onion, cut in pieces, carrots, and leeks. Cover with water, cover, bring to a boil, and then reduce heat to simmer.

Take enough of the *couscous* to cover the bottom of the colander or steamer to a depth of about 1½ inches. Moisten lightly with cold, salted water, tossing the grains with the hands so all are moistened and the grains swell uniformly. Place the colander or steamer on top of the stewing pot, taking care the *couscous* does not come in contact with the cooking liquid. Seal edges by wrapping with a dampened, floured cloth so no steam escapes. (If the colander or steamer holes are too large to contain the *couscous*, wrap *couscous* lightly in cheesecloth before placing in the colander.) Cover and let steam 35 to 40 minutes.

Meanwhile, mince remaining onions and sauté slowly in 4 tablespoons butter until they are soft. Salt lightly. Keep warm. Simmer raisins in 1 cup water about 30 minutes. Drain and keep warm. Season ground beef with salt and pepper. Mix with chopped garlic and egg. Form into small balls, dust lightly with flour, and brown well in butter. Keep hot.

Remove *couscous* from top of stewing pan (re-cover pan and continue simmering stew while proceeding with next steps). Wet *couscous* well with cold water, then drain. Stir through with a wooden spoon. Put in a bowl and add ½ cup water salted with 1 teaspoon salt. Work with hands, pulling apart and tossing lightly so the water penetrates each grain and the *couscous* swells. Repeat process with more salted water until semolina is well saturated. Set aside.

Cook remaining semolina as before, adding the first batch of semolina in four or five portions and mixing well after each addition.

When stew has been simmering 1 hour, add the turnips,

zucchini, green peppers, tomatoes, cabbage, and chick peas.

When all the *couscous* has been cooked, the vegetables and meat should be tender (total cooking time for the *tajin* is between 1½ and 2 hours). Remove *couscous* from steamer and toss with ¼ pound butter, mixing lightly until butter is melted. Place *couscous* on a large dish, forming it into a mound. Make a good-sized well in the center. Place the chicken and lamb pieces in the well and surround with the sautéed onions. Sprinkle the raisins over all and arrange the meat balls on the *couscous.* Serve the vegetables with the cooking liquid, which has previously been reduced somewhat over a high fire, in a separate dish.

Pass with the *couscous* a sauce made of the chili peppers, cumin, coriander, parsley, and saffron mixed with ½ cup of the cooking liquid, 2 tablespoons olive oil, and 1 tablespoon lemon juice. This sauce is called *Harisa.* It is available canned in some specialty food stores.

Without the hot pepper sauce, the Algerian *couscous* would be very pallid. Here's another version in which the "heat" is cooked in.

## LAMB COUSCOUS

*1 leg of lamb, cut in 2-inch cubes*
*3 cloves garlic, chopped*
*3 chili peppers, chopped*
*2 tablespoons paprika*
*1 tablespoon oil*
*Salt and pepper to taste*
*1 tablespoon parsley*
*1½ teaspoons chopped chervil*
*1½ to 2 pounds* couscous
*6 tablespoons butter*

10 to 12 servings

Place all ingredients except *couscous* and butter in a deep stewing pot. Barely cover with water, bring to a boil, and reduce heat to simmer. Cook for a total of about 1½ hours, preparing the *couscous* as described in *Algerian Couscous.*

When both *couscous* and stew are finished, toss *couscous* with butter and some of the cooking liquid. Arrange the *couscous* on a large dish, place the meat on top, and pass the cooking sauce separately.

You may, of course, add any vegetables you wish to the stew.

## FISH

Fish is not terribly popular in North Africa. Problems of transportation and refrigeration limit the consumption of fresh fish to the coastal areas or along rivers. Even along the miles of the Atlantic and Mediterranean shores, it's not exactly a best-seller.

Frying is a favored cooking method when fish is served.

### FRIED MULLET

*12 small red mullets or other fatty fish, cleaned but left whole*
*1 to 2 tablespoons flour*
*1 egg, beaten*
*Oil*
*Salt and pepper to taste*
*1 pound tomatoes, peeled and halved*
*2 cloves garlic, minced*
*2 lemons, sliced* — 6 servings

Roll fish in flour and then in egg. Fry in hot oil until golden brown and cooked through. Drain and season with salt and pepper.

Meanwhile sauté tomatoes and minced garlic in 4 tablespoons oil. Place tomatoes on a plate, top with fried mullets, and garnish with lemon slices.

## FRIED SHAD

*1½ pounds shad, cod, sea perch, whitefish, or catfish fillets*
*1 teaspoon salt*
*2 cloves garlic, chopped*
*½ tablespoon dried coriander or ½ teaspoon ground coriander*
*1 tablespoon paprika*
*⅛ teaspoon cayenne*
*1 teaspoon cumin*
*4 tablespoons lemon juice*
*Flour*
*Oil or fat* 6 servings

Cut the fillets into pieces. Combine salt, garlic, coriander, paprika, cayenne, cumin, and lemon juice. Marinate fish in this mixture several hours.

To cook, drain fish pieces well, roll in flour, and fry in hot fat until well browned.

Serve hot or cold.

In Egypt, hake or cod is sometimes served cold in an aspic made of the cooking liquid.

## FISH IN ASPIC

*2 pounds hake or cod*
*3 or 4 tablespoons oil*
*1 clove garlic, sliced*

*1 cup water*
*3 tablespoons lemon juice*
*Chopped parsley*
*Salt and pepper to taste*

6 to 8 servings

Cut fish into slices 1-inch thick. Heat oil in a shallow frying pan. Brown garlic, then lightly brown fish. Add water mixed with lemon juice and parsley. Season to taste. Cover and simmer about 25 minutes. Cool and chill in refrigerator until the cooking juices jell.

A whole fish filled with stuffed dates is an unusual combination. The dates available in Fez, where this dish is popular, are large and very dark and marvelously tasty. Use the largest you can find.

## BAKED SHAD WITH STUFFED DATES

*1 pound large dates*
*½ cup rice or semolina, cooked and cooled*
*¼ pound almonds, chopped*
*1 tablespoon sugar*
*6 tablespoons butter*
*½ teaspoon cinnamon*
*½ teaspoon pepper*
*Pinch ginger*
*1 large whole shad (or other fatty fish)*
*⅓ cup water*
*Pinch salt*
*½ medium onion, finely chopped*

8 to 10 servings

Pit dates. Combine cold rice, almonds, sugar, 2 tablespoons butter, cinnamon, pinch each pepper and ginger. Stuff dates with this mixture. Fill cavity of whole fish with stuffed dates. Sew up or fasten opening carefully.

Place fish in baking dish and pour over it a mixture of ⅓ cup water, pepper, salt, ginger, and chopped onions. Bake in a slow oven (325° F.) until fish is done, about 40 minutes. Undo cavity, carefully remove dates, and arrange around the fish. Dust all with cinnamon and return to oven until fish is crisp and brown, the water has evaporated but the pan juices remain, and the dates are soft. It may be necessary to increase oven heat.

A thick chowder of fish, similar to bouillabaisse, is sometimes served in Tunisia. It is much more peppery than the French counterpart; adjust the cayenne and pepper amounts to suit your taste.

## MARGAT EL HOUT

*2 teaspoons salt*
*2 tablespoons cumin*
*2 cloves garlic*
*½ cup oil*
*1 large onion, sliced*
*1 to 2 tablespoons cayenne, or to taste*
*1 pound tomatoes, peeled and quartered*
*2 to 4 cups water*
*2 pounds fish, boned*
*1 tablespoon pepper, or to taste* 6 servings

In a mortar, crush salt, cumin, and garlic together.

Heat oil in a stewing pan and brown onion until golden. Add cayenne moistened with 2 tablespoons water and the garlic mixture. Add tomatoes and stir. Sauté at a moderate heat until tomatoes are well cooked. Add water and bring to a boil. Add fish and pepper. Simmer over a low heat just until the fish is tender.

## SALADS AND VEGETABLES

For the vast majority of North African housewives, tomatoes, onions, and dried legumes are about the only vegetables to bother about. The tomatoes and onions, as you've noticed, are present in almost every *tajin*.

Most of the Maghreb is extremely arid, if not downright desert, a condition inhospitable to farming. The nomadic life of most of these people doesn't lend itself to frequent stocking of fresh produce, either.

Salad greens and vegetables are grown in the fertile coastal crescent, which is where the heaviest concentration of European colonials was. It's not surprising that under the French influence, particularly, a greater variety of vegetables found their way into North African kitchens. However, vegetables and salads as separate courses are still not wildly popular even in the coastal regions.

At large feasts, salads are passed so the palate can be cooled and soothed between the rich main dishes as well as for a change in texture (to feed the sense of touch). Some are designed just to stress the texture difference, since they can be highly seasoned, too.

Some of these combinations of ingredients and seasonings may seem distressingly odd, but they are surprisingly tantalizing and, red and black pepper notwithstanding, refreshing.

### BLACK OLIVE SALAD

*7 ounces pitted Moroccan-style olives*
*3 lemons or 3 oranges, peeled, seeded, and diced*

*Cayenne to taste*
*Pinch cumin* 6 to 8 servings

Combine olives and lemons or oranges. Mix a pinch of cumin with cayenne to taste (North Africans would use a lot, at least ½ teaspoon). Toss in the spices carefully just before serving. No dressing of any kind is needed.

## SALAD MÉLANGE

*½ pound onions*
*¾ pound tart apples (optional)*
*¾ pound tomatoes*
*½ pound green peppers*
*¾ pound cucumber*
*2 tablespoons lemon juice*
*Olive oil*
*Salt to taste*
*Dried mint, powdered, to taste*

8 to 10 servings

Peel onions and apples. Wash but do not peel tomatoes, peppers, and cucumbers. Seed the peppers. Cut all into 1-inch cubes. Mix and toss with lemon juice and a little oil. Season with salt and dried mint to taste.

## RADISH SALAD

*1 bunch radishes*
*Sugar*
*1 orange, peeled, seeded, and cut into small pieces*
*Lemon juice*
*Pinch salt*

4 to 6 servings

Grate unpeeled radishes. Sprinkle well with sugar. Mix in orange pieces. Just before serving, toss with lemon juice and season with a pinch of salt.

## COOKED CARROT SALAD

*1 pound carrots*
*3 cloves garlic*
*Pinch salt*
*Pinch sugar*
*Lemon juice*
*¼ to ½ teaspoon cayenne*
*¼ teaspoon cumin*
*Chopped parsley*

6 servings

Scrape carrots and quarter lengthwise. Cook in a little water with garlic and pinch each salt and sugar, for 15 minutes. Drain and chill.

Just before serving, cover with lemon juice, about ¼ teaspoon salt, cayenne, and cumin. Sprinkle with chopped parsley.

## ORANGE SALAD

*3 oranges, peeled, seeded, and cut into large pieces*
*2 teaspoons distilled orange flower water*
*Cinnamon*

4 servings

Toss orange pieces with the flower water. Sprinkle lightly with ground cinnamon. Serve immediately.

## LETTUCE SALAD

*1 small head lettuce, shredded*
*¾ cup orange juice*
*Pinch salt*
*1½ teaspoons pepper, or to taste*

6 to 8 servings

Toss lettuce with orange juice. Season with a pinch of salt and pepper.

## MARINATED CUCUMBER AND PEPPER SALAD

*2 pounds cucumbers*
*Salt*
*5 green peppers*
*Pepper to taste*
*2 tablespoons lemon juice*
*Olive oil*
*2 hard-cooked eggs*

8 to 10 servings

Peel cucumbers. Seed and cut into very thin slices, season with salt, and let stand in a colander to drain over a bowl in the refrigerator 12 hours.

Press out all remaining water gently and pat dry with a towel. Seed green peppers and cut into thin slices. Mix cucumbers and peppers and toss with pepper, lemon juice, and a little oil. Let marinate 2 hours.

To serve, place vegetables on platter and garnish with eggs, quartered.

Vegetables, when they *are* served as a separate course, are also well spiced.

## LOUBIA (SPICED BEANS)

*2 pounds dried beans (lima, great northern, or navy), soaked overnight and drained*
*Salt to taste*
*½ teaspoon cumin*
*1 tablespoon paprika*
*½ teaspoon cayenne*
*¼ teaspoon cloves*
*2 cloves garlic*
*1 tablespoon olive oil*

8 to 10 servings

Place beans in a large pot and cover with cold salted water. Bring to a boil slowly, skim, and simmer until done, about 2 hours. Time cooking so beans are ready about 20 minutes before serving; drain. Combine cumin, paprika, cayenne, cloves, garlic, and oil. Mash until garlic is crushed. Combine with beans, tossing well to mix.

*Foul* (pronounced "fool") is an Egyptian dish, calling for a spicy sauce to dress up the beans. *Foul* is a broad bean and may be bought canned at specialty food stores. If unavailable, use dried lima beans, soaked overnight, then cooked until very soft. Should the canned *foul* be too firm, cook them in stock made of boiling water and a chicken or beef bouillon cube until they are soft.

## FOUL

*1 can* foul *beans*
*3 onions, finely chopped*
*1 clove garlic, chopped*
*4 tablespoons oil*

*2 tablespoons catsup*
*1 tablespoon flour*
*4 tablespoons lemon juice*
*½ teaspoon paprika*
*Pinch cayenne*
*Salt to taste*
*Stock (from cooking the beans)*

4 to 6 servings

Cook *foul*, if necessary, until very soft. Drain, reserving the liquid.

Sauté onions and garlic in hot oil until golden. Remove from heat. Combine catsup, flour, and lemon juice. Add to onions. Return pan to heat and stir in paprika, cayenne, and salt to taste. Bring to a boil, stirring constantly. Add enough stock (or liquid from the canned *foul* if they didn't need further cooking) to make a sauce that's creamy but not too thick. Combine sauce and beans and mix well. Serve hot or cold.

The long, slow *tajin* cooking method is sometimes carried over to vegetable cookery. This virtually reduces the vegetables to a mush which is often served cold—almost what we'd consider a relish.

## VEGETABLE MÉLANGE

*1¼ pounds eggplant*
*½ pound zucchini*
*1 pound tomatoes*
*½ pound green peppers*
*1 clove garlic*
*⅓ cup olive oil*
*Salt and pepper to taste*

*2 tablespoons capers*
*Black and green olives*

6 to 8 servings

Peel eggplant and zucchini. Plunge tomatoes and peppers into boiling water a few moments until skin loosens. Peel and seed both.

Slice the vegetables into uniform slices. Place in a large heavy pan which has been rubbed with the garlic. Drizzle with oil and season with salt and pepper. Cover and cook over a very low fire 1½ hours. (Note: Vegetables are to cook in their own juices and the oil. Add water *only* to prevent scorching.) Add capers and olives and mix. Refrigerate. Serve cold.

In certain parts of North Africa, rice is more popular than semolina. Egypt is one place this is so, and that's where the mixture known as *Pacha Rice* comes from.

## PACHA RICE

*1 onion, finely chopped*
*3 tablespoons butter*
*1 clove garlic, chopped*
*¼ teaspoon turmeric*
*Pinch each thyme, coriander, basil, and cayenne*
*Salt and pepper to taste*
*6 tablespoons each chopped almonds and seedless raisins*
*1¼ cups rice*
*¼ pound vermicelli or spaghetti*
*1 tablespoon oil*

6 servings

Sauté onion in butter until golden brown. Stir in garlic, turmeric, thyme, coriander, basil, cayenne, and salt and pepper to taste. Add chopped almonds, raisins, and rice. Add enough water necessary to cook the rice, 1½ to 2 cups. Cover and simmer on a low fire until rice is done, 30 to 40 minutes.

Meanwhile, break up vermicelli into pieces. Cook very briefly, about 3 minutes, drain, and rinse under cold water. Heat oil in pan and sauté vermicelli over low heat until golden, about 5 minutes. Stir vermicelli into cooked rice and continue cooking 5 minutes to blend.

Leftovers are a mark of an affluent society; it's rare indeed to find recipes using leftover meat in the developing nations. Occasionally, though, the North African housewife will have a little lamb left over when a whole one has been roasted for a ceremonial occasion. In Tunisia she frequently uses it to make vegetables more palatable, as in this casserole.

## CASSEROLE OF EGGPLANT WITH TOMATO

*1¼ pounds eggplant*
*4 tablespoons olive oil, divided*
*1 cup chopped leftover roast lamb*
*1 large onion, chopped*
*¾ pound tomatoes, peeled, seeded, and diced*
*Salt and pepper to taste*
*1 clove garlic, crushed*
*1 tablespoon each dried parsley and dried celery or to taste*
*½ teaspoon dried rosemary*
*1 8-ounce can tomato sauce*
*2 eggs, hard-cooked and quartered*

6 servings

Peel eggplant and slice thinly lengthwise. Heat 2 tablespoons oil in a saucepan and brown the eggplant. Drain on paper towels.

Combine chopped meat and chopped onion. Add diced tomatoes. Add remaining oil to the pan used for browning eggplant and sauté meat mixture until brown. Season with salt and pepper.

Grease a casserole dish and layer the eggplant and meat mixture alternately, starting with eggplant, until all is used up.

Mix garlic, parsley, celery, and rosemary into the tomato sauce. Bring just to a boil. Pour over casserole and bake in a slow oven (300° F.) 1 hour.

Garnish with quartered eggs.

## CAKES AND PASTRY

North African cakes and pastries are every bit as rich and voluptuous as the rest of the cuisine. And they're generally very sweet. North Africans have a passion for the sugary that easily rivals that of a Viennese matron.

Almonds, ground into paste, are a favored filling for cookies and small cakes that may be baked or fried in deep fat. A fried cake similar to our doughout is found all across the Maghreb, dripping with sugar or honey syrup and the remains of the frying oil. Many of the confections contain the juicy dates that grow there. In the eastern regions, they gobble *Konafa,* a mixture of nuts, sugar, and what looks like shredded wheat.

Gazelle Horns—*Kab el Ghzal*—are a crescent-shaped, filled cooky traditionally served to guests at the end of dinner. Custom demands that the offering be accepted, even if it means taking it home for later munching.

## KAB EL GHZAL

*½ to 1 cup confectioners' sugar*
*Orange flower water*
*2½ tablespoons butter*
*½ pound almond paste*
*3¼ cups sifted flour (about)*
*4 ounces (1 stick) butter, melted*
*1 egg, beaten*
*Pinch salt*
*Sugar*

3 to 4 dozen

Work confectioners' sugar, a little orange flower water for perfume, and 2½ tablespoons butter into almond paste. Mix well into a smooth, oily paste. (Add more butter if paste is too dry.)

Combine flour, melted butter, egg, a little salt, and enough water to make a supple dough about the consistency of bread dough (add more flour if necessary). Knead well.

Lightly grease a pastry board, rolling pin, and fingers. Take a piece of the dough and roll out with the pin, then stretch with the hands until the dough is quite thin, about like thin cardboard. Cut into about 4-inch squares. Roll some of the almond paste between the palms into a sausage shape and lay on the square diagonally. Roll up pastry and form into a crescent. Each crescent should be about the thickness of a finger. Regrease hands, pin, and board between each rolling-out. Lay crescents on ungreased baking sheets and bake in a moderate oven (350° F.) until the pastry is lightly browned, 20 to 30 minutes. Should the dough puff up too much in baking, prick with a pin.

If desired, roll in granulated sugar when still warm.

*El Menenas* are another kind of almond-paste cooky. This recipe comes from Egypt.

## EL MENENAS

*½ pound almond paste*
*¾ cup sugar*
*2 teaspoons orange flower water*
*Ground cinnamon*
*⅔ cup butter, melted*
*2 cups sifted flour*

about 4 dozen

To the almond paste add sugar and mix well. Add 1 teaspoon orange flower water and cinnamon to taste (at least ½ teaspoon). Blend well into a smooth paste.

In a bowl, combine melted butter and flour. Add 1 teaspoon orange flower water and knead into a dough that holds together. Do not add any water unless absolutely necessary. Form dough into balls about 1½ to 2 inches in diameter. Make a depression in the center of each ball with the thumb. Fill hole with almond paste. Place cookies on a greased baking sheet and bake in a moderate oven (375° F.) 30 minutes or until nicely browned. Sprinkle with granulated sugar.

VARIATION: A date filling may be substituted for the almond paste. Chop finely ½ pound pitted dates and combine into a paste with 4 tablespoons soft butter.

In Morocco, a popular almond-paste delicacy is called *Mhanncha,* which means snake. The origin of the name is obvious since the pastry is formed into a large coil.

## MHANNCHA

*½ pound almond paste*
*½ to 1 cup confectioners' sugar*
*1 teaspoon orange flower water*
*2½ tablespoons butter*
*1 teaspoon cinnamon*
*Frozen strudel dough, thawed*
*5 tablespoons melted butter*
*Cinnamon sugar*

3 5-inch rolls

To almond paste, add confectioners' sugar, orange flower water, butter, and cinnamon. Work with hands into a smooth, oily paste.

Spread sheets of pastry on a table overlapping to form a 24-inch square that is 2 or 3 layers deep at all points. Form the paste into long rolls about ½-inch thick. Place almond-paste roll in center of pastry, fold pastry over and roll up. Coil filled pastry around itself as tightly as possible. Place on greased baking sheet and drizzle generously with melted butter. Bake in a moderate oven (375° F.) until brown, about 30 minutes. Garnish with cinnamon sugar (1 tablespoon cinnamon to 4 tablespoons sugar).

This will keep several days, but brief heating in the oven before serving may be necessary for proper crispness.

*Sebaa el Aaroussa*—the Fiancée's Finger—is the sentimental name of these fried cookies. Perhaps the name comes from the shape or maybe it's because they drip with honey.

## SEBAA EL AAROUSSA

*3½ cups sifted flour*
*½ teaspoon salt*

*⅓ cup sugar*
*2 eggs, beaten*
*Oil*
*⅔ cup honey*

about 3 to 4 dozen

Place flour in a bowl and make a well in the center. In the well, place salt, sugar, and eggs. Mix with a spoon, then with the hands to make a firm dough. Add a little water *only* if necessary. Roll out on a floured board to about ¼-inch thickness. Cut into strips about 2 inches long. Roll each piece on a floured board into a finger shape. Fry in hot, deep fat just until golden, turning to brown on all sides. Drain briefly, then roll in honey.

These may be served hot or cold.

Dates and almonds are sometimes used together. Here are two versions of a popular cake-like treat.

## DATE CAKE

*1⅓ cups chopped dates*
*2 cups finely chopped almonds (packaged in some stores as almond meal)*
*4 eggs, separated*
*1 cup sugar*

2 8-inch cakes
or 1 9-by-13 cake

Toss chopped dates with almond meal until dates are well coated and don't stick together.

In a bowl start beating egg yolks and then slowly add sugar and then almond-date mixture. Beat egg whites until firm peaks form. Gently fold into date mixture. Bake in two well-greased 8-inch cake pans or one 13-by-9-inch pan in a slow oven (275° F.) until cake shrinks from side of pan, 1 to 1½ hours. Cool in pan 15 minutes, then turn out and cool on racks.

This next recipe sounds like simply a richer version of *Date Cake,* but its texture is more cake-like.

## DJAMILAH

*1½ cups chopped dates*
*1 cup almond meal*
*4 eggs, separated*
*1⅓ cups confectioners' sugar*
*¼ teaspoon vanilla*
*4 tablespoons butter, melted*
*¼ cup flour*

1 8- or 9-inch cake

Toss chopped dates with almond meal until dates are well coated and don't stick together.

Combine egg yolks, sugar, and vanilla and beat well, about 5 minutes. Add melted butter and date-and-almond mixture and mix well. Mix in flour. Fold in egg whites which have been beaten until firm peaks form. Bake in a well-greased 8- or 9-inch cake pan in a hot oven (425° F.) 20 to 30 minutes or until cake shrinks from edge of pan.

Across North Africa, you'll find many versions of doughnuts. Most often they're glazed with honey and sometimes further embellished with chopped nuts.

As with almost all their confections, North African doughnuts are sweet. However, one variety, *Sfenj,* which is a breakfast favorite in Fez, is completely unsweetened bread dough fried in deep fat. *Sfenj* are bought by weight each morning and packaged by stringing on a length of cord. They're eaten by dunking in hot mint tea, which is sweet enough in itself.

## SFENJ

*4 cups sifted flour*
*Pinch salt*
*1 cake yeast*
*½ cup lukewarm water*
*Oil*

*1½ to 2 dozen*

Mix flour, salt, and yeast which has been dissolved in ½ cup lukewarm water. Knead well, adding water to make a very soft dough. Set aside to rise several hours.

Grease hands. Break off an egg-sized piece of dough and make a hole in the center with the finger, twirling the dough as you punch through. Drop into deep hot oil. Fry on both sides until brown. Drain.

These recipes are for the sweet varieties:

## MESSELMEN

*3 cups sifted flour*
*⅔ cup sifted confectioners' sugar*
*¼ cup olive oil*
*1 tablespoon vanilla*
*4 teaspoons baking powder*
*Oil*
*Honey*
*1 cup ground almonds*

2 to 3 dozen

Combine flour, sugar, olive oil, vanilla, and baking powder. Work carefully with hands, adding water as needed to form a very pliant dough. Roll out on a pastry board to about ¼-inch thickness. Cut into triangles or 2-inch circles. Drop into hot deep fat (375° F.) and fry until both sides are golden. Drain.

Dip drained cakes in honey and then dust with ground almonds.

## DEBLA

*3 eggs*
*⅔ cup water*
*3¼ cups sifted flour (about)*
*Oil*
*¾ cup honey*
*1 teaspoon lemon juice*

about 3½ dozen

Beat eggs in a bowl, add water, and then slowly add the flour to obtain a dough thick enough to knead and then roll out. Flour a pastry board and roll out dough, portion by portion, until it is very thin. Cut into strips and roll up. Fry in deep hot fat (375° F.) until golden. These cakes cook fast; fry a few at a time and remove from fat as soon as they are golden. Drain well.

Make a syrup of honey, a little water, and lemon juice. Heat. Dip the drained cakes in the syrup and cool.

## MAKROUD

*1 pound pitted dates*
*Cinnamon*
*Peel of ½ orange, very finely chopped*

*1 pound semolina flour*
*⅓ cup lukewarm water (about)*
*2 teaspoons baking soda*
*Oil*
*Honey*

about 4 to 5 dozen

Chop the dates and sprinkle with cinnamon. Combine with chopped orange peel. Mix into a smooth paste.

Place semolina flour in a large bowl. Heat ⅔ cup oil and pour over. Cut in oil with a fork until the grains are impregnated with the oil. Add warm water and baking soda. The dough should be soft; add more water if necessary.

On a pastry board, pat out the dough with the hands to a square about ¼-inch thick. Cut into strips about 3 inches wide. Spoon some of the date mixture along one side of each strip; fold each strip over and press down firmly with the hand. (Each strip will now be 1½ inches wide.) Cut slantwise into 2-inch pieces. Fry in very hot oil until golden. Drain and dip in warm honey.

*Konafa* gets its name from the long, thread-like noodles used for the crust. It is a confection enjoyed widely all over the eastern Mediterranean. (In Greece, it is called *Kateifi.*) The *Konafa* noodles look a great deal like shredded wheat. In fact, the English translations of menus in Greece and Turkey often list "shredded wheat" under desserts, and some version of the Egyptian *Konafa* is what is meant.

There's more to it than the noodles, of course. Sandwiched in between the crusts is a chewy layer of nuts and cinnamon. The North African housewife rarely makes the noodles herself. They're sold in the market place from pushcarts heaped high with the yellowish-white threads. As supplies dwindle, the *Konafa* seller bakes some more on a large griddle, dribbling the dough in long, snaky patterns from a batter container with holes in the bottom.

Shredded wheat, however, is an acceptable substitute for those who wish to make *Konafa* here. Or, if they are obtainable, try the very thin Japanese noodles available at some Oriental food shops.

## KONAFA

*2½ cups sugar*
*1 cup water*
*½ teaspoon lemon juice*
*2 cups finely chopped walnuts*
*2 tablespoons cinnamon*
*12 shredded-wheat biscuits (10-ounce box)*
*1¼ cups unsalted butter*

one 9-inch *Konafa*

Combine 2 cups sugar and water in a small saucepan. Bring to boiling and cook over low heat until syrup is slightly thickened, 15 to 20 minutes. Remove from heat and add lemon juice. Cool.

Mix walnuts, cinnamon, and remaining sugar in a bowl.

Crumble shredded-wheat biscuits. (If they do not break up easily, dip biscuits in warm milk briefly and then mash up.) Melt 7 tablespoons butter in a large frying pan and lightly sauté shredded wheat. Add more butter if necessary to make sure shredded wheat becomes limp. Into a 9-inch cake pan which has been *generously* greased, press half the shredded wheat firmly to form a crust. Spread walnut mixture over crust, then form remaining shredded wheat over the walnuts to make a top crust, pressing well with hands. Pour over remaining butter, melted. Bake in a moderate oven (375° F.) 30 to 35 minutes or until edges are nicely browned. Remove from oven and pour half the cooled sugar syrup over.

This may be served warm or cold with some of the remaining syrup spooned over each slice. This is extremely rich, so don't be too generous in your servings.

A while back, Alice B. Toklas caused a bit of a stir at Kaffeeklatsches on several continents because her cookbook included a cooky recipe calling for hashish. I doubt that recipe was purely a product of the unique imagination of Gertrude Stein's friend. She probably picked up the idea, if not the recipe itself, during her travels in North Africa. There, certain confections are designed to provide both sweetness and a bit of euphoria. In a culture that prohibits alcohol, these goodies serve the function that, say, a bourbon and water does in the Western world.

In Fez, this delicacy is called *Majoun*, a round, slightly gooey candy. It's supposed to lift not only the spirits but the libido as well. The recipe includes hashish plus cantharides, the supposedly aphrodisiac Spanish Fly. How much of a glow you get depends on how potent a *Majoun* you can afford.

Availability of ingredients being what they are, this treat would be hard to duplicate here—not only for the hashish and cantharides but for the special *Ras el Hanout* and shelled acorns. For the record, though, it goes something like this:

## MAJOUN

*1 pound almonds browned in butter*
*½ pound walnuts*
*¼ cup shelled acorns*
*Several cantharides*
*1 pound seeded raisins, finely chopped*
*½ teaspoon ginger*
*1 teaspoon special* Ras el Hanout

*½ pound honey*
*½ pound butter*
*Hashish (to taste)*
*Sesame seed*

Combine almonds, walnuts, acorns (you need special ones; many ordinary acorns are toxic), and cantharides and pound into a fine powder. Add chopped raisins, ginger, and special *Ras el Hanout*. Mix and mash well. Add honey and butter and cook over a low fire until thick, like jam. Add hashish to taste. Cool enough to handle and form into walnut-sized balls. Roll in sesame seed.

Yield: enough.

## BEVERAGES

Generally, North Africans do not drink anything with their meals, except perhaps water occasionally. As would be expected in arid areas, plain water, well chilled, is a treat. The water seller is a fixture in the market places of the *medinas*. He circulates through the crowds, festooned with hammered brass cups, dispensing water from a sheepskin container which cools the water by condensation.

Since the Koran expressly prohibits the drinking of alcohol in any form, Moslems are teetotalers, and in North Africa, certainly, they "total" a lot of tea. Cafés and bars dispense teas in various forms, and men congregate to chat and sip at all hours. These bars and cafés serve the same social function as our taverns, except that rarely is the clientele other than entirely male. In Egypt, tea is most often served flavored just with sugar. Algerians largely prefer green tea with a slight flavoring of mint. In Morocco, green tea is brewed with a heavy dose of fresh mint.

In fact, the making of mint tea is a highly formalized art in Morocco. It's usually the host's prerogative to make the tea at the end of the meal; in restaurants, one man (it's always a man) does nothing but sit in a place of honor in the middle of the room making tea for the diners. Host or specialist, he performs the task with great ceremony and serious concentration.

The equipment consists of a samovar of hot water, a teapot, separate containers of tea, loaf sugar, and mint, and a small hammer for breaking up the sugar pieces. All the pots and containers are of brass or, preferably, silver, and heavily chased. The tea, mint, and sugar are combined and brewed, and the host continuously tastes and adjusts until he feels the infusion is just right. And for Moroccans, "just right" is a fragrant mixture that is as sweet as possible but with the blended taste of tea and mint still discernible, if only barely.

## MINT TEA

*Boiling water*
*1½ tablespoons green tea*
*1 handful fresh mint leaves and stalks*
*1⅓ cups sugar cubes*

for 4 persons, 3 servings each

Rinse out a 3-cup teapot with hot water. Add tea. Pour in ½ cup boiling water, swish around in pot quickly, and empty water (leaving the tea in the pot, of course). This is supposed to remove any bitterness from the tea. Stuff mint leaves and stalks down into the pot and add sugar. Fill pot with boiling water. Let steep 5 to 8 minutes, checking occasionally to be sure the mint doesn't rise above the water. Stir, taste, adding sugar if necessary. Serve traditionally in small glasses set in silver holders.

For second helpings, the Moroccan would leave the mint and the tea in the pot, add a teaspoon of tea and several mint leaves, plus about a cup of sugar cubes and fill again with boiling water. When the mint rises to the surface, it's ready to stir and taste for sugar and serve. The same process is repeated for a third pot; custom requires three helpings be offered and three helpings accepted.

Fruit juices are also popular. Grape juice, lemon juice sweetened with sugar, orange juice, and pomegranate juice diluted with water are particular favorites. All are usually perfumed with several dashes of orange flower water. Chilled coconut milk is also seasonally available.

Something called *Almond Milk* is particularly refreshing in hot weather. It's always served very cold.

## ALMOND MILK

*1 pound blanched almonds*
*1 cup sugar*
*4 cups water*
*Several dashes orange flower water*

4 servings

Reduce almonds to a paste. Combine in a blender with sugar, water, and orange flower water. Process until well mixed. Strain and chill until very cold.

# WEST AFRICA

WHENEVER I THINK ABOUT AFRICA, I realize it's West Africa that always pops to mind first. For me, West Africa is more "African" than the rest of the continent. Perhaps that's because it is more like what I imagined all of Africa to be before I went there.

West Africa can be hot—blasted hot. The humidity can be horrendous. Many places along the coast are thick with rain forests and palm trees. The West African scene is colorful and lively. Both men and women adore color and choose riotous prints, mixed and matched, for their clothes. There's always a lot of movement in the streets and the market places, and yet it's a relaxed, easy going sort of business atmosphere punctuated with humor, high spirits, and much laughter.

The ambiance varies, of course. In Dakar, the capital of Senegal, most of the population are Moslems, who tend to be more reserved, dignified and aloof. But the farther south you go (actually east, since the West African states lie on the underside of the bulge), the more relaxed and friendlier everything seems to become.

Lagos, Nigeria, typified West Africa for me. It's a great, sprawling city, a jumble of modern, elegantly designed buildings sprouting tall from a thick underbrush of ancient one-storied structures and sagging lean-tos. There's a main part of town, but no real center of town; Lagos gives the impression of being laid out by someone who merely dropped ink on a map and let it spread.

All during the day, the streets are alive with activity as crowds of people jostle each other at the edges of the streets (sidewalks are found only along a very few of the streets in the main part of town). There are modern stores and markets, but most of the action is in the traditional market, an area of about eight or ten square blocks, choked with tin-roofed, bamboo-sided shanties that spread out behind some of the town's newest buildings housing things like the Bristol Hotel and the Bank of America. There, it is not at all unusual to see children running around naked or, deep in the portions where people live, to see women cooking over open fires while shooing away flocks of chickens.

In terms of food, the imprint of the former colonial traditions is quickly apparent to the visitor. In West Africa particularly, the tourist is perforce restricted to hotels and "safe" restaurants.

In the former French areas, this makes dining a usually delightful experience; French cuisine has exported quite well and prospered nicely. In some instances, the crispy, chewy French bread and flaky, light croissants are even better than you can buy in Paris these days. One of my favorite sights of Abidjan, the capital of the Ivory Coast, is of the tall, slim women in colorful native dress pedaling bikes down the main street with several long French loaves balanced on their heads.

The English-speaking countries tend to eat pallidly British, except for the traditional weekend curry lunch. This institution was firmly established all over former British Africa—East and West—by the long-ago colonial officers, many of whom had served in India before being assigned to an African post. So today, at any large hotel—be it in Accra, Lagos, Freetown, Lusaka, or Nairobi—the sweet-spicy smell of curry fills the dining rooms at midday on Saturday and Sunday. Some hotels offer a regional dish at noon, too—one of the endless varieties of starches and stews, the area's dietary staple. The vast majority of people in that developing part of the world live on subsistence agriculture, eating what they grow on the usually poor soil. Theirs is a monotonous diet, generally quite deficient in protein. Tropical fruits—papaya, pineapple, mangoes—are easily available in many places, but some peoples are denied their benefits because of superstitions and food taboos.

These fruits, fortunately, are not denied the visitor. At breakfast, he may be offered pineapple, *pawpaw* (the word for papaya), and mangoes, and if he likes all three as much as I, he will sample them all.

Our interesting gustatory experiences in West Africa are still remembered as sharp, vivid vignettes. Two were in Sierra Leone, and both involved lazy afternoons on the truly magnificent beaches around Freetown. The sands along the sheltered side of the peninsula on which the capital is built are extremely fine—so fine you make squeaky sounds like an unhappy puppy when you walk. And they are dazzingly white, a wide strip separating the deep blue (and warm) water from the dark green of the palm groves.

One Sunday, a young couple took us to a beach about ten miles out of Freetown. It was hot and the sun was bright and we had the beach to ourselves. We had come out for a quick swim and hadn't brought any refreshments along.

But just as thirst was driving us from that idyllic spot, a Sierra Leonean came along selling coconuts. He may even have picked them from the trees behind us, I don't know. Handling a murderous-looking machette as if it were a paring knife, he sliced off the top of the coconut and waited patiently while we drank the milk. Then he whacked up the shell so we could easily eat the sweet, moist nutmeat. It was the perfect snack for that perfect setting.

Another day we were guests at a picnic with the Gus Williams family. The Williamses are Creoles, descendants of the freed West Indian slaves who founded Freetown in the eighteenth century and a highly educated and sophisticated people. Mrs. Nerissa Williams was a former student of my husband and works in the Ministry of Information.

Nerissa, incidentally, epitomizes the best of Creole womanhood. She's not only a wife and mother, but a career woman as well. She's well educated and has traveled extensively in Europe. By any standards, she'd be considered handsome of face, but in American terms her ample figure would be kindly described as Wagnerian. However, in Sierra Leone (as well as in many other parts of Africa) her tall stature and generous proportions marked her as a real beauty. In fact, a well-fleshed-out woman (I hate to use the culture-bound word "fat") is so much admired that those not naturally endowed are not above padding themselves at bust and hips with layers and layers of turkish toweling.

Perhaps it is misleading to say we were on a picnic. This was no light repast; Nerissa had prepared a complete Sierra Leonean dinner and transported it intact in pots and colorful tinware swaddled in towels and newspapers to keep the hot food hot.

There was a salmon salad to start and then *Jollof Rice* (reminiscent of Spanish rice), *Garri*, and *Okra Stew*. *Garri* is grated, roasted cassava root made into a thick porridge;

cassava is quite tasteless and filling since it's largely cellulose without much food value. Unfortunately from the nutritional point of view, it is the staple for many people because it's extremely cheap and grows all over tropical Africa. *Garri* is always served with a stew of some kind, and *Okra Stew* is popular everywhere in West Africa. There's meat in it, and it's made with palm oil, which gives it the characteristic orangy-red color.

Nigeria had its moments, too. There was the evening at the home of another of my husband's former students. This was a post-dinner party, but even so, his wife provided cold roast chicken and cold roast pork, rice seasoned with thyme, fried plantain, *Moinmoin* (mashed beans, highly seasoned, and steamed), and fruit.

That night we also had our first taste of palm wine, which is the sap from one of the many varieties of palm tree that grow in Africa. (Africans, we were told, make 127 uses of palm trees—everything from eating to clothing to building.) The sap comes out of the tree, our friends insisted, already alcoholic; that particular palm contains a lot of natural yeast. The time of day the tree is tapped influences the taste and potency of the wine. Fresh from the tree, it's sometimes fed to babies because it's considered nutritious. The longer it stands, the more fermented, potent, and vinegary it becomes. Our sample had been standing awhile.

Then there were the pleasant Saturday afternoons at the Lagos Island Club, where government workers, newspapermen, lawyers, and intellectuals—almost all male—gathered on the veranda to drink Star beer and talk. There were, however, a few women, mostly female "beentos." "Beento" is a slang expression meaning someone who has *been to* the United States or Britain for schooling or work experience. Women beentos are extremely Westernized and favor European clothes, beehive wigs, and emancipated ways. In a society that is changing slowly from traditional to modern, women beentos are frequently criticized. Newspapers periodically carry pro and con stories about whether beentos, "corrupted" by Westernized societies, can possibly make good wives.

Along with the Star beer were served platters of *Pepper Chicken* and *Moinmoin. Pepper Chicken* can be made in several ways; as a snack, as it was served at the Island Club, it was roasted or charcoal-broiled. The pepper, of course, refers to the ubiquitous red pepper which is used with a heavy hand all through the western area of Africa.

We also enjoyed a memorable *Pepper Chicken* in Zaria in the Northern Region of Nigeria. It was served at Ma Bigger's, a popular night spot and one of the few such places in town. *Pepper Chicken* was the specialty of the house, and it was served along with Star beer and a charmingly inept troupe of performers from neighboring Niger.

Star beer, incidentally, is *the* drink in the former British areas of West Africa. It is light, milder than American varieties, and less bitter. The world-famous Dutch firm Heineken brews Star beer in several cities in West Africa. So widespread is its use that the Star beer bottle has become a standard of measure in West African recipes. "Add one Star beer bottle of palm oil," for instance, is a frequent direction. (On my last trip, I measured a Star beer bottle; it comes to 2¾ cups.) Another uniquely West African unit of measure is the "Player's No. 3 cigarette tin." (That's equal to about 1 cup.)

In developing countries, nothing is ever thrown away. It's merely put to another use. Cigarette tins (because of the humidity, cigarettes in any quantity were packaged in tins) and beer bottles become units of measure, storage containers, stoves, even jewelry. The people of Bida in the Northern Region of Nigeria make interesting beads from melted-down Star beer bottles—as well as milk bottles, Coke bottles, and milk-of-magnesia bottles. They're known as Bida beads, and in 1965 in an antique shop in London I saw a strand priced at $21!

As I've indicated, West Africans are extremely fond of highly seasoned food. Most often the heat is generated by red peppers, used in quantities hard to believe. A home economics teacher in Lagos gave me her recipe for *Pepper Chicken,* which calls for 4 large red peppers or 1 *tablespoon* cayenne. I need hardly add that I've cut down on the red pepper quantities in the recipes you'll find on the following pages. Red peppers have medicinal uses in West Africa, too. They are widely regarded as a cold remedy, eaten whole and uncooked, like an apple. This undeniably flushes out all eight sinus cavities as well as the tear ducts.

The preference for the spicy makes all the more puzzling the African acceptance of Anglicized cuisine, which can be experienced at its less flavorful renditions in the first-class dining cars on the Nigerian railroad. We traveled (on our first trip) by rail from Lagos to Kaduna, the capital of the Northern Region, so had experience with English-type meals that lost considerably in the translation.

The lunch and dinner menu was always the same (as it was on the return trip five days later): tepid cream-of-something soup, limp fried fish, roast chicken with roasted potatoes and overcooked Brussels sprouts, a rather dry cake inundated with custard sauce, and hard yellow cheese and crackers. Most of the passengers, however, dine during the lengthy stops at each station. When the train comes to a halt, the third- and second-class coaches empty in seconds and passengers either buy prepared *garri* and stews from the townswomen doing business at tables set up on the platform, or purchase dried fish, rice, vegetables, and fruit from women circulating through the crowds carrying their wares on their heads, and do their cooking en route on small portable stoves.

I remember the train ride, too, for my first view of a mango tree. I'd always thought mangoes grew like other tropical fruits, such as papaya or pineapple, on bushes or small trees. But at Ilorin, where the train waited out an eight-hour delay, there was a beautiful mango tree beside the platform. The station master said it was at least thirty years old—unusual for a mango, whose shallow roots make it an easy prey to winds and storms. It was over fifty feet tall and perfectly proportioned, the thick, dark green foliage forming a rounded, slightly pointed silhouette against the cloudless blue sky. The clusters of yellowish fruit at the end of the branches were just beginning to ripen.

Though fresh mangoes might be hard to come by for these recipes, they are available canned in most specialty food shops, so I've not substituted for mangoes when called for. However, I do recommend using peanut oil rather than palm oil, which is obtainable only in very well-stocked foreign food stores anyway. I doubt it would appeal to most American tastes. It's heavy, with a distinctive, strong taste which would be strange to a country where cooking oil companies vie with each other to produce a product that is lighter and more taste-free than its competitors. Also, many would find unappetizing the orangy-red color it imparts to food.

Peanut oil is widely used in West Africa, where peanuts are one of the biggest cash crops. In some circles it is preferred as being more "refined." So its use won't sacrifice too much in authenticity. However, where palm oil would be used by the average African housewife, I have listed it in the ingredients as an alternative.

As for the hot red pepper, I've included quantity for both the fresh peppers and the crushed or ground red pepper equivalent. However, I have adjusted the amounts downward, to the point where these dishes will be edible by most Americans. For greater authencity, increase the red pepper dose to your own level of tolerance. Maybe my taste buds burn out faster than yours. Actually, the ground or crushed pepper is easier to use; and in most of these recipes the fresh peppers must be ground, mashed, or finely chopped anyway.

Peppers, incidentally, come in several sizes in Africa. Generally, the smaller the pepper, the hotter it is. Some recipes require both large peppers *and* small ones. I've substituted bell peppers for bulk. The crushed red pepper or cayenne dosage will be sufficient to give the proper effect.

Courses are a luxury the average West African cannot afford, so in this chapter you'll find only a little beyond stews, starches, and vegetables. When some variety and multiplicity of dishes is available, everything is served at once, anyway. Some dishes, however, would serve very nicely as appetizers or first courses, and I've included them there.

Appetizers and cocktail party fare, incidentally, are known in West Africa as "small chop." "Chop" means food in pidgin English, a dialect still widely used in the former English areas of the region. "Palava"—to talk or discuss—also is part of the culinary lexicon. *Spinach Stew* often goes by the name of *Palava Sauce*, and a stomach upset is "tummy palava." And if a hostess asks if you wish some "small-small," she's offering you a second helping.

## APPETIZERS

One meat dish that can double as first course or entree is from Ghana and is called *Tsitsinga.* The recipe was given me by Miss Barbara Baeta, the dietician for the YWCA in Accra and the city's most successful caterer. She prepared the buffet dinner given by the American Ambassador when then Vice-President Hubert Humphrey visited Ghana in 1967.

Miss Baeta is a tall, handsome, sophisticated woman,

widely traveled, and educated in Britain. (Women "beentos" are more accepted and encouraged in Ghana and Sierra Leone than in some other countries; there is a group, comparatively sizable but still small by American standards, of professionally and politically oriented women in Ghana.) Miss Baeta is a member of a distinguished Ghanaian family, and her aunt is a judge and active in the movement to promote equality and opportunity for women.

*Tsitsinga* calls for roasted corn flour, called *ablemanu*, which is used in numerous dishes. To make your own, cut kernels from the cob and roast in a moderate oven until quite dry. Whirl in a blender until a little finer than cornmeal. Or you could toast cornmeal in a slow oven—the taste would be almost the same.

## TSITSINGA

*1 pound round steak, cut in 1-inch cubes*
*1 pint salad oil*
*2 tablespoons vinegar*
*Salt to taste*
*Tomatoes, peeled*
*Onions*
*Fresh ginger*
*3 chili peppers, or ½ to 1 tablespoon crushed red pepper, or ½ to 1 teaspoon cayenne*
*½ cup roasted corn flour*

4 to 6 servings

Marinate meat in a combination of ½ to 1 cup oil, the vinegar, and salt for at least 1 hour. Skewer meat and grill over charcoal until half done. Grind or blend enough tomatoes, onions, ginger, and peppers to make about 1 cup in all. (If using crushed red pepper or cayenne, add after grinding vegetables and ginger.) Remove meat from skewers and coat well with the vegetable mixture. Skewer meat again and roll in roasted corn flour. Dab generously with remaining oil and return to grill until done.

May be served cold with a salad for a light meal. As an entree, serve hot with rice and an *Ata* sauce.

*Moinmoin* is another dish that could begin a meal. There are many versions of *Moinmoin*—with or without tomatoes, more or less oil, hot or hotter. This recipe was given me by Mrs. Akinbehin, a home economist who was senior education officer with the Ministry of Education in Lagos. The ground dried crayfish or shrimp can be obtained in Oriental food stores. Some recipes eliminate it entirely.

## MOINMOIN

*2 1-pound cans black-eyed peas*
*2 chili peppers, or ½ tablespoon crushed red pepper, or ½ teaspoon cayenne*
*1 medium onion*
*1 tomato (optional)*
*1 tablespoon ground dried crayfish or shrimp (optional)*
*2 tablespoons palm or peanut oil, heated*
*1½ cups boiling water (about)*
*Salt to taste*

8 to 10 servings

Drain beans well and mash in a mortar or blender. Add peppers, onion, and tomato and blend until smooth. Add crayfish. Mix in heated oil and enough of the boiling water to make a soft consistency. Add salt. Place in small greased molds or baking dishes, cover tightly with foil, and steam

30 minutes to 1 hour, depending on size of the mold. When turned out, mixture should be stiff enough to hold its shape.
VARIATIONS: *Moinmoin Elede (Shrimp Moinmoin)*—add fried shrimp, minced, to bean mixture before steaming. Omit dried shrimp.

*Meat Moinmoin*—add chopped meat to bean mixture before steaming.

*Kuduru*—substitute black beans (kidney or pinto) for black-eyed peas.

*Akara* (bean cakes) is another dish in which individual tastes determine the amount of onion and pepper added. The size of the *Akara* balls or cakes will depend on whether they are to be an appetizer or a main dish.

## AKARA

*2 1-pound cans black-eyed peas*
*1 onion*
*1 teaspoon cayenne*
*Salt to taste*
*Palm or peanut oil*

8 to 10 servings

Drain peas well and mash in a blender. Place in a bowl and toss a bit to fluff. Add warm water slowly, beating constantly until the mixture is light and drops easily when shaken from a spoon, about the consistency of a thick cake batter. Mince onion very fine (or put through food grinder) and add to beans along with cayenne and salt to taste, mixing well without much further beating. Heat oil, drop mixture in by spoonfuls and fry evenly until brown. These may be deep-fat fried or shallow fried, as you prefer.
VARIATIONS: *Rich Akara*—add 2 eggs to the mashed peas

after some of the water has been added. Continue as directed, but shorten beating time.

*Akara Awon*—add 4 okras, finely minced, to the batter.

*Akara Ijesha*—cut down on the amount of water, using only enough to make the vegetables and seasonings hold together. Beat well and fry in big lumps.

*Akara Eggs*—make a thick *Akara* mixture somewhere between normal *Akara* and *Akara Ijesha.* Form mixture around whole, shelled, hard-cooked eggs. Mixture should be just thick enough to hold shape around the eggs without falling apart. Place on a spoon and lower into hot deep fat (375° F.). Fry gently until brown and drain. To serve, cut each egg in half.

*Akara Meatballs*—make a thick *Akara* mixture as for *Akara Eggs.* Combine with 1 pound ground beef and 1 egg, beaten. Form into balls and fry in oil.

Peanuts are one of Africa's largest export crops and are grown in most of the semi-dry areas all over the continent. They're called groundnuts over there and appear in many dishes.

In northern Nigeria, the Hausa people call these groundnut balls *Kulikuli,* eaten as a snack or a main dish with coconut or *Garri.*

## KULIKULI

*2 cups shelled roasted peanuts, unsalted*
*Salt to taste*
*Peanut oil*

about 46 1-inch balls

Grind the nuts very fine. Place in a clean dish towel and squeeze out as much oil as possible. Mix the nuts with salt to taste and enough warm water to make a stiff but pliable dough. Form into balls, rings, or any shape desired and fry in hot oil until golden brown.

Ibos sometimes prepare peanuts mixed with dried crayfish.

### OSE OJI

*2 cups shelled roasted peanuts, unsalted*
*1 teaspoon ground dried crayfish or shrimp*
*¼ to ½ teaspoon cayenne*
*Salt to taste*

4 to 6 servings

Process nuts in blender until finely ground. Combine crayfish and cayenne and add to nuts with salt to taste. Blend until smooth.

This is traditionally served with kola nuts.

## STEWS, SOUPS, AND SAUCES

The foundation of West African meal planning is what we'd call a stew. In West Africa it is variously known as sauce, soup, or stew—depending on the ingredients used, the number of ingredients that go into the pot, the amount of water used, whether the ingredients are fried in oil first or boiled first. The line between them is hardly firm. For instance, if root vegetables or beans or even several greens are added to a soup, it becomes a stew.

Sauces are generally cooked in oil with little or no water added. They always include hot peppers and usually tomatoes, onion, and crayfish as well. The proportions determine what sort of sauce it is—lots of pepper makes a pepper sauce;

a generous addition of crayfish makes it crayfish sauce; tomatoes, tomato sauce. Fresh, cooked fish or pieces of meat may also be added to sauces which are usually served with boiled root vegetables, plantains, or bean dishes.

Soups, on the other hand, usually have a water base, but none are as thin as our soups. They are always thickened—with okra or various edible seeds or nuts—and are never drunk. And they're served with some sort of starch dish.

A West African stew is a combination of soup and sauce. In a stew the meat or fish is first simmered in water, then browned in oil with the other ingredients, then cooked in the stock again until done.

Perhaps the stew best known outside Africa is *Groundnut Stew*. This dish is widely prepared in West Africa from Senegal to the Congo. There are hundreds of ways of preparing it —with fish or meat or chicken, with one vegetable or many—depending on the availability of food and the cook's budget. It always, naturally, contains peanuts. In Africa the cook starts with whole peanuts and grinds them to a paste. If you don't feel like going to the trouble, use peanut butter.

This groundnut recipe, from Dahomey, is a basic one.

## GROUNDNUT SAUCE

*2 pounds beef or chicken*
*½ cup peanut oil*
*1 pound soft tomatoes, peeled, seeded, and well mashed*
*1 onion, finely chopped*
*1 teaspoon ground dried shrimp*
*½ to 1 teaspoon cayenne*
*Salt to taste*
*1 cup peanut butter*
*2 cups water*

6 servings

Cut the meat into 2-inch cubes or the chicken into parts. Slowly brown in one-half the oil. Heat remaining oil in a stewing pan; add mashed tomatoes, chopped onion, ground shrimp, cayenne, and salt to taste. Simmer about 15 minutes. Add browned meat or chicken. Dilute the peanut butter with the water and add to the meat mixture, mixing well. Cover and simmer over a moderately low fire until the meat is cooked, 20 minutes to 45 minutes depending on cut of beef used or size of chicken pieces.

Serve with mashed yams, *Yam Balls*, *Boiled Plantain*, or *garri*.

More elaborate versions would contain a greater variety of vegetables and both chicken and beef or perhaps chicken and shrimp. This particular recipe was given me in Ghana.

## GROUNDNUT STEW

*1 2-pound frying chicken, cut into small pieces*
*1 pound beef, cut in 1½- to 2-inch cubes*
*Salt and white pepper to taste*
*Peanut oil*
*1 teaspoon salt*
*1 cup chopped onions*
*1 green pepper, chopped*
*2 large tomatoes, peeled and cut up*
*1½ to 2 teaspoons cayenne*
*2 cups water*
*1½ cups peanut butter*

8 to 10 servings

Season chicken pieces with salt and white pepper. Set aside. Brown beef cubes in hot oil. Add 1 teaspoon salt, ½ cup of the onions, half the green pepper, half the tomatoes, the cayenne, and the water. Simmer gently 30 minutes.

Combine 1 cup of the cooking liquid with the peanut butter, mixing into a smooth paste. Add to the beef mixture and cook 15 minutes more. Add chicken pieces and remaining vegetables. Continue simmering until chicken and meat are tender.

Serve with boiled rice, mashed yams or potatoes, or plantain.

VARIATION: This same recipe may be used for a chicken and shrimp combination. Use 2 cut-up fryers and ½ pound cleaned and cooked shrimp; omit beef. Brown chicken in oil. Add the chopped onions and cook until browned. Add tomatoes, green pepper, cayenne, 1½ teaspoons salt, and ½ teaspoon white pepper. Cover and simmer over low heat about 20 minutes. Mix water and peanut butter into a smooth paste and add to the chicken. Cover and simmer until chicken is tender. Add shrimp and return to fire until shrimp are hot.

In Senegal, *Groundnut Stew* is called *Mafé* and calls for a variety of vegetables that clearly shows the residual Gallic influence in that former French colony.

## MAFÉ

*2 pounds beef, cut into 10 or 12 pieces (or 1 fryer chicken cut in pieces)*
*½ cup peanut oil*
*½ pound onions, finely chopped*
*½ pound tomatoes, peeled, seeded, and cut in half*
*2 cups water*
*Salt and cayenne to taste*
*2 green peppers, seeded and cut in pieces*
*½ pound acorn squash, peeled and diced*
*1 pound cassava root, diced (if available)*
*2 sweet potatoes, peeled and diced*
*1 turnip, diced*

*1 cup peanut butter*
*2 small eggplants, peeled and diced*
*1 head cabbage, cut in eighths*

6 servings

Brown the beef in the oil in a stewing pan. Remove meat and set aside. Sauté onions and tomatoes in the oil until onions are golden. Return meat and add water, salt, cayenne to taste, green peppers, squash, cassava root, sweet potatoes, and turnip. Cover and simmer 45 minutes. Mix peanut butter with about 1 cup of the cooking liquid into a smooth sauce. Add to pot with eggplants and cabbage. Cover and simmer 30 minutes more.

Serve with boiled rice.

A basic *Pepper Sauce* is the starting point for various stews with meat, fowl, fish, or green vegetables. In Africa, the meat would be cooked especially for the dish, but *Pepper Sauce* would be ideal as a zesty way to serve any leftovers.

This is the way to prepare *Pepper Sauce* as it's made in Nigeria, where it's called *Ata Sauce* (*ata* means hot). It's a *very* hot sauce, so proceed with caution.

## ATA SAUCE (PEPPER SAUCE)

*5 red bell peppers*
*1 large onion*
*2 large tomatoes*
*3 to 5 chili peppers, or 1 to 2 tablespoons crushed red pepper, or 1 to 2 teaspoons cayenne*
*½ to 1 cup palm or peanut oil*
*Salt to taste*
*1 teaspoon ground dried shrimp*

4 to 6 servings

Seed bell peppers. Grind all the peppers, onion, tomatoes, and chilies in a blender, or grind half the vegetables and slice or chop the other half. Heat oil in a heavy frying pan and sauté vegetables (and cayenne if it's being used instead of chilies). Cook until peppers are done. Add ground shrimp and simmer until all ingredients are brown but not burned.

Notice that no water is required—the vegetables will cook in the oil and their own moisture.

To this may be added any meat, chicken, or fish. Usually meat and chicken is simmered in a very small amount of water, then browned in oil before adding to the sauce.

Serve with boiled, stewed, or fried starch.

(One recipe I have for *Ata Sauce* points up cultural differences between countries; it suggests *Ata Sauce* be served with a boiled starch for breakfast!)

VARIATIONS: *Tomato Sauce*—reduce the number of bell peppers and chilies and increase the number of tomatoes. Proceed as above.

*Onion Sauce*—reduce the number of peppers and chilies and increase the number of onions. Proceed as above.

Spinach added to a rich (that is, made with little or no water) sauce very much like *Ata Sauce* is a widely served dish. Generally, the amount of pepper is reduced to avoid overwhelming the more delicate flavor of the spinach.

According to Miss Baeta, many Ghanaians use very little pepper.

## PALAVA SAUCE

*1½ pounds cubed beef*
*1 onion, sliced*
*2 tomatoes, peeled and sliced*
*Fresh ground ginger to taste*

*Red pepper to taste*
*¼ to ½ cup peanut oil*
*2 pounds fresh spinach, cooked, drained and chopped, or 2 10-ounce packages frozen chopped spinach, cooked and drained*

4 servings

Boil meat in a small amount of water until tender; drain. Fry onion, tomatoes, ginger, and red pepper in oil until onions are golden. Add cooked, drained spinach and meat and sauté a few minutes to lightly brown meat and blend flavors.

Another Ghanaian recipe I have is very heavy on the onions, producing more of a general vegetable stew.

## SPINACH-VEGETABLE STEW

*4 tomatoes, peeled*
*8 onions*
*1 tablespoon finely minced green pepper*
*½ to ¾ cup palm or peanut oil*
*2 pounds stewing beef, cut in cubes*
*1 cup water*
*¾ teaspoon salt*
*½ to 1 teaspoon cayenne*
*¼ teaspoon fresh ground ginger root*
*2 pounds fresh spinach or 2 10-ounce packages frozen chopped spinach, thawed*

6 to 8 servings

Grind or process in blender tomatoes, onions, and green pepper. Heat oil in a stewing pan and briefly sauté meat and processed vegetables. Add water, salt, cayenne, and ginger and simmer 2 hours or until meat is tender.

If using fresh spinach, clean and shred. Add spinach to meat, adjust seasoning, and simmer gently until water has evaporated and spinach is done.

*Nigerian Spinach Stew* is spicier.

## NIGERIAN SPINACH STEW

*2 pounds spinach or 2 10-ounce packages frozen chopped spinach, cooked and drained*
*Meat or fish as desired*
*½ to 1 teaspoon cayenne*
*1 tablespoon ground tomatoes*
*1 tablespoon ground onion*
*¼ to ½ cup palm or peanut oil*
*½ tablespoon ground dried crayfish*

4 to 6 servings

If using fresh spinach, cook, drain, and chop. Boil meat or fish in a little water until tender. Drain. Combine cayenne, tomato, and onion and cook in hot peanut oil until done. Stir in dried crayfish. Add chopped spinach and meat or fish and stir well. Simmer briefly to heat and blend flavors.

Okra is another popular vegetable on which to build a stew. As with spinach, okra is combined with either meat or fish.

## OKRA STEW

*1 pound meat, cubed*
*3 or 4 red bell peppers*
*1 small onion*
*½ to 1 tablespoon crushed red pepper or ½ to 1 teaspoon cayenne*

*¼ cup palm or peanut oil*
*2 10-ounce packages frozen okra, cooked and cut into pieces*
*1 tablespoon ground dried shrimp*

4 to 5 servings

Simmer meat in a little water until tender and only juices from the meat remain. Grind or chop peppers and onion. Mix with cayenne or crushed pepper. Heat oil and add to meat, along with vegetable mixture. Sauté gently until meat is nicely browned and vegetables are tender. Add cooked okra and stir well. Stir in ground shrimp and simmer 2 minutes.

Serve hot with boiled or mashed yams, potatoes, or plantain.

*Pepper Chicken*, as I mentioned before, can be made many ways. One version, by roasting, is served dry. But usually *Pepper Chicken* is a stew—either actually cooked by stewing or fried or roasted and served with an *Ata Sauce* over it.

*Pepper Chicken* has become a great favorite with my children, particularly prepared according to this recipe, given me by a home economics teacher in Lagos.

## PEPPER CHICKEN

*1 frying chicken, cut up*
*Salt and white pepper to taste*
*Peanut oil*
*2 onions, sliced*
*8 tomatoes, peeled and sliced*
*2 chili peppers, or 1 tablespoon crushed red pepper, or 1 to 1½ teaspoons cayenne*
*2 tablespoons catsup*
*½ teaspoon thyme*

4 to 6 servings

Season chicken with salt and pepper. Fry in hot oil until golden brown. Drain.

In a heavy stewing pan, heat ¼ cup peanut oil. Sauté sliced onion until transparent. Add sliced tomatoes and peppers (if using fresh ones) and sauté. Add catsup, thyme, and crushed red pepper or cayenne (if using). Mix well. Add chicken and simmer until chicken is tender. (No added water is necessary; the chicken cooks in the oil and juice from the tomatoes.)

Serve over rice.

For the times when fresh tomatoes are too expensive, I've developed a *Pepper Chicken* recipe which is similar to that served at the Ikoyi Hotel in Lagos. Actually, it's chicken served with my own version of *Ata Sauce,* using canned tomatoes.

## BAKED PEPPER CHICKEN (ADAPTATION)

*1 fryer chicken, cut up*
*Salt to taste*
*Cayenne to taste*
*2 onions, sliced*
*½ green pepper, diced, or 1 tablespoon dehydrated green pepper*
*Peanut oil*
*1 1-pound can stewed tomatoes*
*½ to 1 tablespoon crushed red pepper or ½ to 1 teaspoon cayenne (or to taste)*
*Tomato or vegetable juice (optional)*
*1 cup rice*

4 servings

Season fryer with salt and a generous amount of cayenne. Place in a single layer in a baking pan and bake uncovered in a hot oven (400° F.) until done, 45 minutes to 1 hour. (I never add butter or oil when baking chicken this way because my family likes the skin to be very crisp. If you wish, you may brush with melted butter or oil before seasoning chicken pieces.)

About 30 minutes before chicken is done, sauté onions and green pepper in a small amount of oil until golden. If using dehydrated green pepper, add when onions are almost done. Add tomatoes and red pepper or cayenne. If you like a wetter sauce, add tomato or vegetable juice as desired. Simmer 5 to 10 minutes.

Cook rice as directed on package, but add ¼ teaspoon cayenne to water.

Serve chicken with rice, with sauce poured over each portion.

## FISH STEWS

In many of the preceding recipes, fish may be substituted for meat or chicken. However, some West African dishes are always made with fish.

The consumption of fresh fish is largely confined to the areas surrounding the source of supply. Problems of storage and transportation are the limiting factors. Even so, much nutritional missionary work needs to be done to increase the use of fish in this protein-poor part of the world. At present, unfortunately, even the available catch is not used as widely as it should be.

In arid, inland regions, dried fish is generally distributed, as is smoked fish.

From the Ivory Coast comes this particularly tasty fish stew made with okra and eggplant.

## FISH CALALOU

*2 large tomatoes*
*1 pound eggplant*
*1 large onion, finely chopped*
*2 tablespoons peanut oil*
*1 pound fresh fish fillets, cut in pieces*
*1 10-ounce package frozen okra, thawed*
*½ to 1 teaspoon cayenne*
*½ green pepper, sliced*
*¼ cup very finely chopped peanuts or chunk-style peanut butter*
*Salt to taste*

6 servings

Peel tomatoes and eggplant, but leave whole.

In a stewing pan, brown half the chopped onion in oil. Add fish fillets and brown. Reduce heat and simmer 15 minutes. Remove fish and set aside. Add whole vegetables, cayenne, green pepper, and chopped peanuts or peanut butter. Add enough water to cover. Simmer, covered, on a low fire about 30 minutes. Remove whole vegetables and mash together into a purée. Return vegetable purée to stewing pot, along with remaining chopped onions and fish. Season with salt and simmer a few minutes to heat and blend flavors.

Shellfish is included in a fisherman's catch at some places along the coast. Both crab and shrimp are used in this okra sauce from Dahomey.

## SHELLFISH OKRA SAUCE

*4 crabs*
*½ pound shrimp*

*1 pound okra or 1 10-ounce package frozen okra, thawed*
*6 spinach leaves*
*½ pound smoked fish*
*1 tablespoon ground dried shrimp*
*1 large firm tomato, peeled and diced*
*4 green peppers, quartered and seeded*
*1 large onion, chopped*
*½ to 1 teaspoon cayenne*
*Salt and pepper to taste*

6 servings

Cook crabs and shrimp in salted water. Shell.

Cut okra into slices. Cook, uncovered, in a saucepan with just enough water to cover, until soft. Continue boiling, uncovered, 5 minutes longer. Remove from fire and mash the okra with any remaining cooking liquid and beat 2 or 3 minutes. Add spinach leaves, shrimp, crabs, and smoked fish. In a bowl, mix dried shrimp with a little water and add the tomato, green pepper, onion, cayenne, salt, and pepper. Add this mixture to fish mixture and cook over a low fire 10 minutes. The sauce should then be smooth and rather thick.

Serve with a *foofoo*.

Another Dahomeyan favorite combines spinach and smoked fish.

## SMOKED FISH SAUCE

*2 pounds spinach or 2 10-ounce packages frozen chopped spinach, thawed*
*1 pound smoked fish (eel or herring)*
*½ to 1 cup peanut oil*
*½ pound soft tomatoes, peeled and cut up*

*4 green peppers, cut up*
*2 tablespoons dry mustard*
*Salt to taste*
*1 large onion, chopped*

6 servings

If using fresh spinach, wash, drain, and chop. Fillet the smoked fish and cut into 1½-inch pieces. Heat oil in a stewing pan. Add tomatoes, peppers, mustard, salt, ⅔ of the onion, and smoked fish. Cover and simmer 15 minutes. Add spinach and remaining onion and stir well. Simmer, uncovered, 5 to 15 minutes more or until all vegetables are cooked.

May be eaten hot or cold with a *foofoo*.

A spicy *Ata Sauce* seasons fresh fish in Nigeria.

## FRESH FISH STEW

*3 tablespoons palm or peanut oil*
*2 green peppers, minced*
*2 small onions, minced*
*2 large tomatoes, peeled and diced*
*1 tablespoon catsup*
*½ to 1 teaspoon cayenne*
*About 1 cup boiling water*
*1 pound fresh fish fillets*
*Salt to taste*

4 to 5 servings

Heat oil in a stewing pan. Combine peppers, onions, tomatoes, catsup, and cayenne. Fry until vegetables are soft, stirring frequently to avoid scorching. Add boiling water and stir thoroughly. Add fillets which have been seasoned with salt. Simmer until fish is tender. Adjust seasoning.

*Frejon* is an unusual Nigerian fish dish that's traditionally served on Good Friday. A paste of coconut-flavored beans is combined with *Fresh Fish Stew* and then sprinkled with fine *garri* for thickening. I suggest Instant Cream of Wheat as a substitute for the *garri*.

## FREJON

*1 cup shredded fresh coconut*
*2 cups cold water*
*2 1-pound cans pinto or kidney beans or black-eyed peas, drained*
*Sugar*
*1 recipe of* Fresh Fish Stew (*page* 95)
Garri *or Instant Cream of Wheat*

4 to 6 servings

Soak coconut in cold water about 30 minutes. Strain coconut, mashing out all water possible, reserving the liquid. Set coconut strands aside.

Process drained beans or peas in a blender until they form a fine, smooth paste. In a saucepan, place coconut water and beans. Sweeten as desired (many Nigerians like this dish very sweet). Cook bean paste over a low fire, stirring frequently until of the consistency of a very thick soup. Taste—the coconut flavor of the beans should be apparent. If it's not coconutty enough, stir in a little of the coconut strands and cook a little longer.

Add *Fresh Fish Stew* carefully, taking care not to break up the fish too much. Stir in enough *garri* or Instant Cream of Wheat to thicken.

Smoked fish combined with beans and corn is another Nigerian version of fish stew.

## ADALU

*1 cup canned whole-kernel corn or 1 cup corn cut from the cob or frozen corn, cooked*
*1 No. 2 can beans (kidney or black-eyed peas)*
*¼ to ½ cup palm or peanut oil*
*6 red bell peppers, diced*
*2 medium tomatoes, peeled and diced*
*1 large onion, chopped*
*½ to 1 teaspoon cayenne or ½ to 1 tablespoon crushed red pepper*
*2 medium-sized smoked fish (herring or chubs, etc.)*
*1 teaspoon dried ground shrimp*

5 servings

Combine cooked or canned corn and beans with a little of the canning or cooking liquid. Simmer until both corn and beans are soft and pulpy. Add oil, peppers, tomatoes, onions, and cayenne or crushed red pepper. Stir well. Cook 5 minutes over low heat, stirring occasionally.

Skin fish, remove bones, and break meat up into small pieces. Add to saucepan with dried ground shrimp. Stir well and heat.

Serve with a *foofoo*. Sometimes *Adalu* is served with *Ata Sauce* as well.

Steamed bean paste similar to *Moinmoin* is the basis for another fish stew called *Ekuru*. Shrimp or small whole fish like smelt or perch may be used.

## EKURU

*1 1-pound can black-eyed peas, well drained*
*Salt to taste*

*¼ to ½ cup palm or peanut oil*
*½ teaspoon cayenne*
*2 tablespoons minced onion*
*2 tablespoons minced tomato*
*1 pound cooked shrimp or small fish*

4 servings

Process drained peas in a blender until very smooth. Salt to taste. Stirring constantly, add warm water gradually until mixture thickly coats the back of a wooden spoon. Pour bean mixture into greased custard cups or a mold. Cover with foil and steam until firm, 30 to 60 minutes, depending on size of containers.

In oil, sauté cayenne, onion, and tomato until soft. Add shrimp or fish and simmer until heated and flavors are blended. Mash the steamed beans and mix thoroughly with the fish sauce.

Serve with a starch.

## ONE - DISH STEWS

All the preceding sauces, soups, and stews are made separately from the starch dish which accompanies them. And they are served with whichever carbohydrate is available—yams, cassava, plantain, etc.

Some West African starch-stew combinations are always served with the same starch—rice, say, or cornmeal—which is frequently cooked right in the stew itself.

The best known of these is *Jollof Rice,* common all along the coast. The name indicates it originated in Senegal—some say it was named after the *Jollof* region of Senegal while others think it is a corruption of *Wolof,* the name of one of the peoples of that country. In any event, rice is grown in

Senegal and so is fairly common and easily available there. In many other places along the west coast, rice must be imported and can be comparatively expensive.

In some parts of Senegal, *Jollof Rice* made with fish is the basic diet, served every day. The seas off Cape Verde, the westernmost part of Africa, abound in fish and shellfish most of the year. In its travels down the coast, *Jollof Rice* becomes a meat or chicken offering, as in the Ghanaian and Nigerian renditions.

This is the classic Senegalese dish.

## THIEBOU-DIEN (RICE AND FISH)

*2 onions, chopped*
*2 tablespoons parsley*
*Pinch cayenne*
*Pinch salt*
*2 pounds fish fillets (choose lean fish such as hake)*
*¼ to ½ cup peanut oil*
*½ of a 6-ounce can tomato paste*
*1 green pepper, cut in half and seeded*
*1 head cabbage, cut in half*
*3 carrots, peeled*
*2 sweet potatoes, peeled*
*1 turnip, peeled*
*1 small eggplant, peeled*
*¼ pound dried fish, cut in pieces*
*Pepper to taste*
*2 chili peppers, or ½ tablespoon crushed red pepper, or ½ teaspoon cayenne*
*1½ cups rice*

6 servings

Combine 1 tablespoon of the onions, parsley, and pinch of cayenne and salt. Mash together well and rub fish slices with this mixture.

In a heavy stewing pan, heat oil and sauté fish slices, turning, until they are golden on both sides; remove and set aside. To pan add remaining onions and tomato paste diluted with an equal amount of water. Bring to a boil and simmer 2 or 3 minutes. Add all the vegetables and the dried fish. Cover with water, and season with salt, pepper, and chilies, crushed red pepper, or cayenne. Cover and simmer 20 minutes.

Place rice in a colander or steamer and fit over stew in pan. Cover and let steam 30 to 35 minutes. Add fish pieces to stew, replace rice steamer, cover, and continue simmering 5 minutes or until fish and rice are cooked.

Pass rice in one dish, fish and vegetables in another, and the cooking liquid as a sauce.

Rice may be cooked right in the cooking liquid. After vegetables have been simmering 30 minutes, stir in rice. Cover and continue simmering 30 minutes, adding water if necessary; add fish about 5 minutes before rice is tender.

In neighboring Mali, the rice is combined with a lamb-tomato sauce.

## JOLLOF RICE MALI

*1 pound tomatoes, peeled*
*2 tablespoons tomato paste*
*Peanut oil*
*2 large onions*
*1 pound lamb, cut in 1-inch cubes*
*2 cloves garlic, sliced*
*1 chili pepper or ½ teaspoon cayenne*

*Salt and pepper to taste*
*1 cup rice*

4 servings

Cut tomatoes into quarters and mash well with a fork. Add tomato paste.

Heat ¼ to ½ cup oil in a stewing pan. Mince 1 onion and brown. Add meat cubes and brown. Add mashed tomatoes and garlic.

Slice second onion, brush with oil, and broil until brown. Process broiled onions in blender with chili pepper or cayenne until ground. Add to meat mixture and season with salt and pepper. Add about 1 cup of water, stir well, and simmer over a low fire 45 minutes or until meat is tender.

Meanwhile, cook rice as directed on package until firm but not soft.

Serve with meat sauce poured over the rice.

VARIATION: Other vegetables as available may be added to this dish. Peel and cut in pieces 3 carrots, 1 turnip, 1 large potato, and 1 small cabbage. Add along with the ground grilled onion mixture. If necessary, add a little more water.

The Ghanaian version of *Jollof Rice* is a chicken dish, and the rice is cooked in the stew.

## JOLLOF RICE GHANA

*1 fryer chicken, cut up*
*Salt to taste*
*Pepper to taste*
*4 tablespoons peanut oil*
*6 onions, diced*
*8 tomatoes, peeled and diced*
*½ to 1 tablespoon crushed red pepper or ½ to 1 teaspoon cayenne*

*1 8-ounce can tomato sauce*
*2½ cups water*
*1 cube chicken bouillon*
*1 cup rice*

4 servings

Brown chicken, seasoned with salt and pepper, in hot oil in a stewing pan. Remove and set aside. In same pan, sauté onions, tomatoes, and red pepper or cayenne. Add tomato sauce. When vegetables are half-cooked, add browned chicken and 1 cup of water. Simmer over low heat until chicken is tender, about 45 minutes. Dissolve bouillon cube in 1½ cups boiling water; add to stewing pan and bring to a fast boil. Add rice and stir well. Cover, reduce heat, and simmer until liquid is absorbed and rice is tender.

One Nigerian recipe I have uses meat or chicken which has been slightly marinated with lime or lemon first. I've lowered the amount of rice from the original recipe; Nigerian cooks often allow as much as 1 cup of uncooked rice per person.

## NIGERIAN JOLLOF RICE

*1 fryer chicken or 2½ to 3 pounds meat, cut in pieces*
*1 lime or lemon, cut in half*
*Salt to taste*
*1 clove garlic, minced*
*1 cup water*
*2 tomatoes, peeled*
*2 onions*
*4 red bell peppers*
*½ cup peanut oil*
*1 8-ounce can tomato sauce*

*1 to 2 tablespoons crushed red pepper or 1 to 1½ teaspoons cayenne*
*2 bay leaves*
*½ teaspoon thyme*
*1½ cups rice*

6 servings

Rub meat or chicken pieces with cut sides of lime or lemon. Season with salt and sprinkle with garlic. Let marinate at least 1 hour.

In a stewing pot, simmer chicken or meat with about 1 cup water until tender. Drain, reserving stock.

Mince 1 tomato, 1 onion, and bell peppers. Heat oil in stewing pot and fry meat or chicken until golden. Add minced vegetables, tomato sauce, and crushed red pepper or cayenne. Stir in bay leaves and thyme. Sauté until vegetables are soft. Add rice and cook over medium heat for a few minutes, stirring constantly. Add reserved stock, slowly, stirring constantly. Cover and cook over low heat until rice is almost soft, stirring occasionally to keep rice from sticking. Slice remaining onion and tomato. Add to rice and continue cooking over low heat, well covered, until rice is tender. It may be necessary to add small amounts of boiling water to keep the rice from sticking.

Other rice-stew combinations are prepared in West Africa, too. Here are two from Senegal—one with fish and one with meat. In both recipes the meat or fish is marinated first. And unlike the *Jollof Rice* recipes, there are no tomatoes included.

## FISH YASSA

*1 teaspoon salt*
*1 teaspoon cayenne*

*1 red bell pepper, seeded and sliced*
*½ cup lemon juice*
*2 tablespoons vinegar*
*Peanut oil*
*1½ pounds fish fillets*
*½ pound onions, sliced*
*1 cup water*
*1¼ cups rice, cooked*

6 servings

Combine salt, cayenne, pepper slices, lemon juice, vinegar, and 1 tablespoon peanut oil. Pour over fish and sliced onions in a bowl. Marinate 6 hours.

Oil a broiler pan and broil fish until golden on both sides, but not entirely cooked.

Heat ¼ to ½ cup oil in a stewing pan and slowly sauté marinated onions until golden. Add the marinade, grilled fish, and water. Cover and cook over a low fire about 10 minutes.

Serve over rice cooked very dry.

## LAMB YASSA

*1¼ cups lime juice*
*1 pound onions, sliced*
*1 green pepper, chopped*
*½ teaspoon thyme*
*2 bay leaves*
*Salt and pepper to taste*
*6 large lamb chops*
*¼ to ½ cup peanut oil*
*1 cup rice, cooked*

6 servings

Combine lime juice, onions, chopped pepper, thyme, bay leaves, and salt and pepper to taste. Pour over chops and marinate 12 hours. Drain chops, reserving marinade.

Broil chops in a heated broiler. Meanwhile, heat oil in a stewing pan. Brown marinated onions. Strain marinade and add to pan. Bring to a boil and add grilled chops. Cook over medium heat 15 to 20 minutes.

Serve over rice.

Curries must be included in this section. They have become very much a part of the culinary scene in former British West Africa. They are always served with rice, of course.

The curries themselves are not particularly unusual. They are largely straight renditions or adaptations of Asian curries of lamb, beef, chicken, or seafood. However, they are served with an unusually enormous array of accompaniments—many, many more than I've ever encountered anywhere else even in Indian restaurants in Europe or America or at the homes of Indian friends.

At the Ikoyi Hotel in Lagos, for instance, the accompaniments were wheeled to each table on a three-tiered serving cart. Each shelf was crowded with square serving dishes heaped with all manner of diced, chopped, or shredded fruits, vegetables, nuts, fish, spices, and preserves.

There was chutney of course—several kinds of varying degrees of hotness—and raisins and fresh shredded coconut. There was also: toasted coconut, chopped onions, chopped fried onions, chopped green onions, diced tomatoes, diced green pepper, ground dried chilies, diced mangoes, powdered ginger, diced bananas, diced fried plantain, peanuts, diced pineapple, diced cucumber, diced grapefruit, diced oranges, diced pawpaw (papaya), ground dried shrimp, curry powder, diced guava, diced apple, crumbled bacon, seeded grape halves, chopped dates, diced red peppers, plus several other dishes I didn't recognize. Nigerians and old African hands spoon out a portion of everything so their plates become a mound of curry and rice completely hidden by a patchwork of color and tastes.

Try as many of these side dishes as you like on this version of curry. The tomatoes and okra stamp it as clearly West African.

## CURRY

*1 fryer chicken, cut up, or 2 pounds lamb or beef, cut in pieces*
*1 cut lime or lemon*
*Salt to taste*
*1 clove garlic, minced*
*1 cup water*
*¼ to ½ cup peanut oil*
*2 onions, sliced*
*1 or 2 chili peppers, processed in blender until ground, or ½ to 1 tablespoon crushed red pepper*
*6 tomatoes, peeled and sliced*
*1 tablespoon Madras-type curry powder (strong)*
*½ cup tomato sauce*
*1 small potato, peeled and diced*
*½ teaspoon thyme*
*1 10-ounce package frozen okra, thawed and sliced*
*¾ cup evaporated milk*
*1½ cups rice, cooked*

4 servings

Rub chicken or meat pieces with cut lime or lemon. (Lime or lemon is used this way not only as a seasoning, but as a tenderizer. Meat and fowl, as I've mentioned, are much scrawnier and tougher than in the United States.) Season with salt and sprinkle with minced garlic. Let stand 1 hour.

In a stewing pan, simmer chicken or meat in water until tender. Remove and drain, reserving stock.

Heat oil in a frying pan and gently brown chicken or meat. Add onions, peppers, tomato, curry powder, tomato sauce, potato, thyme, and the stock. Simmer until meat is tender and vegetables are almost cooked. Add okra and simmer until soft. Add milk and heat to serving temperature.

Serve with rice and an array of accompaniments.

In some areas, the starch involved is cornmeal. The cornmeal is cooked in the stewing liquid in both the following examples.

The first, a chicken dish, is from Dahomey.

## AMIWO

*1 fat stewing chicken (or duckling or broiling turkey)*
*2 cloves garlic, minced*
*2 onions, chopped*
*1½ teaspoons salt*
*1 pound very soft tomatoes, peeled*
*¼ teaspoon pepper*
*½ to 1 teaspoon cayenne*
*¼ teaspoon ginger*
*2½ cups water*
*1½ cups white cornmeal, lightly toasted in the oven*
*Peanut oil*
*1 pound firm tomatoes*
*2 tablespoons vinegar*

8 servings

Cut chicken into pieces and combine in a saucepan with garlic, 1 tablespoon chopped onions, and 1 teaspoon salt. Add enough cold water to cover. Bring to a boil, skim, then simmer over low heat about 50 minutes or until chicken is tender. Remove chicken pieces and drain.

Purée the soft tomatoes in a blender or vegetable mill. Add to the stewing liquid and season with ½ teaspoon salt, pepper, cayenne, and ginger. Add ½ of the remaining chopped onions and 2½ cups water. Bring to a boil.

Meanwhile in a bowl toss ¾ cup of the cornmeal with a little cold water until the grains are moistened. When tomato mixture has boiled smooth, add dampened cornmeal, stirring constantly until liquid begins to thicken. Stir in ¼ cup oil. Cook over moderate heat 10 minutes, covering for the last 5 minutes.

Add remaining cornmeal in small quantities, stirring constantly. The mixture should become very firm and will become increasingly hard to stir. Cook another 5 minutes.

In a frying pan, heat 2 tablespoons of oil and brown pieces of cooked chicken.

To serve, spoon out mounds of the cornmeal mixture with an oiled ladle onto a serving plate and place browned chicken around them.

Dice the firm tomatoes and combine with remaining onions. Toss with the vinegar and pass this mixture as a relish.

*Agala Dzemkple,* a shellfish version, is one of the recipes Miss Baeta gave me in Ghana.

## AGALA DZEMKPLE

*6 crabs (the soft-shelled variety would probably work best)*
*1 piece fresh ginger root*
*¼ to ½ cup palm or peanut oil*
*½ cup chopped onions*
*½ cup chopped tomatoes*
*½ cup tomato sauce*

*2 tablespoons ground dried shrimp*
*½ teaspoon ginger*
*1 teaspoon salt*
*½ to 1 teaspoon cayenne*
*1½ cups white cornmeal lightly toasted in the oven*
*Hard-cooked eggs*

6 servings

Boil crabs in salted water with the fresh ginger until cooked. Remove crabs and keep warm; discard ginger, and reserve stock.

In hot oil, sauté onions and tomatoes until onions are golden. Add tomato sauce, dried shrimp, ground ginger, salt, and cayenne. Cook well. Reserve and set aside 3 tablespoons of this mixture.

Add 2 cups of the fish stock to remaining vegetable mixture and bring to a boil. Remove from heat and gradually add cornmeal, stirring vigorously and constantly. Return to moderate fire and cook, stirring constantly until soft and firm but not stiff. Reduce heat to low, cover, and let cornmeal firm up further, but do not burn.

Serve decorated with reserved gravy, hard-cooked egg halves, and the cooked crab.

*Couscous* also properly belongs in a chapter on West Africa. It is frequently made in Senegal and other countries bordering North Africa.

Mrs. Edris Makward, wife of the distinguished Senegalese who is a professor of African languages and literature at the University of Wisconsin, contributed this recipe. As you can see, the stew is much hotter than the North African counterpart.

## SENEGALESE COUSCOUS

*1½ fryer chickens, cut up*
*4 medium onions, chopped*
*½ cup peanut oil*
*3 bay leaves*
*1¼ teaspoons turmeric*
*2 chicken bouillon cubes dissolved in 2 cups boiling water*
*2 carrots, cut up*
*1 turnip, cut up*
*1 small cabbage, cut up*
*1 to 2 teaspoons cayenne*
*Salt to taste*
*3 or 4 zucchini, cut up*
*1 eggplant, peeled and cut up*
*1 1-pound can chick peas, drained*
*1 pound instant* couscous
*¼ cup butter, melted*
*5 tablespoons raisins*

6 servings

Brown chicken and onions in hot oil until golden. Add bay leaves, 1 teaspoon turmeric, bouillon and enough water to barely cover. Simmer 20 minutes. Add carrots and turnip and continue simmering 15 minutes. Add cabbage, cayenne, salt, zucchini, and eggplant and simmer 20 minutes longer or until all ingredients are tender. (Add bouillon or water as needed.) Add chick peas. If sauce is too watery, reduce over high heat, stirring frequently.

Meanwhile cook *couscous.* First, wash grains very quickly with only enough water to barely wet. Strain very carefully in a clean, soft kitchen towel.

Melt butter and add ¼ teaspoon turmeric. Mix with

*couscous* in a bowl along with the raisins which have been softened in hot water and drained.

Line a *couscous* steamer (or colander that will fit into a large dutch oven) with a dry cloth. Add *couscous* mixture and place colander over boiling water in the dutch oven so the *couscous* is steamed without getting wet. Cover and steam about 15 minutes.

Serve *couscous* on a large dish with chicken around it, and garnished with a few vegetables. Pass the sauce separately in one bowl and the rest of the vegetables in another.

## OTHER WAYS TO COOK MEAT AND FISH

On occasion, meat or fish is prepared by frying, roasting, or grilling.

*Pepper Chicken* in Nigeria, for example, is sometimes roasted rather than stewed.

### ROAST PEPPER CHICKEN

*1 broiler-fryer chicken, cut up*
*¼ to ½ cup peanut oil or melted butter*
*Salt to taste*
*½ to 1 teaspoon cayenne*
*1 4-ounce can or jar pimiento, diced*
*1 onion, diced*
*1 tomato, peeled and diced*

4 servings

Brush chicken pieces on both sides with oil or melted butter. Season well with salt and cayenne. Put in baking pan and sprinkle with pimiento, onion, and tomato. Bake in a hot oven (400° F.) until cooked and golden brown, 45 minutes to 1 hour.

From Mali comes a recipe for chicken that would be ideal for charcoal broiling. The chicken is first well marinated in a generous amount of lemon juice.

### GRILLED CHICKEN

*2 small whole fryers*
*1 to 1½ cups lemon juice*
*Oil*
*Salt*
*Cayenne*

4 to 6 servings

Cut chickens open but do not separate. Flatten gently and cover with lemon juice. Marinate several hours, turning occasionally. Brush chicken with oil, season with salt and cayenne, and grill over charcoal, on a rotisserie, or in the oven, until nicely brown on both sides and cooked through. (You should use at least 1 teaspoon cayenne for authenticity when seasoning the chicken.)

Cooked fish combined with mashed yams—African yams, that is—makes a modest amount of food go a long way. In Nigeria, these *Fish Cakes* are often served with *Ata Sauce.*

### FISH CAKES

*1 cup flaked, cooked fish*
*2 cups cooked, mashed African yams or potatoes*
*2 tablespoons melted butter*
*Salt to taste*

*½ teaspoon cayenne*
*1 egg, beaten*
*Peanut oil*
Ata Sauce

4 servings

Combine fish, yams, butter, salt, and cayenne. Add egg and mix well. Form into cakes and fry in oil until brown on both sides. The cakes may also be deep-fried or baked.

Serve with *Ata Sauce.*

Miss Baeta developed a baked fish recipe which, while not really traditionally Ghanaian, captures the flavor of the cooking. It was one of the dishes she prepared for Vice-President Humphrey's visit to Ghana.

## FISH GHANA

*2 bay leaves*
*2 peppercorns*
*2 cloves garlic*
*Peanut oil*
*1 whole red snapper*
*Salt to taste*
*1 to 2 teaspoons cayenne*
*1½ onions, chopped*
*2 or 3 tablespoons lemon juice*
*2 tomatoes, peeled and chopped*
*2 teaspoons catsup*
*1 teaspoon ground dried shrimp*

servings depend on size of fish

Soak bay leaves, peppercorns, and garlic in peanut oil to cover. Wash and dry fish well and rub with this oil. Season fish with salt and ½ to 1 teaspoon cayenne. Drizzle with ½ chopped onion, lemon juice, and a little more oil. Bake in a moderate oven (350° F.) until done, 40 to 60 minutes.

Meanwhile, sauté in hot oil remaining chopped onion and tomatoes. Add catsup, salt, ½ to 1 teaspoon cayenne, and ground shrimp. Cook until vegetables are done.

Serve fish with sauce poured over.

## STARCHES

West Africans serve a variety of starches with their stews—corn, rice, plantain, yams, cassava. They are the mainstay of the diet; the amount of sauce, stew, or soup accompanying the starch depends on the individual family's economic situation. For most, unfortunately, the daily fare is usually much more starch than stew.

These carbohydrates are prepared in several ways, but not, traditionally, made into bread. Bread, leavened or unleavened, is not the African staff of life, though it has been introduced by the Europeans and is purchased and eaten by those who can afford it.

Probably the most popular way of preparing starches is as what we'd call mush. It's called *foofoo* (or *fuufuu* or *foufou* or *foutou*) and involves making the corn, yams, rice, or whatever into a flour before cooking. One of the most typical of sights in West Africa is of a woman standing at a wooden mortar about two feet high, pounding yam or cassava with a long-handled pestle into flour. It takes considerable time and enormous expenditures of energy.

You must remember that the word "yam" in this context is not the sweet potato we know in this country. In the tropics, yam refers to a large root vegetable (some grow to 18 to 20 pounds each) which, when cut, looks much like a potato but is coarser. There are several varieties of yam—

cocoyam, wateryam, white yam. A large, dry potato may be substituted for yams in any of the following recipes. For the traditionalist, yams are sometimes available in specialty food stores.

Cassava, called manioc in many places, is also widely grown in tropical areas around the world. It is terribly lacking in food value, though, and for that reason—as well as the fact that when cooked it is virtually tasteless—I don't recommend it, except as something to try once or twice. Cassava is available in some southern areas, as it's the plant that also produces tapioca. Also, I've found frozen cassava in imported food shops. In Africa, the leaves of the cassava plant are cooked as a vegetable.

For your information, here's how West Africans make their flours.

*Yam, Plantain, Cassava, Rice, or Corn Flour*

Prepare one of the following: Yams—peel, wash, and dry; slice thinly. Plantains—choose unripe fruit; peel and slice thinly. Cassava—peel, wash, and dry; cut into pieces and soak in water overnight; drain and slice thinly. Corn—remove kernels from cob. Rice—wash and drain.

Spread out yam, plantain, or cassava slices or rice or corn kernels in a single layer on flat sheets. Dry well in the sun. When thoroughly dry, beat or grind into flour. Sieve well.

Most of these flours are then used in making *foofoo*.

## CORN FOOFOO

*1 cup corn flour (or white cornmeal)*
*2¼ cups boiling water*

4 servings

Into 2 cups of the boiling water, slowly add corn flour, stirring constantly with a wooden spoon. Add enough more boiling water to make the *foofoo* thick but not too stiff. Stir well and simmer, covered, over a low fire 5 to 10 minutes.

For *Yam Foofoo,* use 1 cup yam flour and 2½ cups boiling water and proceed as for *Corn Foofoo.*

For *Rice Foofoo,* use 1 cup rice flour and 2 cups boiling water seasoned with 1 teaspoon salt.

*Rice Foofoo* may also be made from whole-grain rice. This is the method often used by the Hausa in northern Nigeria and Ghana, where *foofoo* is known as *Tuwo.* The Hausa also use *Guinea Corn* (sorghum) for *Tuwo.*

## RICE FOOFOO (WITH WHOLE RICE)

*1 cup uncooked rice*
*2½ cups boiling water*
*1 teaspoon salt*

Cook rice in salted water until it is overcooked and mushy. Add more water if needed. With a wooden spoon, press the rice against the sides of the pot until it is well mashed and rather stiff.

*Plantain Foofoo* is made with fresh fruit. In the Ivory Coast it is combined with a bit of cassava.

## PLANTAIN FOOFOO

*1 piece cassava root about as big as a large carrot*
*4 pounds plantain*

Peel the plantain and the cassava. Cut them in slices and cook in unsalted boiling water 15 to 20 minutes. Remove from fire and let plantain cool in the cooking liquid. Meanwhile, drain the cassava and then grind or mash until smooth and free of lumps. Remove plantain from cooking liquid and mash until smooth. Combine with mashed cassava and mix well. Form into oval loaves.

*Cassava Foofoo* is a bit more complicated and time-consuming.

## CASSAVA FOOFOO

Peel 4 pounds cassava, wash, and soak in water 3 days. Drain and grate. Place in a clean sack and weight with something heavy so all the water is squeezed out. Let it remain weighted 3 days. When the cassava is quite dry, grind. Cover with a generous amount of cold water and strain. Leave in strainer overnight.

To cook, add enough cold water to the drained cassava to make into a thick, smooth paste which is not too soft. The amount of water required depends on how wet the cassava is to begin with. Put into an iron pot and stir over medium heat until cooked. When ready, the *foofoo* will be rather transparent and smooth.

Serve as an accompaniment to soups.

In some areas of Cameroon, *Cassava Foofoo* is steamed rather than boiled and is called *Miondo.*

## MIONDO

Proceed as for *Cassava Foofoo* to the point the cassava is ground. Mix ground cassava with enough water to make a batter of fairly stiff consistency. Place in greased molds, cover, and steam until cooked. (In Africa the batter is tied up in greased plantain leaves and steamed.)

Another form of mush made from cassava root is *garri*, which is eaten all over West Africa. *Garri* is cassava that has been grated and then roasted. It is available in some American specialty food stores.

## COOKED GARRI

*1 cup* garri
*2 cups water*

4 servings

Bring water to a boil. Pour in *garri*, then pour off surplus water if any. Stir with wooden spoon until smooth. If too stiff, add a little boiling water. Cook for 2 minutes. *Garri* should be fairly soft but hold its shape. For a more elegant *garri* add some seasonings and meat or fish.

When the African family tires of *foofoos* and *garri*, the housewife can prepare rice, yams, and plantain in other ways. Plantains, for instance, may be boiled, baked, or fried.

## BOILED PLANTAIN

*6 medium plantains*
*Boiling salted water*
*Dried ground red chili peppers*

4 servings

Peel plantains and cut into 4-inch pieces. Cook in boiling salted water until done. Drain and sprinkle with ground chilies.

Baked plantains are a favorite with a meal or as a snack. Every market place in West Africa has at least two women, frequently sitting side by side, baking plantains over a charcoal fire and selling them hot off the grill.

## BAKED PLANTAIN

Have 1 plantain for each person. Choose barely ripe fruit, not overripe or soft. Carefully slit open the skin along one side and free the fruit without damaging the skin. Return plantain to the skin. Bake in a slow oven (300° F.) until the skin definitely changes color and the fruit itself shrinks a little. The plantain may also be roasted unpeeled and on a baking sheet. By this method, the outside will harden somewhat.

For charcoal roasting, peel plantain and place on the grid. Turn frequently while cooking.

Plantains are delicious fried in deep or shallow fat much like French-fried or cottage-fried potatoes. When fried in palm oil, the plantain slices take on a rich red color. *Fried Plantain* is also a popular snack available from street-hawkers.

## FRIED PLANTAIN

*1½ ripe plantains per person*
*Palm or peanut oil*
*Salt to taste*

Remove plantain from skin. Cut in slices crosswise, diagonally, or lengthwise (as for French fries). Slice thin or thick, as desired. Season with salt to taste. Fry in hot deep or shallow fat until lightly browned. When frying in deep fat, brown a few at a time to maintain the cooking temperature. Keep cooked slices hot until ready to serve.

*Fried Plantain* is usually served with an *Ata Sauce*.

In western Nigeria a fried plantain dish called *Dodo* is considered so tasty, it's about as popular as candy is with American children.

## DODO

After frying, the plantain pieces are dipped in beaten egg and refried. They may also then be tossed in an *Ata Sauce* made with equal amounts of tomato and onions.

Nigerians in the Eastern Region cook rice in coconut milk as is sometimes done in the Far East. The West African touch is the addition of tomatoes and onions.

## COCONUT RICE

*Meat from 1 fresh coconut, grated*
*2½ cups water*
*Dried ground crayfish to taste*
*1 cup rice*
*3 or 4 small tomatoes, peeled and diced*
*¼ cup chopped onion*
*Salt to taste*
*Cayenne to taste*

4 to 6 servings

Cover grated coconut with water. Let soak 20 to 30 minutes. Place in colander and drain over a bowl, squeezing out as much liquid as possible. You should have about 2 cups coconut milk. If not, add a bit more water to the grated coconut and drain again. Bring coconut milk to a boil. Add ground dried crayfish (about 1 teaspoon) to taste. Stir in rice, cover, reduce heat, and simmer until rice is almost cooked. Stir in tomatoes, onion, salt, and cayenne. Cook until water is completely absorbed and rice is quite dry.

Yams, too, are often boiled or fried as you would potatoes and served with stews. Sometimes they are mashed and mixed with a tasty combination of ingredients, then fried as balls or cakes.

## YAM BALLS

*2 pounds cooked African yam*
*1 large onion, finely minced*
*3 fresh tomatoes, peeled and finely diced*
*1 teaspoon cayenne*
*1 pint peanut oil, divided*
*¼ to ½ teaspoon dried thyme*
*Salt to taste*
*2 eggs, beaten*
*1 tablespoon flour*

4 to 6 servings

Mash yam until smooth. Fry half the onion and tomatoes, seasoned with cayenne, in ¼ cup peanut oil. Season with thyme and salt. Combine fried mixture, remaining onions and tomatoes, and mashed yam. Add eggs and mix well. On a pastry board sprinkled with flour, form yam mixture into balls. Heat remaining oil and deep-fry yam balls until golden brown. Drain.

*Yam Balls* may be garnished with hard-cooked eggs.

## DESSERTS

The dessert repertoire in West African cookery is generally meager—a situation not unusual in poorer areas. Whatever fruit is available is eaten, not necessarily to round out a meal, but rather to assuage hunger. Where mangoes grow, they are plentiful and popular. Pawpaw and pineapple are, too.

Among the more affluent and the educated in metropolitan areas, the desserts favored by the former colonialists have been adopted, along with the rest of the cuisine. French pastries, fresh fruit tarts, liqueur-soaked fruit, and crepes suzette are executed most creditably in the big hotels and restaurants in former French Africa. They're expensive, of course, but delicious.

The most memorable crepes suzette we had in Africa were at the N'Gor Hotel in Dakar—not because they were absolutely the very best, but because we were enjoying food and lodging at a hotel which may be *the* most expensive hostelry in a continent known for its high hotel prices—and it wasn't costing us anything. The bill was being paid by the airline because we were forced to layover there nine hours.

The N'Gor is about 15 miles out of the city, right on Cape Verde. It's a big, modern hotel with huge lounge rooms, poolside terraces, a riding corral, and a small, sandy beach tucked in a little cove along the rocky shore. The dining room overlooks the Atlantic, and we had a table by the window. The only trouble was we arrived after dark on a moonless night and couldn't see a thing out the window. What's more, we knew we'd have to leave before the sun rose to catch our 5:00 a.m. plane. So we soothed our frustrations by ordering crepes suzette for a late evening snack at something like $4 a serving.

The British dessert inheritance seems to be custard sauce. You can't escape it. Delicious fresh pineapple—with custard sauce. Cake—with custard sauce. Gelatin—with custard sauce. Stewed fruit—with custard sauce. And not just a daub, you understand. Slathers and slathers of it. Obviously many—if not most—people don't share my dislike of this custom; few ever refused the dessert. As far as I'm concerned, it made everything taste rather alike, no matter what was hiding under that slithering yellow mass. And for me, that intense yellow color faintly tinged with green was downright offensive. The taste, in my opinion, wasn't much better, since the custard frequently asserted its cornstarch thickening. If you like custard sauce, hunt up an English cookbook; I'm not going to include a recipe here. Anyway, though it's accepted in former British Africa (East, South, Central, *and* West), it's not traditional.

A few sweets and savories, however, are a part of the West African cuisine.

Peanuts are the base for some of them.

*Kulikuli,* the Hausa dish listed as an appetizer on page 81, can also be considered a dessert snack.

Another peanut confection the Hausa like is somewhat similar, except that the peanut mixture is not fried.

## DANKUYA BOATS

*1 cup unsalted roasted peanuts*
*½ cup homemade corn flour*
*½ cup sugar*
*Hot water*

about 12

Grind peanuts to a fine meal. Roast the corn flour in a slow oven until slightly golden. Mix peanuts and corn flour. Add sugar and enough hot water to make a firm, pliable paste. Form walnut-sized pieces into small boat shapes.

Many West Africans make a peanut mixture similar to our peanut brittle.

## GROUNDNUT CAKES

*½ cup sugar*
*1 tablespoon water*

*1 cup roasted peanuts, unsalted*
*Pinch caraway or anise seeds*

about ½ pound

Dissolve sugar in water and boil without stirring until golden brown and thick. Add nuts and seeds and mix well. Pour into a greased pan and score into squares when partially cooled. Break up after completely cooled.

As in this country, coconut is sometimes used for sweet treats. *Gurudi* is Nigerian.

### GURUDI

*1 cup cassava flour*
*3 tablespoons sugar*
*2 cups grated coconut*
*Pinch salt*

about 4 dozen 2-inch squares

Combine flour, sugar, coconut, and a little salt. Add enough water to form into a paste. Spread the mixture as thinly as possible on a greased jellyroll pan. Bake in a hot oven (400° F.) about 8 minutes. Remove from oven and cut into sections or squares without removing from the pan. Return to oven and continue baking until done, 2 to 5 minutes. Cool, then remove from pans. These cookies are soft fresh out of the oven, but get crisp on standing. Store in airtight containers.

In northern Nigeria, *Chinchin* vendors are a fairly common sight. Their deep-fat fried cakes may be made in any shape, though the traditional one is a sort of bow.

## CHINCHIN

*1 cup butter*
*1 cup sugar*
*4 eggs, beaten*
*4 cups flour (about), sifted*
*½ teaspoon baking powder*
*Pinch salt*
*Peanut oil*

about 3 dozen, depending on size

Cream butter. Cream in sugar and beat well. Add eggs and beat well. Add flour mixed with salt and baking powder, a little at a time, mixing well after each addition—enough flour to make a thick dough. (If dough should become too stiff, add a little milk.) Knead lightly until smooth. Roll out onto a floured board to about ¼-inch thickness. Cut dough into rectangular strips about 2 by 5 inches; cut a slit in the center of each strip and pull one end through to form a loop. Fry a few at a time in deep hot fat until nicely browned. Drain well.

VARIATION: *Chinchin* are sometimes flavored with nutmeg, caraway seed, or grated orange rind. These flavorings are combined with the flour before it is added to the egg mixture.

They may also be cooked in shallow fat, but will require turning.

It is interesting to note that chocolate or cocoa in any form is not found in traditional West African cooking even though cocoa beans are one of the area's largest cash crops. As far as I was able to find out, the beans are not processed in West Africa at all—certainly not into candy, since that requires a good milk supply, something West Africa does not have. Also, chocolate candy isn't very stable in the heat of the tropics—another reason, perhaps, that it is found only in the big cities and largely sold to Europeans.

In West Africa, chocolate is not used in meat cookery (as it is in Mexico or other tropical Latin American countries), nor is it a popular drink.

# SOUTHERN AFRICA

EVEN WITH A SEEMINGLY nonpartisan subject like cooking, it is virtually impossible to avoid getting involved in politics when discussing South African cuisine.

South Africa may be the richest and most advanced country on the continent, but it is also the place where the tourist will have the hardest time finding the opportunity (outside a private home) to sample the specialties of the region.

First of all is the barrier of the country's apartheid policy —though invisible, it is as unyielding as the Berlin Wall. So to tourists (all of whom are white, naturally, since only whites get visas) a Durban restaurant catering to third-generation Indians, say, or an African *shebeen* (beer tavern), is strictly off-limits. The racial laws work both ways—the nonwhites are prohibited from using any facilities reserved for whites and whites can't use any for nonwhites.

Then there is the situation stemming from the rivalries between the two dominant white segments of the population, the English speakers and the Afrikaners, the Afrikaans-speaking descendants of the Dutch who began settling at Cape Town in 1652. In the country's formative years the English generally tended to be the city dwellers and the Afrikaners were the farmers. Consequently, the menus handed visitors in hotels and restaurants usually reflect a sort of international cuisine with a strong English accent. Afrikaners, I was told, prefer family dinners to eating out, so restaurants offering the traditional Afrikaner dishes that have evolved over the years just don't exist. At least I was unable to find one, and I had the help of newspaper editors and government information officials. Someone thought there was a restaurant that served Afrikaner dishes in Stellenbosch, about fifty miles from Cape Town, but it was not possible for me to make the detour.

This state of affairs is too bad, because there is an Afrikaner cuisine which is well worth sampling. It is a tasty relic of the days before strict apartheid when there was some cross-culturalization among all peoples in the country. Essentially, Afrikaner cooking is a well-spiced mélange of Cape Malay and Dutch traditions with just a soupçon of seasoning from French Huguenot vintners.

This cuisine is usually referred to as Old Cape Cookery.

That the good things of the South African table should have originated in Cape Town is certainly appropriate. Food was the reason the Dutch decided to found a settlement at the foot of majestic Table Mountain, which rises abruptly 3,500 feet above a great sheltered bay near the Cape of Good Hope. (Cape Town ranks with San Francisco, Rio de Janeiro, and Hong Kong among the world's most spectacular harbor cities.) The first settlers were sent to grow and provide food and water for the ships sailing between Holland and the Dutch holdings in the East Indies. It wasn't long before the Dutch began importing Malay slaves to Cape Town. The spices and condiments these peoples brought with them from the Indonesian archipelago soon overpowered the bland dishes the Dutch *hausfraus* kept simmering at the back of the stove. Among early arrivals at Cape Province were French Protestants fleeing persecution in Catholic France. Their baggage included vine cuttings which blossomed into a wine industry in the mild Cape climate.

Today, Afrikaner cooking clearly shows the Far Eastern influence, particularly in fish, meat, and poultry dishes; the northern European heritage is most evident in vegetable cookery and baking. In addition, as a sort of gastronomic obbligato, there are the preserves of all kinds, mirroring the country's pioneering farmer traditions.

And that frontier flavor is still much in evidence in South Africa. The history of the white segment of the population curiously parallels that of the American West. Even the scenery is similar—great, open, semi-arid plains ringed by distant purplish mountains, a green and fertile strip along one coast. The stern and dour Boer farmers pushed ever north to avoid English rule and to find land. And much land was required; only a large holding of 500 to 1,000 acres of the relatively poor soil was economic. There was even a gold rush (diamonds, too) which changed the country's economic, social, and political course.

So you find certain frontier foods reminiscent of our Wild West, some still popular today. *Biltong*, for instance, is salted and dried meat, just like our jerky. The difference is, it is still popular in South Africa, both as the basis for a main dish and as a snack. Packages of *biltong* are always found right next to the candy bars at refreshment stands in movie theaters and are hawked at horse shows and soccer games like peanuts at Yankee Stadium. You can buy *biltong* of beef or springbok (a South African antelope) or even ostrich. The latter, South Africans will tell you, is the best.

The cookout, too, is as old and established a tradition as in American suburbia. In South Africa this ritual is called a *braai* and purist practioners always start with a wood fire.

Apparently South African appetites are still attuned to the physical exertions of pioneering life. In her book of cookout recipes, Mrs. Leslie Faull, probably South Africa's best-known home economist, suggests these portions for each guest at a *braai:*

"Women's Portions: 1 chop, 1 hamburger, 1 finger of steak, 3 ounces *boerewors* [sausages], 1 buttered roll, ½ tomato, 2 lettuce leaves, 10 chips or crisps [French fries], small slice melon, 3 tablespoons fruit salad.

"Men's portions: 5 ounces steak, 2 chops, 2 hamburgers, 4 ounces *boerewors,* 2 buttered rolls, large slice melon, 4 tablespoons fruit salad."

The pioneer-farmer strain accounts for the country's strong conservatism in food matters, too, a sort of "what was good enough for grandfather is good enough for me" outlook. Only five or so years ago, you could buy just two kinds of bread—white or whole wheat. Now bakeries offer all sorts of loaves to meet the demand of the various European peoples who have been encouraged to immigrate to South Africa. However, bread is still sold unsliced—a good serrated bread knife is included on any list of basic kitchen requirements.

Meat marketing is another illustration of slow-to-change ways. A national law—obviously passed decades before refrigeration—regulates the hours meat may be sold. Butchers open their doors at 5:30 a.m. and close at 1:00 p.m. on Monday, Thursday, and Saturday, at 3:00 on Tuesday, at noon on Wednesday, and at 5:00 on Friday. They never open on Sunday. No doubt there was once a good reason for this checkerboard system—to ensure the consumer fresh meat. But in today's age of modern cold-storage methods, it seems anachronistic to be unable to buy meat anywhere after these stated hours. Even in the self-service supermarkets (this type of store is gradually gaining a foothold in South Africa, though countless specialized stores—dairies, bakeries, butcher shops, nuts and dried-fruit stores, fruitiers, etc.—are still thriving) the prepackaged meat is cut off from the buyer by a locked cover when the closing hour arrives.

And who, you ask, shops at 5:30 a.m.? The servants. Household help is generally available to white people. Since the lady of the house doesn't have to slice the bread, eviscerate and disjoint the chicken, or shell the peas, there aren't the same pressures for convenience packaging of foods there are in the U.S.

Because of the long Cape Malay tradition, the Asian immigrations in the last century didn't have a dramatic impact on South African cuisine. Asians—mostly Indians—were brought into Natal province (on the East Coast) in the 1860s to work on sugar plantations. Their curry spices were already familiar, though their proportions were different from the mixtures concocted by the Cape Malays. A good Durban curry, according to Mrs. Faull, is much hotter than a Malay curry.

Whether because of Cape Malay or Indian influence, curry cooking has so permeated the cuisine that curry and rice is one of the offerings on the breakfast menu of the South African Railways. We never had the stomach for such exotica in the morning so never ordered it. But the train ride we took from Johannesburg to Cape Town did provide some other brief insights into the white South African's eating habits outside the home.

For one thing, even though there seemed to be as many Afrikaans-speaking passengers as English-speaking, the cuisine was essentially English—cream soup, fried or poached fish course, ordinary meat and vegetables, desserts with that custard sauce again, and hard cheese and fruit. Not one item was an Afrikaner specialty. It was also interesting to note that many people packed in their entire food supply for the two-day journey—and my unscientific survey indicated these were mostly Afrikaners. How much or exactly what is cause and effect, I don't know. Do the frugal Afrikaners usually bring their own food since they prefer home cooking anyway, making the English-speakers the most numerous clients of the dining cars? Or do they bring their own food because Afrikaner specialties are not available?

Besides the dessert custard sauce, another relic of the British Empire is firmly entrenched in the South African Railway —tea. Anyone who has traveled in England or former English territories has grappled with the custom of before-breakfast tea served in his room in hotels, in guest houses, in private homes, on trains. For the visitor who doesn't need a cup of tea to start functioning, this custom has many disadvantages —the primary one being that timing is determined by the hotel or host and not by you. No less of a disadvantage is that you cannot turn it off—at least in Africa you can't. No matter how often you tell the hotel desk or the floor steward you don't want to be awakened at 7:00 a.m. for tea, it comes anyway. And if you yell your refusal through the door, another steward comes twenty minutes later to demand the dishes you don't have. Early rising must have been a colonial virtue.

On the South African Railway this tea business is carried to even greater lengths. The tea steward (that's his only job, preparing and serving tea and its accompaniments) comes not only first thing in the morning but at 10:00 a.m., noon, 4:00 p.m., and 6:00 p.m. And "first thing in the morning" proved to be 6:00 a.m. The tea steward's equipment includes not only teapots and cups and saucers, but a special key that opens all locks—even the bolt—on the compartment door. Even if, in search of a bit of privacy, you bolted the door, at the stated hours the steward could unshoot the bolt, pop in his head, and ask "Tea?" There was absolutely no way of keeping him out.

It is interesting how rigid these customs become. Though it was impossible to avoid tea *before* breakfast, it was almost as impossible to get tea *with* breakfast in former British Africa. Tea is for before the meal; coffee is for with the meal —impossible Americans who can't abide English coffee notwithstanding.

There are differences in eating patterns on the other side of South Africa's color line, too. Besides the nearly 600,000 Asians, the other nonwhite groups are, to use the South African terms, Bantus and Coloureds. Bantu refers to peoples who speak the Bantu languages—in other words, the over 13 million blacks. "Coloured" is equivalent to our term "mulatto" and designates the almost 2 million mixed-blood descendants of Hottentots, Cape Malays, blacks, and early white settlers of the Cape Province.

Coloureds and many of the third- and fourth-generation city-dweller Bantus generally follow the area's dominant eating pattern, within their economic limits. Most of the Bantu —the majority of whom live in traditional societies—subsist on the starch-and-stew diet prevalent in the rest of Africa. Corn—they call it *mealie*—is the starch staple. Usually the white field corn is ground into meal and made into a stiff mush like West Africa's *foofoo.* In South Africa this is called *pap* (the Dutch word) or *putu* (in Bantu languages). When they can afford it, the Africans serve a "skillie stew" with the *putu.*

These stews are much blander than West African versions. South African blacks, I was told, traditionally use little seasoning beyond salt, but many peoples have gradually borrowed from Cape Malay or Asian spice shelves.

Next to *putu,* samp corn is the favored way of preparing that starch—corn kernels which have been dried on the cob are stamped in a big mortar but not ground, then cooked a very long time with salt and fat in water. Sorghum—they call it *kaffir corn*—is also widely eaten.

Most of the recipes that follow are in the Old Cape tradition—they make up what is now considered Afrikaner cooking. I'm including *putu* and the like, of course, and some of the more curious modern dishes. But it is the Cape Malay-Dutch-French mixture stirred up in the early days plus frontier necessities that are most interesting.

As is true in less favored places in Africa, there are no traditional beginnings to a typical meal. It is not, however, for poverty reasons; Afrikaners believe in getting to the meat of the subject, you might say, as quickly as possible. Many meat and fish recipes would make excellent appetizers; you can decide for yourself which ones you'd like to use. There are not, you'll note, any traditional South African soups, either.

On to the main courses, then.

## MEAT COURSES

*Sosaties* come from two Malay words—*saté*, spiced sauce, and *sésate*, skewered meat. They are made of lamb which has been marinated in a pungently spiced, slightly sweet sauce for several days. Probably the most popular dish for a barbecue or *braai*, they may also be grilled in an oven or even baked in their marinade sauce.

Each South African cook has her own special recipe for *Sosaties*—and the spice proportions can be varied endlessly. Some prefer lemon juice to vinegar, and many won't make *Sosaties* unless they can get tamarind leaves—a Malay ingredient that imparts the sour note in this sweet-sour dish.

### SOSATIES

*4 large onions, sliced*
*2 tablespoons oil*
*2 tablespoons curry powder*
*½ teaspoon turmeric*

*2 tablespoons flour*
*1 tablespoon sugar*
*1 tablespoon freshly grated coconut*
*1 tablespoon pepper*
*Salt to taste*
*2 cups each vinegar and water*
*½ cup dried apricots (moist pack)*
*½ cup seedless raisins*
*4 bay leaves*
*1 leg of lamb, cut into 1½-inch cubes*

8 to 12 servings

Fry onion slices in oil until golden. Combine curry powder, turmeric, flour, sugar, coconut, pepper, salt to taste, vinegar, and water. Add to onion. Add apricots and raisins and cook about 5 minutes, stirring constantly. Add bay leaves. Pour sauce over meat in a shallow pan so all the meat is covered. Marinate 3 days, stirring mixture a few times each day.

To grill, string meat and apricot slices on skewers, and cook over glowing coals (or in a broiler) until done. Heat marinade and serve as a sauce.

To roast, place meat and the marinade in a shallow pan. Bake, uncovered, in a slow to moderate oven (325° to 350° F.) until meat is done, about 1 hour.

*Sosaties* are traditionally served with boiled rice or *Yellow Rice*, and chutney.

Here's another *Sosatie* marinade that uses different spices —with the exception of the curry powder. All *Sosatie* recipes *must* include curry powder and onions.

## SOSATIE MARINADE

*4 onions, thinly sliced*
*2 tablespoons oil*

*1 tablespoon curry powder*
*3 chili peppers, sliced*
*2 cloves garlic, crushed*
*1 teaspoon coriander seed*
*Lemon juice*

Fry onions in oil until golden. Combine with curry powder, chilies, garlic, coriander seed, and enough lemon juice to cover the meat. Marinate cubed leg of lamb for 1 day. Cook as directed in first recipe, preferably by grilling.

Some *Sosatie* recipes include milk in the marinade liquid. This particular recipe was given me by Mrs. Elsie Pitman, women's editor of the *Sunday Times* of Johannesburg, who writes as Ann Wise.

## SOSATIES

*3 to 3½ pounds leg of lamb, cut into small cubes*
*Salt and pepper to taste*
*1 clove garlic*
*5 onions*
*Fresh lemon leaves*
*1 tablespoon brown sugar*
*½ cup milk*
*Salad oil*
*½ cup vinegar*
*3 tablespoons curry powder*
*1 tablespoon sugar*
*2 tablespoons apricot jam*
*2 bay leaves*
*1 or 2 chili peppers, sliced*

8 to 10 servings

Season lamb cubes with salt and pepper. Place in a deep dish which has been rubbed with the clove of garlic. Mince 1 onion with lemon leaves. Add brown sugar and milk, and mix well. Pour over meat and marinate for 24 hours.

Chop remaining onions and fry in a little oil until golden. Add vinegar, curry powder, sugar, and salt to taste. Add apricot jam and bring to a boil. Remove from heat and cool. When cold, pour over the meat, adding bay leaves and sliced chilies. Cover meat and let stand 1 to 2 days.

To cook, thread meat on skewers and grill over glowing coals. Bring marinade to a boil and serve with the meat.

Stews play a very important part in Afrikaner cuisine, just as they do elsewhere in Africa. Stews that include vegetables are called *bredies*, and what kind of *bredie* it is depends on the dominant vegetable. To make any *bredie*, however, you must have at least one onion on hand.

Traditionally, the meat used in a *bredie* is mutton, and fat mutton at that. I recommend a fat cut of lamb—ribs or shoulder. Water should be added only if necessary, as the meat is supposed to cook in a little oil, its own fat and juices, and the juices of the vegetables. Like the North African *touajen*, this requires a heavy saucepan and low heat.

The method for making *bredie* is generally the same, no matter which vegetable is used. The onion is first browned in a little oil, then the meat is laid on top of the browned onion and sautéed until brown. Lastly, the vegetables are added and the pot is set to cook until everything is done. After the vegetables are added, the stew is never stirred; it is served layered, with the meat and onions on the bottom and the vegetables on top. There are exceptions, of course.

The starch served with *bredie* is always rice.

## TAMATIE (TOMATO) BREDIE

*2 or 3 large onions, sliced*
*2 to 4 tablespoons oil*
*2 pounds ribs or shoulder of lamb, cut in pieces*
*1 clove garlic, minced*
*Salt and pepper to taste*
*8 large tomatoes, peeled and sliced*
*2 potatoes, peeled and cut in eighths*
*1 teaspoon sugar*
*2 chili peppers*
*1 bay leaf*

4 to 6 servings

In a heavy stewing pan, sauté onions in oil until golden yellow, stirring frequently. Add meat, garlic and salt and pepper to taste. When meat begins to brown, cover pan and let meat cook slowly, about 45 minutes or until partially cooked. Add tomatoes, potatoes, sugar, chilies, and bay leaf and continue simmering until meat and potatoes are tender, about 30 or 45 minutes. Add water only if necessary to prevent scorching. Spoon off fat.

(When tomatoes are out of season, I substitute partially drained canned tomatoes.)

## KOOL (CABBAGE) BREDIE

*2 large onions, sliced*
*3 or 4 tablespoons oil*
*2 pounds ribs or shoulder of lamb, cut up*
*Salt and pepper to taste*
*1 large cabbage, shredded*
*2 leeks, cut into small pieces*
*½ cup sliced celery*

*1 chili pepper*
*4 potatoes, peeled and quartered*

4 to 6 servings

In a heavy stewing pan, sauté onions in oil until golden yellow. Add meat seasoned with salt and pepper and sauté until red color starts to disappear. Add cabbage, leeks, celery, and chili. Cover and simmer slowly until meat is almost done, about 1½ hours. Add potatoes and continue cooking until everything is tender, about 30 minutes more. Spoon off fat.

VARIATION: *Blomkool (Cauliflower) Bredie* is made just like *Kool Bredie*. Just substitute 1 large cauliflower, or 2 small ones, broken into flowers or shredded into strips, for the cabbage.

## GROEN ERTJIES (GREEN PEA) BREDIE

*2 pounds ribs or shoulder of lamb, cut into small pieces*
*1 onion, sliced thin*
*2 tablespoons oil*
*Salt to taste*
*1 chili pepper*
*¼ cup chopped parsley*
*3 10-ounce packages frozen peas, thawed*
*1 tablespoon sugar*

4 to 6 servings

Wash meat; drain but do not dry.

In a heavy stewing pan, brown onion in oil until golden yellow. Add meat, season with salt, and sauté until brown. Cover and simmer until meat is almost cooked. Add chili, parsley, peas, and sugar. Cover and simmer until peas and

meat are tender, 20 to 30 minutes. Spoon off fat.
VARIATION: Carrots substituted for green peas make *Wortel Bredie*. Replace peas with 6 or 8 large carrots, shredded. Instead of chili pepper, season with ½ teaspoon nutmeg and 2 to 3 whole cloves. Increase sugar by 1 teaspoon.

The word *bredie* actually comes from the Malagasy word for spinach. In its South African transformation, it came to mean any vegetable. *Spinach Bredie*, however, is one popular variety.

## SPINASIE (SPINACH) BREDIE

*3 10-ounce packages frozen chopped spinach*
*¼ cup chopped sorrel*
*2 large onions, thinly sliced*
*2 or 3 tablespoons oil*
*2 pounds ribs or shoulder of lamb, cut into pieces*
*Salt and pepper to taste*
*Lemon juice*

4 to 6 servings

Cook spinach with sorrel in a small amount of water; drain.

In a heavy stewing pan, brown onions in oil until golden yellow. Add meat. When red color begins to disappear, cover and simmer until meat is tender and brown. Add cooked spinach and season with salt and pepper. Heat to serving temperature and add lemon juice to taste. Spoon off fat.

Usually chili peppers are used for *bredie* seasoning, but this recipe spices up beans with curry powder.

You may, of course, start with dried beans—any kind will do. Soak them overnight, then cook until almost soft. You'll need about ½ pound of dried beans. For faster preparation, I prefer canned beans.

## KERRIEBOONTJIES (CURRIED BEANS) BREDIE

*3 onions, thinly sliced*
*2 to 3 tablespoons oil*
*2 pounds ribs or shoulder of lamb, cut into pieces*
*Salt and pepper to taste*
*1 teaspoon curry powder*
*1 green chili pepper*
*2 cloves garlic*
*2 1-pound cans kidney, pinto, or navy beans or black-eyed peas, well drained*
*Lemon juice*
*Sugar to taste, optional*

4 to 6 servings

In a heavy stewing pan, brown onion in oil until golden yellow. Add meat, seasoned with salt and pepper. Sauté until meat begins to lose its red color. Cover and simmer until meat is about half-cooked. Add curry powder and chili which has been crushed with the garlic. Continue cooking until meat is almost tender. Add beans and continue simmering until meat is tender and flavors are blended. Before serving, drizzle with lemon juice and add sugar to taste if desired. Spoon off fat.

For *Pumpkin Bredie*, be sure to choose a rather dry pumpkin. If it is too moist, it becomes mushy on cooking; it is supposed to hold its shape. Acorn or banana squash may be substituted for the pumpkin.

## PAMPOEN (PUMPKIN) BREDIE

*4 large onions, sliced*
*4 tablespoons oil*
*2 pounds shoulder or ribs of lamb, cut into pieces*

*3 cloves garlic*
*1-inch piece fresh ginger root*
*Salt to taste*
*3 pounds pumpkin, peeled and coarsely diced*
*2 2-inch sticks cinnamon*
*2 tablespoons sugar*
*3 chili peppers*
*4 whole cloves*

4 to 6 servings

In a heavy stewing pan, sauté onions in oil until golden yellow. Add meat and sauté 10 minutes. Process garlic and ginger in a blender until mashed, then stir in salt. Add garlic-ginger mixture to meat with pumpkin, cinnamon, sugar, chilies, and cloves. Cover and simmer very slowly until meat and pumpkin are tender. Add water if needed to prevent scorching. Spoon off fat.

## GROEN BOONTJIE (GREEN BEAN) BREDIE

*2 large onions, finely sliced*
*Oil*
*2 pounds ribs or shoulder of lamb, cut in pieces*
*2 10-ounce packages frozen French-cut green beans, thawed*
*4 potatoes, peeled and thickly sliced*
*1 cup water*
*½ teaspoon thyme*
*½ cup chopped parsley*

4 to 6 servings

Brown onions in oil in a heavy stewing pan. Add in layers meat, green beans, and potatoes. Combine water, thyme, and parsley and pour over the layers. Cover and simmer very slowly until done. This may also be cooked in a slow to moderate oven (325° to 350° F.) about 2 hours. Spoon off fat.

## LENSIES (LENTIL) BREDIE

*1 pound lentils*
*3 onions, thinly sliced*
*2 tablespoons oil*
*2 pounds ribs or shoulder of lamb, cut into pieces*
*1½-inch piece fresh ginger root*
*2 cloves garlic*
*½ teaspoon salt*
*½ teaspoon nutmeg*
*2 chili peppers*
*2 tablespoons lemon juice*

4 to 6 servings

Wash lentils; cook in six cups water until almost soft.

Brown onions in oil until golden yellow. Add meat and sauté until red color disappears. Process ginger and garlic in blender until well mashed. Add to meat, cover, and simmer until meat is nearly soft. Add lentils. Season with salt and nutmeg; add chilies. Continue simmering until meat and lentils are cooked. Add lemon juice and simmer several minutes longer. Spoon off fat.

Not all meat braised or stewed for a long time is made into a *bredie*—that is, with vegetables. *Denningvleis,* for instance, is simmered with a variety of seasonings and then served with rice. True, there are onions in this dish, but they're just another seasoning, not a vegetable.

## DENNINGVLEIS (SPICED MEAT)

*2 pounds fat leg or shoulder of lamb, cut into pieces*
*4 onions, sliced*
*4 cloves garlic, minced*
*8 whole allspice*
*3 bay leaves*
*¼ teaspoon nutmeg*
*2 tablespoons oil*
*2 or 3 chili peppers*
*3 whole cloves*
*2 tablespoons lemon juice*

6 servings

Wash meat and place, without drying, in a heavy stewing pan, along with all other ingredients except lemon juice. Simmer slowly, covered, adding water only as needed to keep the meat from scorching or drying out. Cook until done, about 1 or 1½ hours. Five minutes before serving, add lemon juice. Spoon off fat.

Serve with rice and an *Atjar*.

*Beeriani* also requires long cooking, but is not really a stew. The Eastern origins of this recipe are clearly evident, and one version or another of this savory mixture is found all across the Middle and Far East.

## BEERIANI

*2 pounds rice*
*¼ cup butter*
*2 pounds fat leg of lamb, cut into small pieces*
*3 onions, thinly sliced*
*1-inch piece fresh ginger root, grated and mashed*

*1 teaspoon dried fennel*
*2 cloves garlic, minced*
*1 teaspoon cumin seed*
*2 tomatoes, peeled and sliced*
*2 hard-cooked eggs, sliced*
*Pinch saffron*
*½ cup boiling water*

8 to 10 servings

In a heavy stewing pan, cook rice in salted water, using method requiring least amount of water. When almost done, add butter. Set aside.

Meanwhile, wash meat and put, without drying, into a heavy stewing pan along with onions, ginger, fennel, garlic, and cumin seed. Lay tomato slices on top, cover, and simmer until meat is nearly cooked. Add water only if necessary to prevent scorching.

Remove rice from cooking pot, but leave a layer of rice on the bottom. Alternate layers of meat mixture and the cooked rice, placing egg slices on top of meat in each layer. End with rice. Steep saffron in boiling water, then pour over top layer of rice. Cover tightly—pot should be well sealed. Simmer over an extremely low flame or in an oven set at lowest heat necessary to just simmer. Cook 1 to 2 hours. When finished, the flavors should be well mingled and the meat and rice should be neither moist nor dry.

Curries are as much a part of Malay cooking as they are of Indian. In South Africa numerous curry blends—hot to hotter—produce for the connoisseur subtly different tastes. These curries—as well as some other Cape Malay recipes—include, in addition to the curry powder, another spice blend called *mussala* (also spelled *massala*), an Indian term meaning *spices*. It contains many of the spices used in the curry mixture, and this reinforcement heightens the flavor of the dish. *Mussala* can be bought in Indian or Oriental food stores. Or you may make up some of your own: combine equal parts of fennel seed, cumin seed, coriander, and cinnamon. Pound or process in a blender until ground.

## CURRY

*3 large onions, thinly sliced*
*Oil*
*1 small piece ginger root*
*5 or 6 cloves garlic*
*Pinch salt*
*1 tablespoon* mussala
*5 cardamon seeds, ground*
*3 large tomatoes, peeled and thinly sliced*
*1 tablespoon each turmeric and curry powder*
*1 cup lukewarm water*
*4 to 6 pounds leg of lamb or rump of beef, cut in cubes*
*1 potato, peeled and diced*

10 to 12 servings

Brown onions in oil. Mash ginger and garlic together with a little salt until well mixed. Add to onions and continue sautéing a few minutes. Add *mussala* and cardamon and mix well. Add sliced tomatoes and simmer until tomatoes become soft. Combine turmeric and curry powder and add to tomatoes along with water. Simmer 15 to 20 minutes.

Meanwhile, wash meat and place, without drying, in a heavy stewing pan. Brown in its own juices over moderate heat, then cover and simmer until almost done. Add meat and potato to curry sauce and simmer until all is tender.

Serve with rice or *Roti* and one or more *Sambals*.

VARIATION: Another version of this curry calls for cooking the meat in the sauce. In that case, add the meat, after it has been browned in its own juices, to the curry mixture along with the tomatoes, following all other procedures as given.

In the rural areas, venison—from springbok or kudu—isn't the rarity it is in this country.

Mrs. Pitman gave me her father's method of roasting venison. She said, incidentally, that most South Africans don't skin venison until they are ready to cook it. Her father eviscerated the animal and hung it until it was aged; then he cut it into portions, skin and all. His farm, like most, had a cold, underground room where the meat was stored until needed. I don't recommend following this method if you must freeze your venison roast to keep it.

## ROAST VENISON

*1 venison roast*
*Bacon fat*
*Red wine*
*Flour*
*Salt and pepper*

servings depend on size of roast

Skin venison and wipe with a damp cloth. Lard with bacon fat, place in a deep dish and cover with red wine or vinegar. Marinate two or three days.

Make a thick paste of the flour mixed with generous amount of salt and pepper and water. Cover meat with paste and roast in a slow to moderate oven (325° to 350° F.). For the last 30 minutes of roasting, take off the paste and discard and baste frequently with the wine.

This next recipe is not Old Cape or Afrikaner or old English or old anything else. But it does appear on the menus of many restaurants in South Africa. I'm including it mostly because the name fascinated me—Monkey Gland Steak.

This dish is merely beefsteak cooked in or served with a mildly spicy sauce. No food expert I talked with had even a clue as to its origin or etymology. Mrs. Faull said, rather apologetically, that she had thought it was an American dish. A maître d' in an elegant Cape Town restaurant became agitated at my even mentioning it.

"It's on the menu, and I'll have it made if you insist," he hissed. "But *really*. A sauce made of FOUR sauces!"

A personal friend, Mrs. Desmond Kennealy of Johannesburg, gave me her recipe.

## MONKEY GLAND STEAK

*4 serving-size pieces of fairly thin-sliced flank, round, or minute steak*
*Garlic*
*1 large onion, finely chopped*
*Oil*
*1 large tomato, peeled and finely diced*
*1 tablespoon prepared mustard*
*2 teaspoons Worcestershire sauce*
*¼ to ½ teaspoon cayenne*
*1 tablespoon steak sauce*
*Fresh-ground pepper*
*3 tablespoons catsup*
*¼ teaspoon salt*

4 servings

Rub steaks with garlic. Sauté onion in oil until soft but not brown. Add steak and fry on one side. Turn and add tomato, arranging slices evenly on top of meat. Combine mustard, Worcestershire sauce, cayenne, steak sauce, pepper, catsup, and salt. Pour over steak. Cook until done to your taste.

VARIATION: Some people prefer to broil or sear the steaks separately and serve them with the sauce made by sautéing the onions until light brown, then adding remaining ingredients and simmering until tomatoes are cooked. And you may substitute red wine for the tomatoes.

Ground meat is a housewife's best friend, in South Africa as in most other places. The most traditional ground-meat dish is a Cape Malay meat loaf called *Bobotie*. There are many variations on the *Bobotie* theme with curry powder as the basic motif. The meat should be ground lamb, though ground beef works as well.

This first version is from Mrs. Pitman's files.

## BOBOTIE I

*2 pounds ground lamb or beef*
*1 slice white bread*
*Milk*
*2 medium onions, shredded or chopped*
*2 cloves garlic, minced*
*Butter*
*Curry powder*
*1 tablespoon sugar*
*1 teaspoon salt*
*2 tablespoons lemon juice*
*½ teaspoon grated lemon rind*
*2 tablespoons seedless raisins*
*2 tablespoons ground almonds*
*2 tablespoons chutney or apricot jam*
*2 eggs*

8 servings

Mix ground meat with bread which has been soaked in a little milk and then squeezed nearly dry. Fry onions and garlic in 1 tablespoon butter until golden yellow. Mix in 1 to 1½ tablespoons curry powder, sugar, salt, lemon juice and rind, and raisins and simmer 15 minutes. Add meat, almonds, and chutney or jam. Stir in 1 egg and mix well. Place in a buttered baking dish and bake in a moderate oven (375° F.) about 30 minutes. Drain off fat. Beat remaining egg with 1 cup milk and about 1 teaspoon curry powder. Pour over the meat, reduce heat to slow (300° to 325° F.), and continue baking until well set but not dry.

*Bobotie* is always served with rice and chutney, plus any curry-type accompaniments you like.

VARIATION: Substitute 2 lemon, orange, or bay leaves for the lemon juice and rind; reduce curry powder to ½ teaspoon; increase eggs to 4; add ¼ teaspoon turmeric; eliminate raisins. Mix together meat, soaked and squeezed bread, 2 eggs, ¼ pound melted butter, chopped onion, mashed garlic, curry, turmeric, and almonds. Put mixture into greased baking dish and bake in a moderate oven (375° F.) 30 minutes. Drain fat. Beat remaining eggs with ½ cup milk and pour over meat. Stick orange, lemon, or bay leaves into loaf, reduce heat to slow (300° F.), and bake until set but not dry.

Cooked meat may be substituted for raw meat in *Bobotie.*

## BOBOTIE II

*2 onions, finely sliced*
*1 apple, diced*
*2 tablespoons butter*
*2 pounds ground cooked or raw lamb or beef*
*2 slices bread, soaked in milk and squeezed out*
*2 tablespoons curry powder*

*2 tablespoons sugar*
*2 eggs*
*2 tablespoons vinegar*
*2 teaspoons salt*
*¼ teaspoon pepper*
*¼ cup raisins*
*¼ cup slivered blanched almonds*
*6 bay or lemon leaves*
*1 cup milk*
*1 teaspoon turmeric*

8 servings

Fry onion and apple in butter until onion is golden. Mix with meat, bread, curry powder, sugar, 1 egg, vinegar, salt, pepper, raisins, and almonds. Combine well. Place in a greased baking dish. Insert lemon or bay leaves into meat loaf (roll lemon leaves). Bake in a moderate oven (350° F.) 25 minutes for cooked meat, 50 to 60 minutes for raw. Drain fat. Beat second egg with milk and turmeric and pour over meat; continue baking until set.

In our lexicon the word *kebab* refers to cubes of meat grilled over charcoal. The Cape Malays, however, apply the term to a ground-meat dish.

Unless you're the type who really plans ahead, this particular recipe would be hard to duplicate in its original form, since we don't use charcoal-burning stoves. The ground meat is smoked by placing glowing coals on top of the meat after it has been mixed with the spices. The well-organized person could have some ground meat ready-mixed next time there is some charcoal available and smoke the meat for freezing and later use. For the rest of us, I've substituted hickory-smoked salt or liquid smoke.

## KEBABS

*2 onions, finely chopped*
*3 cloves garlic, minced*
*Pepper to taste*
*1½ teaspoons hickory-smoked salt or 1 teaspoon salt plus 1 teaspoon liquid smoke, or to taste*
*2 pounds ground beef*
*3 slices white bread, soaked in milk or water and squeezed out*
*3 eggs, slightly beaten*
*1 teaspoon butter*
*Pinch nutmeg*
*8 hard-cooked eggs, shelled*
*Oil*
*3 bay leaves*
*2 onions, thinly sliced*
*Vinegar to taste*
*Salt to taste*
*Sugar to taste*

4 servings

Mash together chopped onions, garlic, pepper, and salt if using liquid smoke. Mix with beef, bread, 3 eggs, butter, and nutmeg. Sprinkle on hickory salt (or liquid smoke) and mix well again. Let stand 10 to 15 minutes to blend flavors.

To cook, form meat mixture around hard-cooked eggs so they are well covered. Heat enough oil for shallow frying and add bay leaves. Fry *kebabs,* turning to brown on all sides. It may be necessary to baste frequently to prevent drying. As they cook, drain and keep warm.

To remaining fat in the pan, add sliced onions and fry until nicely browned. Season with vinegar, salt, and sugar, tasting to be sure the mixture is sweet-sour. Pour over *kebabs* and serve with rice.

*Pannas* is a relic of Cape pioneer days when housewives helped with the butchering and had all sorts of bits and pieces of meat to use up.

Strictly speaking, *Pannas* is not a ground-meat dish, but I'm including it here because it could be made with ground beef, lamb, or even pork. And it would do for stretching a small amount of leftover meat.

The original recipe calls for *boermeal,* which is a coarse whole-wheat flour or cereal (*boer* means farmer in Afrikaans). I suggest substituting a whole-wheat hot cereal (like Wheatena) or cornmeal. This, incidentally, would make an excellent breakfast or brunch dish.

## PANNAS

*1 pound soup meat, leftover meat, or ground meat*
*Salt and pepper to taste*
*Stock*
*Whole-wheat cooking cereal or cornmeal*
*Butter or oil*

4 to 6 servings

If using soup meat, season with salt and pepper and boil until meat falls off the bone or is very well cooked. Skim and reserve stock. Cut meat into small pieces. Finely dice leftover meat and season. For ground meat, season well with salt and pepper and fry until meat is nicely browned; drain.

Bring 2 or 3 cups of stock to a boil (if using leftover or ground meat make a stock with bouillon cubes). Add meat and then enough wheat cereal or cornmeal to make a very stiff mush. Cook until done. Turn into a greased pan 13 by 9 by 2 inches and cool. Cut into slices and fry in butter or oil until brown.

Stuffed cabbage no doubt was a recipe transported intact from Europe. Sometimes the dish, called *Frikkadel,* is made with grape leaves in the Eastern manner.

Poaching is the usual method for cooking, but I prefer this version, which is fried.

## KOOL FRIKKADEL (STUFFED CABBAGE)

*2 pounds ground lean lamb*
*2 slices bread, soaked in milk and squeezed out*
*1 small onion, finely chopped*
*Salt and pepper to taste*
*¼ cup chopped parsley*
*1 teaspoon nutmeg*
*2 eggs*
*Oil or butter*
*1 head cabbage*

6 to 8 servings

Combine lamb, soaked bread, onion, salt, pepper, parsley, nutmeg, and eggs. Mix well. Form into balls and fry gently in a small amount of oil or butter until well browned and cooked. Remove meat, reserving fat in pan.

Separate leaves of cabbage carefully. Pour boiling water over them, then drain. Roll each meat ball into a cabbage leaf, tucking in ends to form a secure packet. Reheat oil or butter in pan, adding more if necessary. Sauté stuffed cabbage until well browned on all sides.

Serve with rice.

Ground meat is sometimes used for a curry. The term *geema* in the name of this dish is probably a corruption of the Persian *kima,* which means hash.

## GEEMA KERRIE (GROUND-MEAT CURRY)

*2 onions, chopped*
*¼ cup oil*
*1 inch piece fresh ginger*
*3 cloves garlic*
*½ teaspoon salt*
*1 pound tomatoes, peeled and sliced*
*2 chili peppers*
*1 tablespoon curry powder*
*1 tablespoon turmeric*
*1 tablespoon* mussala
*2 pounds ground meat*

6 to 8 servings

Sauté onions in oil until well browned. In a blender, process ginger and garlic until well mashed; stir in salt and add mixture to onions. Add tomatoes, chilies, curry powder, turmeric, and *mussala*. Simmer gently while cooking ground meat separately over a moderate fire until it loses its red color (cook meat in its own juices; do not add any fat). Add meat to curry and continue simmering until all ingredients are well cooked.

Serve over rice.

The Indians have contributed *Samosas* to the South African cuisine just as they have to the cuisine of other African countries in which they've settled in any numbers. (See chapter on East Africa.)

Making the dough for *Samosas* is a tedious process. I have found that frozen egg-roll dough or skin, available in gourmet shops, works just as well.

This is a party-sized recipe which makes about 80 servings. It may be cut in half.

## SAMOSAS

*1 inch piece ginger root*
*6 cloves garlic*
*2 pounds ground lean lamb (or beef if desired)*
*3 large onions, thinly sliced*
*1 tablespoon* mussala
*1 tablespoon curry powder*
*1 tablespoon turmeric*
*Salt to taste*
*2 pounds frozen egg-roll dough, thawed*
*Flour*
*Oil*

80 servings

Process ginger and garlic in blender until well mashed. Combine with meat, onions, *mussala,* curry powder, and turmeric. Sauté in a heavy frying pan, without adding any fat, over a low heat 30 minutes, stirring occasionally and breaking up the meat. Salt well. Spoon off fat.

Cut sheets of thawed egg-roll dough into strips about 3 by 6 inches. Fold one point up to form a triangular pocket. Fold over again and then fill the pocket with some of the meat mixture. Bring down the top and seal all open sides with a paste made of flour and water. You should end up with a neat, secure triangle of meat-stuffed pastry.

Deep-fat fry filled *Samosas,* a few at a time, in oil until golden brown. Drain and keep warm.

After frying and quick cooling, *Samosas* may be frozen. To serve, thaw and place in a hot oven (400° F.) until very hot.

## PRESERVED MEAT AND SAUSAGES

Homemade preserved meat and sausages are still another mark of a rural society that lingers on in South Africa.

*Biltong*, as I've mentioned, is widely regarded as a snack and is made commercially as well as in the home. Coriander is often used to give the salted meat a bit of flavor.

Use *Biltong* also in a sandwich with buttered bread or as you would deviled ham, say, in sandwich fillings. It is good, too, crumbled into scrambled eggs or mixed with cream cheese for a spread or dip.

### BILTONG

*2½ pounds coarse salt*
*⅛ pound saltpeter*
*2 ounces coriander*
*1½ teaspoons pepper*
*50 pounds beef, venison, or large game birds cut into strips with the grain*
*Brine made of 3 gallons water mixed with 1 pound salt*

about 20 pounds

Mix coarse salt, saltpeter, coriander, and pepper together. Rub mixture well into meat. Layer meat in a large tub or crock. Sprinkle all with any remaining salt mixture. Let stand in a cool place 48 (if pieces of meat are small) to 72 hours (for large pieces). Wash meat in brine and hang up in a cool, ventilated place to dry thoroughly.

Another preserved meat specialty is *Soutribbetjies*. These are corned lamb ribs designed to be grilled over charcoal.

## SOUTRIBBETJIES (CORNED LAMB RIBS)

*¾ cup salt*
*1 tablespoon brown sugar*
*½ teaspoon saltpeter*
*4 pounds lamb ribs*

6 to 8 servings

Combine salt, sugar, and saltpeter and rub this mixture well into ribs. Place in an earthware dish 48 hours. Hang the ribs up to dry thoroughly.

To cook, simmer dried ribs in water until tender, then grill over glowing coals until well browned. May be served hot or cold.

Sausage-making isn't as widely practiced in the home these days as in former times, though most modern South African cookbooks include recipes for the old-time Afrikaner sausage, *Boerewors*. The seasonings are somewhat different from the spice blends used in this country.

Combinations of meat are usually specified in *Boerewors*—sometimes just beef and pork, sometimes beef, pork, and lamb. Here are two versions.

## BOEREWORS I

*3 pounds each lamb, pork, and beef*
*1½ pounds pork fat, cut in small cubes*
*2 tablespoons vinegar*
*2 tablespoons salt*
*1 tablespoon pepper*
*4 tablespoons coriander*
*1½ teaspoons ground cloves*
*1 tablespoon allspice*

10 pounds

Grind together beef, lamb, and pork. Put through grinder again with pork fat. Combine with remaining ingredients and mix well. Pipe or stuff into sausage skins or form into patties.

### BOEREWORS II

*10 pounds beef*
*6 pounds pork*
*Fat if needed*
*1 tablespoon each coriander and cloves*
*¼ teaspoon peppercorns*
*½ teaspoon each thyme and sage*
*1 cup vinegar*
*Salt and pepper to taste*

16 pounds

Grind together beef and pork, adding extra pork fat if meat is too lean. Combine with remaining ingredients and mix well. Refrigerate 12 to 24 hours. Mix again and pipe or stuff into sausage skins or form into patties.

## POULTRY

Domesticated poultry was not as plentiful as sheep and cattle in the early days of South Africa. When available, it was usually cooked with a generous dash of seasoning.

This Old Cape recipe for *Spiced Fowl* was used two ways: either passed with rice or baked into a pie.

### SPICED FOWL

*3 onions, sliced*
*2 tablespoons butter*

*1 stewing hen (turkey may be substituted), cut in 8 or 10 pieces*
*Salt and pepper to taste*
*5 peppercorns*
*1 teaspoon coriander*
*2 or 3 whole allspice*
*Pinch mace*
*1 cup boiling water or more*
*1 tablespoon cornstarch*
*½ cup vermicelli pieces*

6 to 8 servings

Sauté onions in butter until golden brown. Add chicken pieces, season with salt and pepper, and brown lightly. Place peppercorns, coriander, allspice, and mace in a cheesecloth bag. Add to chicken with 1 cup boiling water. Simmer slowly, adding water as necessary. When chicken is almost tender, remove spice bag. Combine cornstarch with a little cold water and add to chicken. Stir in vermicelli. Continue simmering until vermicelli and chicken are cooked. Adjust seasoning and serve with rice. There should not be much liquid left when dish is finished.

VARIATION: To make a *Chicken Pie*, when vermicelli is cooked, remove bones from chicken. Place chicken mixture in a pie pan lined with pastry. Top with pastry, seal edges, and prick top with a fork. Brush top with a little beaten egg and bake in a hot oven (425° F.) until pastry is nicely browned.

*Gebraaide Hoender* translates as roast chicken, though most of the cooking is done by steaming.

## GEBRAAIDE HOENDER

*1 2½- to 3-pound broiler-fryer, cut up*
*Salt to taste*
*1 onion, cut in pieces*
*2 teaspoons mussala*
*Pepper to taste*
*½ teaspoon shredded, mashed ginger root*
*2 or 3 potatoes, peeled and sliced*

4 servings

Place chicken in a heavy stewing pan, season with salt, and add a little water. Cover and simmer gently. When about half cooked, add onion and all the spices. Arrange potato slices over the chicken and continue simmering until all is cooked. Brown under a broiler just before serving.

Chicken rather like West Africa's *Pepper Chicken* is popular in present-day South Africa.

This dish appears on menus as *Chicken Peri-Peri*—*peri-peri* being the local name for long, red chilies. (In East Africa these chilies are called *peli-peli.*) Powdered *peri-peri* is a staple on grocery spice shelves. For Americans, cayenne is an acceptable substitute. Don't make the mistake of substituting chili powder for chilies. Chili powder is a blend. However, some specialty food stores stock pure ground chilies which may be used for *peri-peri*.

As with *Pepper Chicken,* there are several ways to cook *Chicken Peri-Peri.* Mrs. Pitman makes hers by broiling.

## BROILED CHICKEN PERI-PERI

*1 broiler-fryer, cut up*
*½ cup melted butter*

*Lemon juice*
*2 to 3 teaspoons* peri-peri *powder or cayenne*

4 servings

Place chicken on broiler pan. Brush with melted butter and drizzle well with lemon juice. Broil, turning chicken frequently and applying butter and lemon each time. When nearly done, sprinkle one side with at least 1 teaspoon *peri-peri* or cayenne and broil about 7 minutes. Repeat for other side.

Serve with French-fried potatoes.

Mrs. Faull recommends marinating the chicken in a sauce heavily spiked with powdered *peri-peri* and then grilling it over coals.

## GRILLED CHICKEN PERI-PERI

*½ cup vinegar*
*½ cup oil*
*½ tablespoon Worcestershire sauce*
*2 tablespoons catsup*
*2 cloves garlic, crushed*
*3 teaspoons salt*
*1 teaspoon paprika*
*½ teaspoon powdered mustard*
*2 teaspoons* peri-peri *powder or cayenne*
*2 broiler-fryers, cut up*

8 to 10 servings

Combine all ingredients except chicken and let stand 12 to 24 hours. Marinate chicken pieces in the sauce at least 4 hours; the longer it marinates, the stronger the flavor. Grill over glowing coals, basting with the marinade sauce, until chicken is browned and well cooked.

## FISH AND SEAFOOD

The rich waters off the southern coast of Africa have provided many ingredients for Cape cookery.

South Africa's lobster tails are exported to all parts of the world. Some other inhabitants of the southern waters are not as well known by their South African names—fish such as kingklip or snoek, for instance.

*Ingelegde Vis*—pickled fish—has been made in the Cape area for centuries. The Cape Malay or Afrikaner housewife would choose snoek, kingklip, or Cape salmon for this, but you may use any firm fish—salmon, sea bass, snapper, haddock, etc. *Pickled Fish* is a cold dish.

### INGELEGDE VIS (PICKLED FISH)

*2 pounds firm fish fillets, fresh or frozen and thawed*
*Salt and pepper to taste*
*Oil*
*6 onions, sliced*
*Wine vinegar*
*2 chili peppers*
*½ teaspoon turmeric*
*½ teaspoon curry powder*
*½ teaspoon shredded ginger root*
*2 bay leaves (optional)*

4 to 6 servings

Fry fish fillets, which have been lightly seasoned with salt and pepper, in a little oil until lightly browned. Set aside.

To the sliced onions in a saucepan, add enough vinegar to cover. Add salt to taste, chilies, turmeric, curry powder, and ginger. Bring to a boil slowly, skimming as scum rises. As soon as the mixture boils, remove from heat; onions should not cook, but should retain their shape and remain crisp.

Arrange layers of fish and onion in a bowl or shallow dish. Pour the liquid over and add bay leaves if desired. Cover and refrigerate for 2 or 3 days. Serve with *Blatjang*.

Dried snoek cooked with onions and potatoes is an Old Cape Malay favorite.

## SNOEKSMOOR

*2 pounds dried snoek (or any dried, firm fish)*
*2 onions, chopped or sliced*
*Oil*
*2 chili peppers, cut up fine*
*4 potatoes, peeled and diced in small pieces*

4 to 6 servings

Soak fish several hours or overnight. Drain well, remove bones, and shred.

Fry onions in oil until golden brown. Add chilies and potatoes. Sauté until potatoes are lightly browned. Add shredded fish and braise until all is browned and potatoes are cooked.

Serve with rice and *Blatjang* and *Sambals*.

VARIATIONS: There are many versions of this dish. Beans are sometimes substituted for the potatoes (1 1-pound can beans, drained). Or add 4 peeled and sliced tomatoes with the potatoes. Or use tomatoes without potatoes. Or eliminate the potatoes or any substitute altogether.

The rice-layered meat dish *Beeriani* is also made with fish.

## FISH BEERIANI

*2 pounds fish fillets, fresh or thawed frozen*
*Oil*
*5 large onions, sliced*
*15 whole cloves*
*4 cloves garlic, chopped*
*1 teaspoon* mussala
*1 teaspoon turmeric*
*3 teaspoons curry powder*
*3 large tomatoes, peeled and thinly sliced*
*¼ teaspoon each cinnamon and cardamon*
*1½ cups rice*
*2 cups water*

6 servings

Lightly brown fish fillets in hot oil. Drain and set aside.

Brown 2 or 3 of the onions in a little oil. Add cloves, garlic, *mussala*, turmeric, and curry powder. Continue sautéing until onions are well browned. Add tomatoes and fish slices.

Meanwhile, in a heavy stewing pan, brown remaining onions in oil. Add cinnamon, cardamon, water, and rice. Cover and simmer until rice is nearly cooked. Remove the rice from the pan, leaving a layer on the bottom. Layer fish mixture and rice alternately, ending with rice. Cover and simmer very slowly until rice is cooked and all moisture is absorbed. If the pot is heavy enough and the fire low enough, this should take at least 30 to 40 minutes. The longer and slower the cooking, the better.

South Africa's famous lobsters are consumed in a number of ways. One Old Cape recipe is for braising the meat.

## GESMOORDE KREEF (BRAISED LOBSTER)

*1 large lobster*
*2 onions, thinly sliced*
*Oil*
*1 chili pepper*
*Salt to taste*

4 servings

Remove the meat of the lobster from the shell and the legs. Use all the green part and the eggs if there are any. In a heavy pan, sauté onions in oil until golden brown. Add lobster and chili and cook slowly until meat is tender. Add a little water if absolutely necessary. Season well with salt and serve with rice.

Sometimes the ever-handy box of curry powder is used with lobster.

## KREEF KERRIE (CURRIED LOBSTER)

*6 lobster tails, fresh or frozen*
*4 onions*
*Oil*
*1 tomato, peeled and sliced*
*2 teaspoons curry powder*
*1 teaspoon turmeric*
*2 cloves garlic, minced*
*1 piece ginger root*

6 servings

Cut up lobster tails (shells and all) into pieces about 2-inches wide.

Brown onions in oil. Then add all other ingredients and

simmer until lobster is cooked. Serve with rice.

The lobster shells give this curry a strong flavor of the sea which Cape Malays and South Africans like.

For the fishermen in the family, here's an interesting tip from Mrs. Faull's repertoire. She says many old-timers save themselves the trouble of scaling fresh-caught fish. Just wrap a gutted fresh fish tightly in a generous amount of wet newspaper. Place the packet right in the campfire coals. When the paper begins to burn and peel, unwrap the fish. The scales will adhere to the newspapers, the skin will come off easily, and the meat, which has cooked in its own juices, will be delicious.

## SAMBALS AND SALADS

Some preceding recipes, you've noted, recommend serving curries with rice and *sambals. Sambal* is the Cape Malay word for curry accompaniments. In this cuisine, though, it means more than coconut, raisins, and the like; it refers to the variety of grated vegetables or fruit, seasoned with vinegar and chili peppers, designed to be a cooling counter to the hot curries.

When the same vegetables or fruit are shredded instead of grated, they are called salads—*slaai* in Afrikaans.

Whatever the fruit or vegetable being tossed into a *sambal*, the method is the same—it is grated, allowed to marinate in a little salt, then flavored with green chili peppers and vinegar. The vinegar is used sparingly; *sambals* should just be moist, not wet.

Whenever it is in season, cucumber is served with curries.

## KOMKOMMER (CUCUMBER) SAMBAL

*3 or 4 cucumbers, peeled and finely grated*
*Salt*
*2 green chili peppers, diced*
*1 clove garlic, mashed*
*Vinegar*

Sprinkle grated cucumber generously with salt and let stand several hours. Drain, pressing out all the water. Add chilies, garlic, and only enough vinegar to moisten slightly.

For *Komkommer Slaai* (*Cucumber Salad*) slice the cucumbers instead of grating them.

VARIATIONS: *Wortel* (*Carrot*) *Sambal*—Choose a bunch of young, sweet carrots, wash them well, and finely grate. Omit garlic.

APPEL (APPLE) SAMBAL—Peel and grate 4 or 5 apples and moisten with either vinegar or lemon juice.

After spiced and slightly sweet curries, Cape Malay salads do an admirable job of refreshing the taste buds, even though they are frequently seasoned with chilies. The reason is that Cape Malays never use oil in salad dressings—just vinegar.

A number of Cape salads include onions treated to improve their digestibility.

## TREATED ONIONS

Slice the onions—thick or thin, according to the recipe—then cover with boiling water. Let them stand a short while, no more than 10 minutes, then drain. If you wish to crispen the onions, place them in ice water for 10 minutes. This treatment is supposed to wash out "onion breath" as well as making them easier on the stomach.

All these salads make 4 servings.

## ONION SALAD

*1 onion, thinly sliced and treated*
*White vinegar*
*2 green chili peppers, mashed*
*½ teaspoon salt*
*½ teaspoon sugar*

Moisten treated onions with vinegar combined with chilies, salt, and sugar. Use only enough vinegar to moisten.

## TOMATIE EN UIWE SLAAI
## (TOMATO AND ONION SALAD)

*1 tomato, thinly sliced*
*1 onion, thinly sliced and treated*
*Vinegar*
*½ teaspoon each salt and sugar*
*2 green chili peppers, mashed*

Combine tomato and onion. Moisten with vinegar mixed with salt, sugar, and chilies.

## KOOL SLAAI (CABBAGE SALAD)

*1 small cabbage, thinly sliced or shredded*
*1 onion, chopped*
*1 chili pepper, mashed*
*½ teaspoon salt*
*Vinegar*

Scald cabbage with boiling water and drain immediately, squeezing out well. Add onion, chili, salt, and enough vinegar to moisten.

### ROOIBEET SLAAI (BEET SALAD)

*¼ pound beets, cooked, peeled, and thinly sliced*
*2 medium onions, thinly sliced and treated*
*Red wine or cider vinegar*
*½ teaspoon each salt and sugar*

Mix beets and onions. Moisten with vinegar mixed with salt and sugar.

### DADEL SLAAI (DATE SALAD)

*½ pound dates*
*Onions, shredded and treated*
*½ teaspoon each sugar and salt*
*Vinegar*

Cut up the dates. Arrange dates and onions in layers in a flat bowl, or toss them together. Use as many or as few onions as desired—some people like lots, some not many. Combine sugar and salt with enough vinegar to moisten dates and onions well.

## VEGETABLES AND STARCHES

In the Cape Malay tradition, vegetables are most typically cooked up in *bredies*. Alone, they are generally prepared by braising in oil or butter and are served with rice. You'll notice the Malays' favorite ingredient—onions—is included with all vegetables.

## BRAISED VEGETABLES

The method of cooking is generally the same for all vegetables. Two onions, finely sliced or chopped, are browned in oil or butter along with 1 mashed clove of garlic, 1 or 2 mashed chili peppers, and 2 or 3 slices of fresh ginger root. When the onions are browned, the vegetables are added along with more oil or butter if necessary, and the vegetables are braised slowly until cooked.

GESMOORDE KOOL (Braised Cabbage): Shred 1 cabbage very fine.

GESMOORDE BRINJALS (Braised Eggplant): Slice rather thickly 1 medium eggplant or several small ones (choose the long, lean variety). Do not peel.

GESMOORDE SNIPPERBOONTJIES (Braised Green Beans): Use 2 10-ounce packages frozen French-cut green beans, thawed.

GESMOORDE SNIPPERBOONTJIES MET WORTELS (Braised Green Beans with Carrots): Use 1 package French-cut green beans, thawed, and ½ pound shredded carrots. Add carrots to browned onions first; when they are partially cooked, add green beans.

GESMOORDE SPINASIE (Braised Spinach): Use 2 10-ounce packages frozen chopped spinach, thawed.

Other South African vegetable dishes are of European origin, frequently with spice contributions from the East.

White potatoes are not quite as widely used as they are in the United States, but sweet potatoes are highly favored. Occasionally they are used for fritters.

## SWEET POTATO FRITTERS

*1 pound sweet potatoes, peeled*
*1 cup flour*

*1 egg*
*¼ cup butter, melted*
*Pinch salt*
*Oil*

4 servings

Grate potatoes. Cover with boiling water and let stand 10 or 15 minutes. Drain.

Combine potatoes, flour, egg, butter, and salt. (If batter is too stiff, add a little warm water; if it is too wet, add more flour.) Drop by tablespoonfuls into hot oil and fry until nicely browned and cooked through.

This *Stewed Sweet Potatoes* recipe goes particularly well with ham or pork.

## GESTOOFDE PATATS
## (STEWED SWEET POTATOES)

*1 pound sweet potatoes, peeled and sliced*
*⅓ cup brown sugar*
*Salt to taste*
*Butter*
*1 cinnamon stick*
*2 slices ginger root, bruised (That is, hit several times with a wooden spoon)*

4 to 6 servings

Layer sweet potato slices in a heavy saucepan, sprinkling each layer with sugar and salt and dotting with butter. Cover with water. Add cinnamon stick and ginger. Simmer slowly until done and all the water has boiled off. (If water hasn't evaporated, increase heat and boil off, taking care potatoes don't scorch.) Increase heat and cook until bottom is nicely browned, adding more butter if necessary.

Corn—*mealie*—grown in South Africa is generally field corn rather than sweet corn and is, of course, much drier than what Americans are used to.

Green corn in this recipe means corn right off the cob as distinguished from the dried corn staple, *samp*. The batter may be steamed instead of baked.

## GREEN CORN BREAD

*3 cups corn, cut off the cob, fresh, frozen and thawed, or canned*
*1 teaspoon salt*
*1 tablespoon corn oil*
*1 tablespoon sugar*
*2 teaspoons baking powder*

1 8-by-3-inch loaf

If using frozen or canned corn, drain it well. If the kernels are exceedingly moist, place on a flat pan in a 250° F. oven for a few minutes to dry them out a bit. They should not be too dry, however.

Mince kernels in a blender. Combine with remaining ingredients. Bake in a greased 8-by-3-inch loaf pan or an 8-inch square pan in a moderate oven (350° F.) 25 to 40 minutes. Turn out carefully and serve sliced with butter.

If desired, add 1 egg for a richer bread. The egg will also bind the bread and hold the batter together better. The finished product's consistency is similar to spoonbread.

*Putu* or *Pap* is the cornmeal mush Africans in South, Central, and some parts of East Africa subsist on. It is similar to West African *Corn Foofoo* and is eaten with stew when available.

Traditionally, this dish is cooked a very long time—several hours.

## PUTU

*4½ cups water*
*1½ teaspoons salt*
*2 cups white mealie meal (cornmeal)*

8 to 10 servings

Bring 4 cups water to a boil in a heavy stewing pan. Add salt. Pour in cornmeal. Do not stir. Simmer very slowly about 15 minutes. Continue simmering 5 minutes, stirring with a wooden spoon to incorporate remaining moisture and until mixture is smooth and thick. Carefully pour ½ cup water along the sides of the pan. Stir well. Cover and cook very slowly about 15 minutes more.

There are several ways to prepare rice for *bredies* and curries, in addition to plain boiling or steaming.

*Yellow Rice* gets its color from saffron or turmeric, and raisins are added for both color and taste.

## GEEL RYS (YELLOW RICE)

*2 cups water*
*1 cup rice*
*1 cup seedless raisins*
*Scant teaspoon turmeric or ¼ teaspoon crumbled saffron*
*1 2-inch stick cinnamon*
*2 tablespoons brown sugar (optional)*
*3 tablespoons butter*

4 servings

Bring water to a boil. Stir in rice and remaining ingredients. Cover and simmer on low heat until moisture is absorbed.

*Spiced Rice* also goes well with curry.

## SPICED RICE

*½ onion, thinly sliced*
*Oil*
*1 cup rice*
*2 cloves*
*Pinch cardamon*
*½-inch stick cinnamon*
*½ cup water or more*

4 servings

Brown onion in a small amount of oil. Stir in rice, cloves, cardamon, and cinnamon. Add water and simmer over a low heat. Continue cooking, adding small amounts of water as needed until rice is cooked. The rice should be very dry.

*Bredies* and curries may be served with *Roti* instead of rice. *Roti* is the Malay word for bread, but we'd call these pancakes.

## ROTI

*4 cups flour*
*2 teaspoons salt*
*¼ pound butter*
*Oil*

6 cakes

Mix together flour, salt, and enough water to make a soft dough. Roll out, dab with butter, fold up as for puff-pastry, and roll out again. Continue buttering, folding, and rolling out until all the butter is used up. Set aside about 3 hours.

Roll out dough into 6 fairly thin rounds. Heat an iron pan or griddle. Brush thinly with oil. Place 1 round of dough in pan; brush top with oil. When underside is nicely browned, turn and bake until brown. When done, remove from pan, fold in half, then loosely in quarters between two pieces of brown paper. Clap quickly between hands; this loosens the layers formed by the buttering-rolling process. Unfold and keep warm. Repeat until all dough is used up. Serve with a curry or *bredie.*

## PRESERVES

Preserves that South Africans consider uniquely theirs fall into two categories. First are the *Blatjangs* and *Atjars*—the spicy condiments served with curries and curry-flavored dishes. Then there are the fruit preserves made so the fruit is crisp and crunchy and the syrup thick and sweet. Both types are of Cape Malay origin or were highly influenced by the cooking methods brought to Cape Colony by the East Indian slaves.

*Atjar* is fruit or vegetables pickled in seasoned fish oil. Fish oil is not available in this country, and I wouldn't recommend it if it were. To anyone in the over thirty-five generation, anything made with fish oil—no matter the fish—inevitably conjures up memories of cod-liver oil. Use salad oil for a dish acceptable to American tastes. The fruit or vegetable is never cooked (though green beans are blanched) so the product has a crisp, firm texture. *Blatjang* is fruit or vegetable in seasoned vinegar.

The proportions in this recipe for the *Atjar* pickling liquid are for one pint of oil; you'll have to make enough pickle to cover your fruit or vegetables well.

## ATJAR PICKLE

*1 pint oil*
*2 cloves garlic, mashed*
*1 teaspoon powdered fenugreek (available in drugstores)*
*1 teaspoon turmeric*
*2 chili peppers*
*2 tablespoons curry powder (more if you like things hotter)*

1 pint

Combine all ingredients and bring to a boil.

Most popular ingredients for *Atjar* are lemons and green mangoes, a fruit that resembles a very large olive.

## GREEN MANGO ATJAR

*6 pounds green mangoes*
*Salted water*
Atjar Pickle

3 to 4 pints

Cut the meat from the mangoes; cover with very salty water (1 tablespoon per quart) and allow to stand 2 days. Drain well until mango pieces are dry.

Place mangoes in sterilized jars. Pour enough boiling *Atjar Pickle* over the fruit to cover completely. Seal. Process 20 minutes in boiling-water bath.

Whenever a serving of mangoes is removed from the jar, be sure the remainder of the fruit is well covered with the pickle.

## LEMON ATJAR

*12 lemons*
*Salt*
Atjar Pickle
*¼ cup mustard seed*

about 1½ pints

Wash lemons and wipe well. Quarter lengthwise without severing skin entirely. Remove as many of the seeds as possible, and return lemons to original shape. Place lemons in a bowl and cover them with salt. Let stand 2 or 3 days.

Remove lemons from salt, but do not wash them off. Place lemons in sterilized jars. Add mustard seed to boiling *Atjar Pickle* and pour over fruit, being sure all the fruit is covered. Seal. Process 20 minutes in boiling-water bath.

To serve, provide a small fork and knife so each diner may cut off as much of the lemon quarters as he wishes. This is eaten skin and all.

## ONION ATJAR

*2 pounds small onions*
*Salt*
Atjar Pickle

about 3 pints

Choose the smallest onions available. Peel but leave whole. Cover with salt and let stand about 12 hours. Remove from salt and wash. Place in sterilized jars and add boiling *Atjar Pickle,* being sure the oil covers the onions completely. Seal. Process 20 minutes in boiling-water bath.

## CAULIFLOWER ATJAR

*1 cauliflower*
*Salt*
Atjar Pickle

1 to 2 pints, depending on size of cauliflower

Break up the cauliflower into flowers. Cover with very salty water (1 tablespoon per quart) for 6 hours.

Remove flowers from salt water without rinsing and place in sterilized jars. Cover with boiling *Atjar Pickle.* Seal. Process 20 minutes in boiling-water bath.

## GREEN BEAN ATJAR

*2 pounds green beans, thinly sliced diagonally*
*Salt*
Atjar Pickle

about 4 pints

Bring green beans to a boil, then immediately drain. Cover with salt and allow to stand 12 hours.

Remove beans from salt but do not wash. Place in sterilized jars and add boiling *Atjar Pickle,* being sure oil covers the vegetables completely. Seal. Process 20 minutes in boiling-water bath.

*Blatjang* is a hot condiment and strong. As with *Atjar,* the seasonings are similar in all *Blatjangs,* but the pickling medium is vinegar, rather than oil.

## APRICOT BLATJANG

*1 pound dried apricots*
*¼ cup dehydrated onion*
*6 dry chili peppers*
*2 cloves garlic*
*½ teaspoon salt*
*2 cups red wine or cider vinegar*

about 1½ pints

Stew apricots in a small amount of water until they are soft enough to mash. In blender, combine onion, chilies, garlic, and salt. Process until puréed. Force apricots through a sieve. Combine apricots, puréed spices, and vinegar. Bring to a boil, then bottle immediately in sterilized jars. Seal. Process 20 minutes in boiling-water bath.

## RAISIN BLATJANG

*1 pound seedless raisins*
*¼ pound garlic*
*¼ pound ginger root*
*¼ pound dry chili peppers*
*½ teaspoon salt*
*2 cups red wine or cider vinegar*

about 1½ pints

Place raisins, garlic, ginger root, chilies, salt, and ½ cup vinegar in a blender and process until minced. Combine with remaining vinegar, bring to a boil, and bottle immediately in sterilized jars. Seal. Process 20 minutes in boiling-water bath.

VARIATION: For *Date Blatjang*, substitute 1 pound pitted dates for the raisins.

Fruits and vegetables can be combined to produce a *Blatjang* rather like chutney.

## MIXED BLATJANG

*1 pound dried apricots*
*1 pound seedless raisins*
*4 large onions*
*1 tablespoon cayenne*
*¼ cup ground almonds*
*1 clove garlic, minced*
*¾ tablespoon salt*
*2 teaspoons ground ginger*
*4 cups red wine or cider vinegar*

3½ to 4 pints

Soak apricots overnight. In the same water, bring to a boil and stew until soft. Chop raisins. Parboil onions. Combine all ingredients and bring to a rolling boil. Continue boiling, stirring constantly until mixture is a smooth paste that is not too runny, about 30 minutes. Bottle immediately in sterilized jars and seal. Process 20 minutes in boiling-water bath.

Chutneys are a part of South African cookery, too, the contribution of the Indian population. This particular recipe calls for peaches instead of the more usual mangoes.

## PEACH CHUTNEY

*50 ripe peaches*
*5 onions*
*1 tablespoon whole allspice*
*¼ cup salt*
*4 cups red wine or cider vinegar*

*5 chili peppers, chopped*
*2 tablespoons curry powder*
*1 teaspoon cayenne*
*4 to 6 cups sugar, to taste*

12 pints

Peel and slice the peaches. Finely chop onions. Tie allspice into a cheesecloth bag. Combine all ingredients and bring to a rolling boil. Boil about 30 minutes, stirring frequently, until mixture is quite soft and thickened. Remove allspice bag and bottle in sterilized jars while still hot. Seal. Process 20 minutes in boiling-water bath.

If you do not want to make quite that much chutney (though you'll wish you had once you've tasted it), use these amounts: 12 ripe peaches, 1½ onions, 1 tablespoon salt, 1 cup red wine or cider vinegar, 1 small chili pepper, chopped, ½ tablespoon curry powder, ¼ teaspoon cayenne, 1 to 1½ cups sugar, and ¾ teaspoon whole allspice. This makes 3 pints.

Europeans were making fruit preserves in the 17th century when the first settlers arrived in Cape Town. However, most authorities agree that the fruit in these *konfyt* was made into a sort of paste. The Far Eastern method of preserving in sugar syrup produced a fruit in translucent, crisp pieces. This is now the preferred method in South Africa.

Most fruit is first soaked in salt or slaked lime water; this is what insures a crisp finished product. The fruit is then slowly boiled in a sugar syrup until the pieces are translucent and clear. Slow cooking is essential for proper results.

These delicacies are served in the European manner—not as jam on bread, but alone as an accompaniment to tea.

## GHERKIN KONFYT

*2 pounds gherkins*
*Salt water (1 tablespoon salt to 3 quarts water)*
*2 pounds sugar*
*6 cups water*
*2 or 3 pieces dry ginger*
*2 sticks cinnamon*

about 4 pints

Make a crosswise cut in the bud end of the gherkins. Prick all over with a fork and soak in salt water overnight. Wash well and drain.

Combine sugar and water and bring to a boil. Boil until syrup begins to thicken. Add ginger tied in a cheesecloth bag and cinnamon. Add gherkins and simmer slowly several hours or until preserved and translucent. Remove ginger and cinnamon. Bottle while hot and seal. Process 20 minutes in boiling water bath.

## RIPE FIG KONFYT

*4 pounds figs*
*4 pounds sugar*
*8 cups water*
*2 tablespoons lemon juice*
*2 or 3 cloves*
*2 pieces ginger, bruised (see page 172)*

about 5 pints

Choose figs that are just ripe but still firm. Peel thinly. Place in a warm oven (200° F.) briefly until underskin hardens slightly. Prick each fruit all over with a darning needle.

Stir water and sugar together and add fruit. Bring to a boil, stirring until all the sugar has dissolved. Boil 1 minute. Add lemon juice. Tie cloves and ginger in a cheesecloth bag and add. Simmer on a slow fire until figs are clear and transparent. Remove cheesecloth bag; bottle and seal while hot. Process 20 minutes in boiling-water bath.

## WATERMELON RIND KONFYT

*5 pounds prepared watermelon rind*
*Lime water (1 teaspoon slaked lime to 6 pints water)*
*5 pounds sugar*
*7½ pints water*
*2 tablespoons lemon juice*
*3 slices lemon*
*5 pieces bruised ginger*

8 to 10 pints

To prepare rind, remove all pink flesh and the green outer skin of the melon. Cut into desired pieces and prick each piece all over both sides with a fork.

Soak rind in lime water overnight. Drain, then wash rind well, changing the water several times. Soak in cold salt water several hours. Drain, then cover with water again and bring to a boil. Drain immediately.

Combine sugar and water and bring to a boil; continue cooking until syrup thickens. Add the rind, lemon juice, lemon, and bruised ginger tied in a cheesecloth bag. Simmer very slowly until rind is clear, about 3 hours. Remove ginger. Bottle and seal while hot. Process 20 minutes in boiling-water bath.

## TOMATO KONFYT

*3 pounds small tomatoes*
*3 pounds sugar*
*6¾ cups water*
*Several pieces dry ginger*

4 to 5 pints

Choose small, firm tomatoes. Prick all over with a darning needle. Soak in salt water (1 tablespoon salt to each 3 quarts water) overnight. Rinse well.

Combine sugar and water and bring to a boil. Slowly add tomatoes to syrup; add ginger tied in a cheesecloth bag. Simmer slowly until well preserved, about 2 hours. Remove ginger. Bottle in hot, dry bottles and seal while hot. Process 20 minutes in boiling-water bath.

## PINEAPPLE AND CARROT KONFYT

*2 cups shredded carrots*
*3 cups shredded fresh pineapple*
*3 cups sugar*
*3 cups water*
*1 stick cinnamon*
*Small piece dry ginger*

4 to 4½ pints

Soak carrots and pineapple separately in salt water overnight (1 tablespoon salt to 3 quarts water). Drain.

Steam or boil carrots for a few minutes. Drain. Combine all ingredients and bring to a boil. Simmer slowly until pineapple is clear and translucent. Remove ginger and cinnamon. Bottle and seal while hot. Process 20 minutes in boiling water bath.

## QUINCE KONFYT

*4 quinces*
*1 pound sugar*
*3 cups water*
*3 cloves*
*Small piece dried ginger*

about 3 pints

Peel quinces. Quarter and remove core. Cut into rather thick slices. Soak in salt water about 30 minutes (1 tablespoon salt to 3 quarts water). Drain. Bring water, sugar, cloves, and ginger to a boil. Boil until syrup begins to thicken. Add quince slices and simmer very slowly until fruit becomes soft, about 1½ hours. Bottle and seal. Process 20 minutes in boiling water bath.

When the recipe calls for dried fruit, the product will be translucent, but not crisp, of course.

## DRIED APRICOT KONFYT

*2 pounds dried apricots*
*2 pounds sugar*
*6 cups water*
*¼ cup whole blanched almonds (optional)*

4 to 4½ pints

Wash apricots. Boil in water until soft. Add sugar and simmer until fruit is translucent. Add almonds if desired. Bottle while hot and seal. Process 20 minutes in boiling water bath.

I am indebted to Mrs. Pitman for these elegant brandied fruit recipes.

## BRANDIED FIGS

*2 pounds underripe figs*
*1 pound sugar*
*Brandy*

2 to 3 pints

Choose figs that are not quite ripe. Peel. Place figs in wide-mouthed pint canning jars, distributing sugar between the layers. Fill bottles with brandy. Place jars in a saucepan with water and boil until brandy begins to simmer. Remove figs carefully and pack into other sterilized pint jars; pour brandy into saucepan. Stir remaining sugar into the brandy until dissolved. Simmer until brandy-sugar forms a thin syrup. Remove from heat and allow to cool. When cold, pour over figs and seal well. Process 20 minutes in boiling-water bath. Let age about 6 months.

## BRANDIED PEACHES

*12 yellow cling peaches*
*Sugar*

about 4 pints

Peel and pit peaches; slice or leave in halves. If using halves, prick all over with a darning needle. Make enough sugar syrup in proportion of 1 cup water to 1 cup sugar to cover the peaches. Cook until peaches just turn soft. Drain peaches, reserving syrup. Pack peaches into pint jars.

Measure sugar syrup and heat to boiling. For each 2 cups of syrup, add 2½ cups brandy. Remove from heat and cool. When brandy syrup is cold, pour over peaches, seal bottles well, and process 20 minutes in boiling-water bath. Age 6 months.

This goes particularly well with ice cream.

## DESSERTS AND CONFECTIONS

European traditions in South African cookery are most evident in the dessert department, particularly in baked things.

Whenever I asked anyone to name the most traditional South African desserts, the first dish inevitably mentioned was *Melk Tert*—Milk Tart. This, I discovered, was little more than plain old custard pie. The second item on everyone's list was *Koeksisters,* which are doughnuts.

The authentic *Melk Tert* is made with a rich, puff pastry, and the shell is never prebaked.

### MELK TERT (MILK TART)

2 8-inch pies

PASTRY: (make it a day in advance)

*1 egg yolk*
*Ice water*
*4 cups flour*
*2 tablespoons lemon juice*
*1 pound butter*

Place egg yolk in measuring cup and add enough ice water to measure ¾ cup. Add to the flour with the lemon juice. Mix and knead well, adding more ice water if necessary to make a smooth paste. Set aside for 20 minutes.

Divide butter into three parts, forming each piece into a small, flat rectangle. Coat butter pieces lightly with flour. Roll out the dough so it is thick but not too large. Place one piece of the butter in center of the dough and fold edges up like an envelope so butter is covered completely. Fold up opposite sides to the middle and roll out again. Repeat folding and rolling several times. Set dough aside 10 minutes. Repeat with second piece of butter and then, after a second

10-minute interval, again with the third. Keep pastry chilled in refrigerator until ready to use.

FILLING

*2 cups milk*
*1 tablespoon butter*
*Small piece of stick cinnamon*
*¼ teaspoon salt*
*2 tablespoons flour*
*4 eggs, separated*
*2 tablespoons sugar*

In top of a double boiler, combine milk, butter, and cinnamon. Scald. Add salt. Make a paste of the flour and a little cold milk or water and add to scalded milk. Continue cooking until mixture thickens. Remove from heat and allow to cool. Beat egg yolks with sugar; add to cooled milk. Beat egg whites until fairly stiff and fold into milk mixture.

Roll out pastry and line a large pie plate or tart tin, or two 8-inch pie tins. Fill with milk mixture and bake in a moderate oven (350° F.) until set, about 35 to 45 minutes.

*Koeksisters* are made in many shapes—balls, braids, twists—but they always end up coated with a thick sugar syrup.

The traditional Dutch *Koeksisters* are entirely unspiced. Cape Malays add cinnamon and ginger.

## KOEKSISTERS

amount depends on size

SYRUP (make it a day in advance)

*2 cups warm water*
*4 cups sugar*
*⅔ teaspoon cream of tartar*

Combine water and sugar. Place over moderate heat until sugar dissolves, then bring to a boil and boil 8 minutes without stirring. Add cream of tartar and boil 3 minutes longer. Divide into two bowls and refrigerate.

DOUGH

*½ pound butter*
*½ cup sugar*
*2 eggs, well beaten*
*7 cups flour*
*2½ teaspoons baking powder*
*1 teaspoon salt*
*½ cup milk*
*4 tablespoons cream*
*Oil*

Cream butter. Add sugar gradually, then stir in eggs. Combine dry ingredients and sift in alternately with milk and cream. Turn out onto a floured board, sprinkle lightly with flour, and roll out until dough is about ¼-inch thick.

Dough may be pinched off into balls. Or cut into strips about 4 inches by ½ inch; braid three strips together, pinching ends to seal. Or cut into strips about 4 inches by 1 inch; cut in half lengthwise without cutting top end; twist each strip several times, pressing ends together well.

Fry *Koeksisters* in hot deep fat (375° F.) until golden brown. Drain quickly, then plunge into ice-cold syrup, holding under for a few seconds. Use the two bowls alternately, returning unused one to refrigerator, to be sure the syrup is as cold as possible.

VARIATION: For the Cape Malay version, add 1 tablespoon each cinnamon and ground ginger and ¼ teaspoon grated orange rind to the dry ingredients. After coating with sugar syrup, roll in coconut.

*Bollas*—an unsweetened version of *Koeksisters*. To the basic recipe, add just cinnamon. After frying, drain well and serve uncoated.

The Northern European penchant for the sweet and starchy is clearly discernible in this old *Dessert Dumpling* recipe. Note that eggs provide all the liquid needed.

### DESSERT DUMPLINGS

*3½ tablespoons butter*
*6 tablespoons flour*
*2 teaspoons baking powder*
*½ teaspoon salt*
*3 large eggs, well beaten*
*Boiling water*
*Cinnamon sugar*
*2 tablespoons sugar*
*2 teaspoons cinnamon*

6 to 8 servings

Cream 2 tablespoons butter into the flour. Mix in baking powder and salt. Beat in the eggs.

Using a fairly large roasting pan on top of the stove, bring about 2½ inches of water to a rolling boil. Add a pinch of salt. Drop batter by teaspoonfuls; when cooked on one side, turn carefully. When the dumpling is completely cooked, drain. Sprinkle generously with cinnamon sugar (3 parts sugar to 2 parts cinnamon) and keep warm.

Measure remaining liquid in pan and add boiling water to make 2 cups. Add 1½ tablespoons butter, sugar, and cinnamon. Cook until thickened, adding a little flour if necessary. Pass this syrup with the dumplings.

The South African version of *Sugar Cookies* is delightfully spicy. The addition of port and brandy lifts them out of the ordinary.

## SUGAR COOKIES

*1 cup shortening (half of it butter)*
*¼ teaspoon cloves*
*½ teaspoon each ginger, cinnamon, and allspice*
*½ teaspoon grated orange peel*
*2 eggs, well beaten*
*1⅔ cups sugar*
*⅓ cup finely ground almonds (optional)*
*4 cups flour*
*½ teaspoon baking soda*
*½ teaspoon salt*
*½ teaspoon baking powder*
*1 tablespoon brandy*
*¼ to ½ cup port wine*

3½ to 5 dozen
depending on size

Cream shortening. Add cloves, ginger, cinnamon, allspice, and orange peel. Beat in eggs, sugar, and almonds. Sift flour, baking soda, salt, and baking powder together and add alternately with brandy and wine. Chill. Turn out on a floured board and roll until dough is very thin. Cut into desired shapes with pastry cutters. Bake on greased cooky sheets in a hot oven (400° F.) 10 to 15 minutes or until nicely browned.

*Krakelinge*, a rich, crisp cooky, is often served with tea.

## KRAKELINGE

*1 cup butter*
*½ cup sugar*
*1 egg, beaten*
*3 cups flour*
*1 teaspoon baking powder*
*Egg yolk*
*Sugar*
*Chopped almonds*

5 to 8 dozen
depending on size

Cream butter and sugar. Beat in egg. Sift flour and baking powder together and stir in. Roll dough to about ¼ inch thickness. Brush with egg yolk, then sprinkle generously first with sugar, then with almonds. Cut into narrow strips and form strips into figure-8 shape. Bake on lightly greased baking sheets in a hot oven (400° F.) 8 to 10 minutes.

Cape Malays contributed a rice cake to the South African dessert repertoire—*Kolwadjik.*

Use only regular white rice for this recipe. Processed or converted rice won't get soft enough for successful results.

## KOLWADJIK

*1¼ cups regular, long-grain rice*
*½ cup sugar*
*1 teaspoon cinnamon*
*¼ teaspoon cardamon*
*Dash of distilled rose water*
*¼ cup butter*
*1 to 2 cups shredded coconut*

3 to 4 dozen

Boil rice until it is very soft. Drain. Combine rice with remaining ingredients. Press into a baking pan (13-by-9-by-2 inches) and cool. Cut into diamonds and serve like cake.

## CANDIES

South African taste in homemade candies tends toward the very sweet. (This is true of all South Africans, black and white. The wife of a distinguished Xhosa scholar living in Wisconsin told me she uses 50 pounds of sugar every four months or so for her family of five. She did no baking; it was mostly stirred into tea.)

These examples illustrate the point well. Two are of European origin and the other a Cape Malay favorite.

*Fruit Rolls* utilize the many fruits grown in the hospitable southern climate. The recipe also highlights the hot, dry atmospheric conditions prevalent in vast areas of South Africa, for it is "cooked" outdoors by the heat of the sun. This recipe, a favorite in Mrs. Faull's Silwood Kitchen, works only if the humidity is practically zero, the sun high in the summer heaven, and all's right in the world. Any sort of fruit may be used, alone or in combination.

### FRUIT ROLLS

*4 cups prepared fruit*
*4 cups sugar*
*½ teaspoon salt*
*2 teaspoons vanilla*
*Butter*

about 3 pounds

To prepare hard fruit such as quince, apples, cling peaches, etc., boil the fruit in a small amount of water until barely tender, but still firm. Drain in a colander. When cold, pit fruit and cut into fine dice.

Soft fruit such as apricots, freestone peaches, plums, figs, etc., do not need parboiling. Merely seed and cut into fine dice.

Mix fruit well with sugar, salt, and vanilla. Line baking pans with brown paper and grease well with butter. Spread the fruit evenly over the paper so it is about ¼-inch thick. Cover pans with nylon net and place in the sun to dry. Bring inside overnight if necessary. Just before fruit is dry, loosen at the edges of paper with a knife. When dry, sprinkle liberally with granulated sugar, then roll up jelly-roll fashion and cut into pieces.

Another fruit candy is called *Mebos*. This particular version of *Mebos* is made of dried apricots which, as you've probably noted, are a highly favored ingredient in South African cookery.

### APRICOT MEBOS

*1 pound dried apricots*
*Sugar*
*4 tablespoons water*

about 3 pounds

Cover apricots with water and soak overnight. Drain well and put through food grinder twice. Combine apricots, 2 pounds sugar, and water. Bring to a boil and continue boiling, stirring constantly, until mixture is thick and leaves the sides of the pan. Pour into greased pans in thin layers and set. Cut into squares or fingers and roll in sugar.

Coconut is the main ingredient of a sticky concoction that satisfies the sweet tooth of the Cape Malays. It is very soft and is necessarily served in little paper containers. Use small cupcake liners. These candies are traditionally colored bright pink or green, but they're just as good in their natural white state.

### LALLIMALA

*4 cups sugar*
*1 pound shredded coconut (about 7 cups)*
*1 cup water*
*1 tablespoon butter*
*½ to 1 teaspoon distilled rose water*
*¼ teaspoon cardamon*
*Red or green food coloring (optional)*

about 3 pounds

Combine all ingredients except food coloring and boil until mixture is fairly thick, about soft-ball stage. Color with food coloring as desired. Portion into small cupcake liners and set.

## BEVERAGES

Tea is unquestionably the most widely imbibed liquid in South Africa, as I mentioned earlier. Not only is this an English holdover, but the result of Malay and Indian traditions as well.

Usually, tea is brewed in a china pot and served in the English manner—with milk and sugar. Cape Malays, however, make tea in an enamel pan, brew it for a while with a spice bag of cardamon seeds and dry ginger, add milk, then pour it into cups in the kitchen.

Milk, unadorned in any way, does not enjoy the standing as a beverage it does in this country. Among the Asians and

Cape Malays, milk is never taken in any form if fish has been on the menu. There's a superstition that fish and milk together cause illness.

However, on other occasions, the Cape Malays favor a milk drink, *Boeboer*, that's something like a thin porridge. Essentially, this is milk or milk and water thickened with pasta and spiced.

## BOEBOER

*1 quart water*
*½ stick cinnamon, broken up and slightly crushed*
*½ teaspoon cardamon*
*¼ cup sultana raisins*
*2 tablespoons coarsely chopped almonds*
*1 tablespoon cornstarch*
*½ to 1 cup vermicelli pieces*
*Milk*

8 to 10 servings

Bring water to a boil. Add cinnamon, cardamon, raisins, and almonds. Mix cornstarch with a little cold water and add along with enough vermicelli to make the mixture about as thick as a good soup. Simmer until vermicelli is cooked. Remove cinnamon. Serve stock in mugs or glasses and pass the milk to be added as desired.

Unthickened but spiced milk is traditionally served at prayer meetings held after Cape Malay funerals.

## SPICED MILK

*½ stick cinnamon, broken into pieces and slightly bruised*
*½ teaspoon cardamon seeds, bruised*

*1 quart milk*
*Sugar*
*Distilled rose water*

4 to 6 servings

Place cinnamon and cardamon seeds in a cheesecloth bag and place in a saucepan. Add half the milk and allow spices to soak 1 or 2 hours. Bring milk in the saucepan to a boil. Remove from heat and remove bag. Add remaining cold milk, sweeten to taste with sugar, and perfume with a few drops of rose water.

The Cape Province's Mediterranean-like climate is ideal for growing grapes, and a respectable wine industry has matured in the three centuries since the first French Huguenots arrived, seeking haven from religious persecution. At first, the directors of the Dutch East Indies Company sourly decided that Cape wine was better for vinegar than for drinking, but that's certainly not the case today. Both very good red and white wines, as well as brandy, are produced in the Cape area. Cape brandy is the base for a liqueur that many housewives mix themselves and keep on hand to pour over puddings and soufflés and for drinking.

This is Mrs. Pitman's recipe for *Van Der Hum Liqueur.*

## VAN DER HUM LIQUEUR

*36 cloves*
*1½ whole nutmegs*
*6 sticks cinnamon*
*¼ teaspoon cardamon seeds*
*6 bottles (fifths) brandy*
*2 tablespoons tangerine peel, thinly sliced*
*½ cup orange blossoms*

*3 pounds sugar*
*6 cups water*
*1 bottle (fifth) rum*

about 9 bottles (fifths)

Bruise spices slightly. Break up cinnamon. Place all spices in a cheesecloth bag. Add spices to brandy along with tangerine peel (be sure all white pith has been removed from the peel) and orange blossoms. Keep well sealed in an earthenware jar or well corked in a small cask. Shake each day for 1 month.

Strain brandy. Boil sugar with water until it forms a thick syrup. Cool. When cold, add to brandy mixture with the rum. Let stand, covered and undisturbed, for 3 to 3½ weeks. If using a cask, tap and draw off the liqueur, bottle, and seal with wax. With an earthenware jar, carefully ladle out liqueur, bottle, and seal. In either case, take care not to disturb any sediment that may have accumulated at the bottom of the container. Allow liqueur to age a few months.

This is excellent for flavoring such things as Bavarian cream, or as a sauce for chocolate soufflé or pudding, or as an after-dinner liqueur.

# CENTRAL AFRICA

THE FURTHER YOU TRAVEL toward the center of the continent south of the Sahara, the more limited the food possibilities become.

Here and there, the high plateau of Central Africa is dotted with the lush growths usually regarded as "typically" African. But in vast areas the soil is poor and the tsetse fly still curtails cattle production. In this region, what riches there are lie beneath the poor soil.

Aside from several one-hour fueling stops in Kinshasa, Congo, and Blantyre, Malawi, we spent time in only one place in Central Africa—Lusaka, the capital of Zambia.

I must admit we didn't see the city in the best of circumstances. Though we had many interesting experiences, most of them were misadventures, mistimings, and bad luck. But, as is the way with such things, we all remember our Zambian experience perhaps more vividly than other stops along the way.

For one thing, there was the weather. It was cold. The rainy season had just ended, but the winds blew steadily, and at 4,700 feet they can bring some mighty cool temperatures. Actually, the wind is *supposed* to blow in Lusaka—that's why the city is where it is. Lusaka and Nairobi, Kenya, are two of the few—if not the only—African capitals built on sites chosen by European colonizers. All others grew out of long-established cities or settlements. One of the attractions of Lusaka's location was that it was a particularly breezy, cool spot (except for several very hot, dry months). One of the city's greatest virtues is that during a goodly part of the year, it is so windy in the higher districts that it's impossible to keep a cigaret lit outdoors. (The facilities for keeping warm reminded me of those prevalent in my youth in Southern California, where heating in houses was nonexistent or markedly inadequate because it was never supposed to get cold there.)

Then there was the gasoline rationing. Zambia, formerly Northern Rhodesia, has suffered more than any other independent African state because of the United Nations' oil and other economic sanctions against Rhodesia. Historically and economically, Zambia was—and, to a great extent, still is—tied to the last white redoubts in Africa—Rhodesia, South Africa, and the Portuguese possessions of Angola and Mozambique. Almost all her imports must travel to this landlocked country by rail through her neighbors to the south. Gasoline, in short supply, had to come over a tortuous road from Tanzania to the northeast. We were granted only eight gallons a week for our rented car. This was a case of poor timing on our part—a month or so after our visit, the overland gasoline pipeline from Tanzania was finally completed and gas was more plentiful.

Our timing was poor, too, in arriving in Zambia. We chose the worst possible time—Saturday afternoon. As in much of former British Africa, everything closes down tight at noon on Saturday and remains firmly shuttered until Monday morning. This isn't so bad when you are staying at a hotel. But we had rented a University of Zambia guest house about 10 miles out of town and were setting up housekeeping for the duration of our stay.

Actually, the house was quite comfortable, and we were provided with all the equipment (except heaters) we could use—even including a collection of paperbacks, magazines, and comic books, a legacy of prior residents. An adequate hodgepodge of furniture was arranged on the red cement floors; we had the impression that we were taking over someone's haphazardly furnished summer cottage.

The expatriate instructor who administered the guest houses had shown up shortly after our arrival with a grab bag of provisions for our evening meal—several potatoes, one dozen eggs, bread, ½ pound of bacon, a stick of butter, a pint of milk, a can of baked beans, a box of chicken-flavored rice, and a package of dehydrated oxtail soup. Clearly he was a bachelor.

Normally, in such circumstances, we would have gone to a restaurant or hotel for meals until we could get set up. But with no car (the car rental places closed down at noon, too, of course, as did the government gas-coupon office) and no phone to call a cab we couldn't have gotten anyway, I satisfied our hunger with a meal of oxtail soup, omelet with bread and butter, coffee (I had a jar of instant in our luggage), and cookies we had picked up several airports back. But after breakfast the next day (Mother's Day, incidentally) we were cleaned out. Our expatriate host kindly used some of his precious gas to take us into town to the sole establishment open, an Italian grocery store. However, the only thing you could get fresh on Sunday was bread (mighty good bread, too), so we stocked in some canned and dehydrated items to see us through.

Once we had access to open stores, we were able to get almost anything we wanted, for a good price. Since most foodstuffs (at least those Westerners were buying) had to be imported, the cost of living was quite high. Some of the meat was locally grown, but much of the beef came from countries to the south, while the excellent lamb was largely from New Zealand. Very little produce was locally grown, at least at that time of the year.

For most Zambians, life depends on the corn crop. Dried corn or cornmeal plus whatever can be afforded by way of greens or meat or fish for a stew is what cooks in most kitchens.

Money usually limits the diet, but not always. Corn and sometimes stew is what most Africans in this part of the world have always eaten, and it is what they prefer. We are all creatures of our training and our habits, and in no area are we all more conservative than in the matter of food. Think back: are you quick to eat something really new and different? Ever had the courage to try raw fish? Grasshoppers? Rattlesnake steak? Fried ants? Sheep's eyes?

This preference for a reiterative diet has been noted before. Daniel Crawford, a turn-of-the-century missionary in Central Africa, commented on "the curious tendency in Africa to enter a long spell of monotony in one kind of food. In the mountains you are dosed with honey, and in the plains the everlasting fowl is your fare right round the clock. . . . So, too, on the Lake here [Lake Mweru on the Congo-Zambia border], it is fish, and fish, and more fish."

Many Africans consider a limited diet has virtue. Elsewhere in his book, *Thinking Black*, Crawford notes: "They challenge all puzzling diseases with the pungent query: 'What has the invalid eaten?' Hence their national saying . . . : 'Eat one thing, and then you'll know what you have died of!'

Thus when he sees a European dip into so many different tins, the sage Negro says triumphantly: 'That is why you whites die off so easily: we Africans eat only one thing, so we know what kills us.' "

Today, too, many Africans approach our tables warily. A young Basuto studying mining engineering at the University of Wisconsin once admitted to me he was somewhat appalled by American food preferences when he first came to this country.

"I was horrified to see people eating crabs," he recalled. "I'd never be able to eat anything like that. But then," he added with a laugh, "we eat rats and you think that is horrifying." He explained that back home in Lesotho, rats were delicious, usually barbecued whole over an open fire. These are not house rats, but field rodents that grow quite large.

Many developing countries are working hard to alter the eating patterns of their peoples, not necessarily to change the diet but to expand it to include nutritious foods often available but unused, like fish and certain greens (for example, cassava leaves rather than the root). They are also preaching the necessity of changing the order of family serving. Generally throughout Africa, men are served first, and they eat their fill; the women and then the children get what's left. This practice probably evolved from an erroneous correlation between stature and required food portions. It is not unusual for African children to suffer from deficiency diseases even when food is not in short supply. In Lusaka, an audience of government and professional women and government officials' wives reacted with amused whisperings and incredulous gasps when the speaker, a nutritionist, said men must be persuaded to let the children and pregnant women eat first.

## STEWS

Usually, the food in Central Africa is bland and unseasoned. The exceptions are the western coastal countries—both Congos and Gabon. There, old African hands insist, the pepper level is even higher than in West Africa.

In the Congo the basic stew in called *Mwamba* and is made with either chicken, beef, fish, or lamb, browned in oil before stewing.

### MWAMBA

*1 chicken, cut up, 2 pounds beef or lamb, or 1½ pounds fish fillets, fresh or thawed frozen*
*Salt to taste*
*Oil*
*2 large onions, cut up*
*2 to 4 chili peppers, mashed, or ½ to 1 tablespoon dried crushed red pepper*
*6 or 7 tomatoes, peeled, seeded, and mashed*

4 to 6 servings

Season chicken, meat, or fish well with salt. In hot oil in a heavy stewing pan, sauté chicken, meat, or fish with the onions until well browned. Add chili peppers, tomatoes, and enough water to barely cover. Simmer until tender and nicely cooked.

Chicken *Mwamba* is usually served with boiled rice. Fish, lamb, or beef *Mwamba* is frequently accompanied by fried plantain.

VARIATION: Some recipes include peanuts in this dish. Mix ¼ to ⅓ cup peanut butter with a little boiling water until smooth and add to stew 15 to 20 minutes before it is done.

In Gabon, chicken stew is also very hot, but the nuts are added to the pot before the meat. In this instance the nuts are palm nuts. Hazelnuts or filberts are an acceptable substitute.

## GABON CHICKEN STEW

*1½ cups palm or hazelnuts*
*1½ cups water*
*¼ to ½ cup palm or peanut oil*
*2 to 3 chili peppers or ½ to 1 tablespoon crushed red pepper*
*1 teaspoon salt*
*1 clove garlic, minced*
*2 medium onions, thinly sliced*
*1 frying chicken, cut up*

4 to 6 servings

Process nuts in blender until very finely ground. In a heavy stewing pan, combine all ingredients (except chicken), and mix well. Add chicken, turning pieces in the liquid so they are nicely coated. Cover and simmer over a low heat until the chicken is tender, 45 minutes to 1 hour, stirring occasionally. If necessary, add water to prevent scorching.

Contrast the Congolese and Gabon stews with this chicken stew from Zambia seasoned only with salt.

## ZAMBIAN CHICKEN STEW

*1 fryer chicken, cut up*
*2 tablespoons oil*
*1 onion, sliced or chopped*
*1 cup water*

*1 teaspoon salt*
*½ cup unsalted peanuts finely ground or ⅓ cup peanut butter*

4 to 6 servings

Fry chicken pieces in hot oil in a heavy stewing pan until well browned. Drain chicken and set aside. In same oil, sauté onion until golden brown. Add water and salt and bring to a boil. Return chicken pieces to pan and simmer 20 minutes. Add ground nuts or peanut butter and continue cooking until chicken is tender.

More often than not, meat stews are also simmered with little or no seasoning.

## STEWED DRIED MEAT

*1 pound dried meat*
*1 onion, sliced*
*2 tablespoons finely ground unsalted peanuts or peanut butter*
*Salt to taste*

4 to 6 servings

Simmer dried meat with onions in a small amount of water until well cooked and tender. Mix peanuts or peanut butter with a little water into a smooth paste. Add to meat with salt to taste. Continue simmering 10 to 15 minutes more.

I don't mean to imply that the chili pepper is unknown or unloved in the interior of Central Africa. In many places bright red mounds of that ubiquitous pod lend color to the market places.

In Zambia's rich copper belt, many cooks add one or two

peppers to their meat stew, even though their countrymen farther south may not.

### FRESH MEAT STEW

*1½ pounds beef, cut in cubes*
*2 cups water*
*3 onions, sliced*
*1 tomato, peeled and sliced*
*¼ to ½ cup peanut oil*
*2 chili peppers or ½ to 1 tablespoon crushed red pepper*

4 to 6 servings

In a heavy stewing pan, combine meat, water, and onions. Simmer 30 minutes. Add tomato, oil, and chili peppers. Continue simmering until meat is tender, 30 to 45 minutes more. VARIATIONS: This same stew may be made with chicken, lamb, or fish. Eliminate the chili pepper for a southern Zambian version.

Both north and south in Zambia, this would be served with cornmeal mush, called *Nshima.*

In Central African areas where they grow, bananas are added to the stewing pot.

As I've noted before, the African housewife has many varieties of bananas available to her besides the golden eating bananas we know so well. For cooking, you need a rather dry, starchy, unsweet variety. Plantains—which are very large—are most familiar on the West Coast of the continent. In Central Africa the bananas are more likely to be a short, fat variety whose skin is green when ripe.

In Rwanda, where this next recipe comes from, the small green ones would probably be used, though plantains work just as well. Green, unripe table bananas will give a similar effect.

## BANANA BEEF STEW

*1½ pounds beef, cut in 1½-inch cubes*
*1 large onion, chopped*
*2 tablespoons oil*
*4 small green bananas or 2 plantains*
*Lemon juice*
*1 large tomato, peeled and sliced*
*1 teaspoon salt*
*½ teaspoon pepper*
*Water*

4 to 6 servings

In a heavy stewing pan, sauté meat and onion in oil until nicely browned. Cut bananas or plantains into chunks and brush with lemon juice. If using plantains, add to pan and sauté with meat over a low heat, stirring constantly. Add tomato, salt, pepper, and enough water to cover. Simmer slowly until meat is cooked, about 1½ hours. If using bananas, sauté in a small amount of oil separately and add to stewing pan in last 15 or 20 minutes. It may be necessary to add water during cooking.

The seasoning contrast between various parts of Central Africa is evident in fish cookery, too. The first of these stews is from the Congo region and the second from Zambia.

The kinds of ingredients also highlight the differences in availability of vegetables.

## MBISI YE KALOU (FISH STEW)

*1½ pounds firm, white fish fillets, fresh or thawed frozen*
*1 large onion, sliced*
*1 green pepper, seeded and sliced*
*4 to 6 tablespoons oil or butter*
*2 chili peppers or ½ to 1 tablespoon crushed red pepper*
*1 pound fresh greens (kale, spinach, collards, Swiss chard, or beet greens) or 1 10-ounce package frozen greens*
*1 cup water*

6 servings

Cut fish into thick pieces.

In a heavy stewing pan, sauté onion and green pepper slices in 2 tablespoons hot oil or butter, about 5 minutes. Add chilies, greens, and water. Simmer, covered, about 10 minutes. Add 2 to 4 tablespoons oil or butter and fish. Continue simmering, covered, until fish flakes easily, about 20 minutes.

*Kapenta* is a perch-like fish found in the Zambezi and other rivers of Zambia. Most of a fisherman's catch is sun-dried and keeps for a long time. Mrs. Gertrude Zulu, who was president of the YWCA in Lusaka when I was there, told me how she prepared *Kapenta.*

## KAPENTA STEW

*1 onion, chopped*
*2 or 3 tablespoons oil*
*2 tomatoes, peeled and cut up*

1 *pound dried* kapenta, *washed well, or* 1 *pound fresh* kapenta *or perch*

4 servings

For dried fish: sauté onion in oil until it starts to brown. Add tomatoes and sauté another few minutes. Add dried *kapenta* and cook 5 to 7 minutes over a hot fire. Water may be added if you prefer a wetter gravy.

If using fresh fish, add the fish after the onions have started to brown and then add the tomatoes in the last 5 minutes.

Serve with *Nshima.*

## VEGETABLE STEWS

Most of the time, stews contain no meat, chicken, or fish at all. The stew consists of just one green and an onion; more vegetables and ingredients are added in proportion to the fertility of the soil and the affluence of the family.

This *Spinach Sauce* comes from the more abundant regions of the Central African Republic.

### SPINACH SAUCE

*2 onions, chopped*
*2 tablespoons oil*
*2 tomatoes, peeled and sliced*
*1 green pepper, chopped*
*2 pounds fresh spinach, chopped, or 2 10-ounce packages frozen chopped spinach, thawed*
*1 teaspoon salt*
*1 to 2 chili peppers or ½ to 1 tablespoon crushed red pepper*
*½ cup peanut butter*

4 to 6 servings

In a heavy sauce or stewing pan, sauté onions in hot oil until tender but not brown. Add tomatoes and green pepper and continue sautéing 1 or 2 minutes. Add spinach, salt, and chili peppers; cover and simmer 5 minutes. Mix peanut butter with a little water into a smooth paste and add to spinach. Stir well and continue cooking on a low heat about 10 minutes. Stir frequently. As no water is called for, a heavy pot and a low fire are essential to prevent scorching. You may, of course, add small amounts of water if you wish.

Serve with a starch dish.

In Zambia, if a soup bone is available, it is added to the pot to flavor *Groundnut Soup*. Here again, seasoning is limited to salt.

## ZAMBIAN GROUNDNUT SOUP

*1 large tomato, peeled and cut in eighths*
*1 large onion, cut in eighths*
*1 large potato, peeled and cut into eighths*
*2 tablespoons rice*
*Soup bones, if available*
*Salt to taste*
*2¼ cups water*
*1 cup finely ground unsalted peanuts*

6 servings

Combine first six ingredients with 2 cups water. Simmer until vegetables are soft. Mix ground peanuts with ¼ cup water and add to pot. Simmer 30 minutes more.

A thick sauce made of beans is a Burundi dish.

## IBIHARAGE (FRIED BEANS)

*1 1-pound can beans (limas, pinto, kidney, or black-eyed peas)*
*3 onions, coarsely chopped*
*1 clove garlic, mashed*
*¼ to ½ cup oil*
*1 to 2 chili peppers or ½ to 1 tablespoon crushed red pepper*
*2 teaspoons salt*

6 servings

Drain beans. Sauté onions and garlic in hot oil until onions are transparent and soft. Add beans, chilies, and salt. Continue sautéing about 5 minutes more.

Dried beans may be used. Soak 1 cup beans overnight. Simmer until tender. Drain.

A combination of peanuts and zucchini (a French import) is sometimes made in Chad.

## GROUNDNUT-SQUASH SAUCE

*3 pounds zucchini or summer squash*
*½ pound unsalted peanuts, coarsely chopped*
*2 tablespoons oil*

6 to 8 servings

Cook the squash, whole and unpeeled, in a small amount of salted water until tender. Drain and mash. Mix with peanuts and oil in a saucepan and simmer 5 minutes to blend flavors. Sauce will be thick. Serve hot.

## STARCHES

Corn in various guises keeps large segments of the Central African population alive.

Stores in Zambia stock mealie meal, which is white cornmeal; breakfast cereal, which is a more highly refined mealie meal; and *samp*, which is dried corn kernels. In the rural areas the wife prepares her own meal and *samp* literally from scratch—starting with the planting of the corn, the tending, the harvesting, and the milling. And she does all this usually carrying a small child in a sling on her back.

The method of making cornmeal is the same all over Africa (see the chapter on West Africa for details). If you hanker for *samp*, here's how it is produced.

### SAMP

Let field corn stand until kernels begin to harden. Remove from the cob. Pound briefly in a mortar and winnow away the husks. In a large pot, cover the kernels with cold water and allow to soak 48 hours. Drain. Place kernels on sheets in a single layer and dry in the sun.

To cook *samp*, cover with salted water and simmer until soft, at least 2 hours.

The kind of dried corn that is sold for popcorn in the United States won't work for *samp*. If you can't make your own, one possible substitution for cooked *samp* is canned hominy (but not grits).

At times, other ingredients are combined with *samp*.

## SAMP AND BEANS

*1 cup* samp *or 1 1-pound can hominy*
*1 cup beans, soaked overnight*

8 to 10 servings

In a heavy pot, cover *samp* and beans with salted water. Bring to a boil, reduce heat, and simmer until soft, about 2 hours. If using canned hominy, cook beans, then combine with hominy and heat.

## SAMP AND GROUNDNUTS

*1 cup samp or 1 1-pound can hominy*
*¼ cup peanut butter*

4 to 6 servings

Cook samp in salted water until soft; or use hominy right out of the can. Combine peanut butter with a little of the cooking water or canning liquid until smooth. Drain samp or hominy and combine with peanut butter.
VARIATION: Rice may be substituted for samp. Add peanut butter, stirred with a little hot water, to rice after all the cooking water has been absorbed.

Zambians call their stiff cornmeal-mush staple *Nshima.*

## NSHIMA

*1½ cups cornmeal*
*3 to 4 cups water*
*Salt to taste*

6 to 8 servings

Dampen cornmeal with 1 cup of cold water. Bring 2½ cups water to a boil; add salt. Stir in cornmeal and cook over a moderately high heat, stirring constantly until thick. Continue cooking about 5 minutes. Add more boiling water, a little at a time, until of desired thickness.

The mixture should be quite stiff and hold its shape when turned out of the pan. In Africa, each diner tears off walnut-sized balls of *Nshima* and dips it into the stew or sauce.

## NSHIMA WITH PUMPKIN

*1 medium-sized pumpkin or acorn squash or 1 1-pound can pumpkin*
*2 cups cooked* Nshima
*1 cup ground unsalted peanuts*
*Sugar to taste (optional)*

8 to 10 servings

If using fresh pumpkin or squash, peel and cut into pieces. Cook in a little water until soft. Mash until smooth.

Combine mashed pumpkin, *Nshima,* and peanuts. Heat to serving temperature. Add sugar, if desired.

Plantains are steamed or boiled, as elsewhere in Africa. In some places in the Congo, ripe plantains are both boiled and steamed, in the following manner:

## RIPE PLANTAINS

Peel plantains and cut in half. Cover with warm water, bring to a boil, and simmer until tender. Drain well. Mash plantains until smooth. Form into balls about 3 inches in diameter. Place in the top of a double boiler and steam until firm and set.

## BEVERAGES

Except among Moslems, homemade beer is the traditional relaxing or social drink throughout Africa. Herding peoples use wild honey or grain acquired by trading to make their brew; in grain-growing areas, it is made with corn, sorghum, or millet; in the rain-forests, mashed bananas are the base.

In some places special trees or plants peculiar to an area provide the makings for the beer. One such is the *Maroela-boom* (Maroela tree) that grows in northern South West Africa, northern Botswana, and in parts of Rhodesia and southern Zambia. A Swedish-born naturalist and explorer, John Andersson, first described the tree to Europeans in a book published in 1875:

". . . a huge-stemmed wide-spreading tree, with small elongated leaves, yielding in ordinary years tons and tons of a small apple-looking fruit; but it is only in appearance, for it contains a strong kernel, surrounded by a fleshy pulp, which defies your utmost efforts to detach it. By removing the skin, however, an agreeable, sweet, acidulous flavour is obtained. As the fruit begins to ripen it falls to the ground, where it is carefully gathered by the natives who convert it into a kind of beer. This is done by simply removing the peel, and then throwing it into some vessel partially filled with water. In a day or two it is fit for use, and is said to be very intoxicating."

A friend who has lived in South West Africa told me he once tasted *Maroelaboom* beer in Ovamboland in northern South West Africa and, as he said, "found its sourish taste refreshing and for sure, intoxicating."

It isn't only the people who prize the *Maroelaboom* fruit. In season when the fruit falls to the ground and begins to ferment, it is relished by elephants who become quite drunk on it and can become dangerous.

Some kind of grain, however, is most widely used for beer. This recipe came to me from Neil Skinner, professor of African languages and literature at the University of Wisconsin and previously a long-time British colonial officer in northern Nigeria. He got it from a Hausa-speaker and translated it literally for me:

## GIYA (BEER)

First day: start this morning to soak 10 *tia* (1 *tia* is about 2 pints) of *dawa* (sorghum) in water for a whole day.

Second day: pour off the water and spread the seed on mats early in the morning. Then cover the seed and allow it to ferment in this cool and shady place.

Third day: in the morning take out 1 *tia* of this *dawa* that is fermenting, allow it to dry and then grind it up. From a *tukunya* (cooking pot) which holds a *tulu* (3 gallons) of water take out enough water to add to the ground-up *dawa* so as to cook it something like *tuwo* (thick porridge or *foofoo*). This work would normally be done sometime in the afternoon. When this mixture begins to boil, take it off the fire and add it to the rest of the water in the *tukunya*. This part of the *giya* is called the male.

Fourth day: in the afternoon, cook the male brew for the second time.

Fifth day: take the remaining 9 *tia* of *dawa*, which is to be considered the female part of the brew and which has been standing all this time, and place this in a drum containing 5 *tulu* of water (15 gallons). Cook this slowly all day until afternoon. Then add the male part of the brew to this female part and put it aside to cool overnight.

Sixth day: drink the brew.

Seventh day: sleep.

# EAST AFRICA

OF ALL THE REGIONS of the continent, East Africa is unquestionably the most familiar to Americans even if they've never left home.

This is the area so loved and so lovingly described by Ernest Hemingway, Isaak Dinesen, Elspeth Huxley, and Robert Ruark. Its endless plains of green-tinged beige grass dotted with thorn trees have been the setting for countless movies about safaris and lions. And more recently film and television personalities have led millions on conducted tours of East Africa's numerous touristic high points through the medium of prime-time television specials. It is a rare person indeed who does not know what *safari* means or has not heard of Mount Kilimanjaro, the extravagantly exotic Masai, or Elsa, the lion who was born free.

Undeniably, the varied but spectacular scenery and the bountiful game parks rank among the outstanding natural wonders of the world (although emphasis on the wild animals and the colorful primitives markedly distorts a visitor's view of the modern nations of Kenya, Uganda, and Tanzania). The vistas and the wildlife of East Africa offer indelible memories. Gastronomically, however, a trip to East Africa is less than exciting, for this is another region with a British colonial food heritage, enlivened only a little by Indian cuisine.

The growing influx of American tourists to East Africa is making some small impact on the dining scene, however. In the three years between our first and second visits to Nairobi, I noted two marked changes. One was the appearance of the steak-house phenomenon, featuring that standard American menu—steak, tossed salad, and baked potato. The other came because Hilton bought the famous New Stanley Hotel; the coffee shop now offers hamburgers, tunafish sandwiches, and even iced tea. I'm making no judgments as to whether this represents culinary progress. I merely note the change.

The weekend curry lunch is standard here as it is elsewhere in former British Africa. This tradition is reinforced, perhaps, by the large Asian population in Kenya, Uganda, and Tanzania. The Asians—mostly Moslem Indians from the Bombay area—were brought into the region in the early days of British rule to build the railroad that runs from Mombasa on the Kenyan coast to Kampala in Uganda. There are some Indian restaurants in the capitals, but the uncertainty of food-handling standards keeps most tourists away.

As for African food, it is almost invisible to the visitor. I saw an African dish on a menu at the Pan-Afric Hotel in Nairobi. It was served, we were informed, only at dinnertime. In Uganda, *Matoke* and a stew were one of the courses at the curry lunch at the Lake Victoria Hotel in Entebbe.

I never encountered an African dish at any of the several game-park lodges we visited (although more recent visitors tell me some lodges now offer daily African specialties). The cuisine in these establishments was strictly colonial English.

A conflict nearly all American tourists become embroiled in when visiting England, or points north, south, east, and west where the course of British Empire wended its way, has to do with the cooking of bacon. The British serve bacon in a state most Americans consider virtually raw—cooked only until the fat is just turning translucent. All over anglophonic Africa, I had to send the bacon back at least once to get it to the point I'd consider edible.

I remember a meal at a Ugandan game lodge for other reasons. It was at Mweya, overlooking Lake Edward on the Congo border, and it was the night the bat got into the dining room.

Now, Uganda has many bats, and they are rather well-regarded beasts. For one thing, they are a most effective insecticide. And, at least in Kampala, they are a sort of totem or charm. Thousands of bats spend their days hanging in clumps from a double row of eucalyptus trees that grow in a dry wash at one end of Kampala Road, the city's main thoroughfare. This stretch is known as Bat Valley. Bats are noisy sleepers; those gray-black blobs that decorate the branches and sway gently in the breeze give off unusual and loud chirping sounds.

At sunset it's quite a sight to watch them take off in great flocks in all directions to search out and eat insects and do whatever else bats do at night. Periodically, the bats disappear for weeks at a time, which Kampala residents consider an evil omen, a prediction of disaster of some sort—an earthquake, political upheaval, crop failure, or the like.

I, on the other hand, do not look kindly on bats. Like many Americans (women, anyway), I was traumatized early in life by stories of bats getting into your hair or tales of vampires. And my girls become slightly unhinged by almost anything that flutters or flaps, even moths and bees.

This misdirected bat at Mweya entered the dining room at the height of the dinner hour through the French doors (unscreened, naturally; the English didn't believe in screens even in places like Africa), which had been opened wide to catch the evening breeze. Most of the guests were Europeans or Americans, and they couldn't keep their eyes off this creature crisscrossing the long room seeking an exit, wheeling and swooping lower and lower as it became more and more tired. The Ugandans—guests and personnel—were oblivious.

There was a time when we—the females of the family—would have bolted, even though we were only halfway through dinner. But by then (Uganda was our last stop) we were experienced African hands, and we stayed. We didn't exactly linger over the meal, savoring every bite. But we finished our meal, and we made a dignified exit despite the pass the bat made over our heads as we threaded our way among the tables.

The British were only the latest people to leave a culinary mark on East Africa. Long before they came, Arab slavers and traders regularly traversed the interior, bringing their spices with them. Arabs heavily colonized the coast, and the clove island of Zanzibar was an Arabic sultanate (under British protection) until 1964. While the modern sector has followed along the English kitchen path, the traditional peoples have kept to their old recipes, spiced sometimes with Arabic and particularly Indian seasonings. Curry powder is frequently included in African recipes.

However, the overall flavor of East African food is as bland as in Central Africa. Occasionally, chili peppers enliven things a bit, but in many places in this part of the continent, red peppers are not considered good for children, so they are passed separately as a pepper mill is in the States.

More than a few Indian dishes have become standard fare for many city dwellers. *Pilau*, a rice and meat dish, is one, and *samosas* are usually passed at government cocktail receptions in Kenya. Curry, of course, is another.

Here, too, the basic starch is determined by the soil conditions. Field corn is widely grown, and the porridge made from the meal is known as *Ugali* in most places. *Ugali* may also be made with millet. Rice is grown here and there along the Indian Ocean and the shores of Lake Victoria. Women plant cassava and yams in their *shambas* (Swahili for small farms), and in the moist, lush areas the banana is plentiful. Most are *Matoke* bananas—short, fat in shape, very starchy, and green when ripe.

*Coconut Milk*, as in Asia, is often the required liquid for cooking meat or starches. East Africans make coconut milk with boiling water instead of cold water as is usually done on the west coast. For recipes listing coconut milk, follow this procedure:

## COCONUT MILK

*1 fresh coconut*
*3 cups boiling water*

Coarsely grate coconut meat and place in a bowl. Pour boiling water over coconut and let stand 20 to 30 minutes. Strain into a colander placed over a bowl, squeezing the coconut meat against sides of strainer with a spoon to be sure of extracting all the water. This first pressing will give a rich, flavorful coconut milk.

If more liquid is required, repeat process, using only enough boiling water to make up the deficit. This pressing will be thinner, of course. Strain second and any subsequent pressings into separate containers so as not to dilute first pressing.

The liquid found inside the coconut is not the milk in this context. Don't try using that natural product for cooking; it develops a tinny taste when heated.

In a pinch, commercial shredded coconut can be used, though it is not too satisfactory because it has been sweetened. However, if there is an Oriental food store in your vicinity, you can buy unsweetened shredded coconut, which gives very good results.

## APPETIZERS

What we call the cocktail party is one of the trappings of Western modernity that many of the independent African nations have enthusiastically embraced—along with big new airports and Hilton and Inter-Continental hotels. Large, official affairs are usually called *receptions*, while smaller, more social gatherings are called *sundowners* because the British felt it was unhealthy or at least not good form to start drinking hard liquor before sunset.

The food at these affairs is as international and institutionalized as the event itself—cheese, canapés, fresh vegetable nibbles, etc. However, occasionally a specialty of the region appears on the serving trays.

The first time I tasted *Samosas*, in fact, was at such a reception in Kenya hosted by the minister of information in the beautiful gardens of the Parliament Building for the members of the International Press Institute. *Samosas*, of course, are Asian in origin, but have become a general favorite in urban Africa.

As I mentioned in the chapter on southern Africa, making *Samosa* dough can be a bit of a task and frozen egg-roll dough works just as well. For those who want to take the time, I'm including the dough recipe for this version of *Samosas* made with ground beef. (For a ground-lamb recipe, see page 156.)

## SAMOSAS

*2 cups flour*
*2 teaspoons salt, divided*
*3 tablespoons salad oil*
*Cold water*
*1 pound ground lean beef*
*4 cloves garlic, crushed*
*1 teaspoon chopped fresh mint or ½ teaspoon dried mint*
*2 green chili peppers, sliced*
*3 large onions, finely chopped*
*¼ teaspoon each cardamon and cloves*
*½ teaspoon cinnamon*
*Flour-water paste*
*Oil*

20 to 40, depending on size

Sift flour and 1 teaspoon salt together into a bowl. Add oil and enough cold water to form a stiff dough. Knead well. Divide the dough into walnut-sized balls. Working with three balls at a time, roll out each ball into a 3-inch circle. Brush two of the circles with oil on one side and flour well; brush remaining circle with oil and then flour on both sides. Stack the three circles, floured sides together and roll out until the stack is about ¼-inch thick. Fry dough lightly on a griddle or in a frying pan (greased very lightly) about 2 minutes on each side. Remove from pan and carefully peel the three rounds apart. Cut into strips about half as wide as long. Repeat until all dough is used up.

In a heavy stewing pan or frying pan, sauté beef, garlic, and remaining salt until beef is cooked and quite dry. Add mint, chilies, onions, cardamon, cloves, and cinnamon. Mix well and cook several minutes longer to blend flavors. Cool.

Fold a strip of dough on a diagonal twice to form a pocket, sealing edge with flour-water paste. Fill pocket with meat mixture, fold top over, and seal with paste. You should have a neat, triangular package. Fry slowly in deep fat until lightly browned; drain well. Serve hot.

*Samosas* may be frozen. After frying, cool quickly and freeze. To serve, thaw and heat in a hot oven (400° F.) to serving temperature.

Curry-spiced meat balls often show up on East African cocktail buffets.

## KABABS

*1 pound ground lean beef*
*1 slice bread, soaked in water and squeezed out*
*2 onions, finely chopped*
*2 cloves garlic, crushed*
*2 teaspoons chopped fresh coriander or ½ teaspoon ground coriander*
*¼ teaspoon cayenne*
*2 teaspoons curry powder*
*1 teaspoon salt*
*1-inch piece ginger root, chopped*
*1 to 2 green chili peppers, thinly sliced*
*¼ teaspoon cloves*
*½ teaspoon cinnamon*
*Oil*

about 1½ dozen
1-inch balls

Combine all ingredients except oil and mix well. Form into small meat balls and fry in deep fat until nicely browned and cooked through. Drain well.

These may also be made into large balls and served as a main dish.

## SOUPS AND STEWS

This part of Africa is no different from others in that the nature of the stew depends on the local crops and the condition of the pocketbook.

When there is meat in the larder, it goes into the pot; otherwise the stew consists of just greens or legumes or other vegetables. All of the following recipes are usually served with a starch (see pages 246–250).

*Matoke* bananas or plantains are the basic starch in many places, but where maize or rice is grown, bananas become another stew ingredient and are tossed in with the meat.

### BANANA AND MEAT STEW

*1 pound beef, cut in cubes*
*2 medium plantains or 4 small green bananas, peeled and cut into 1-inch pieces*
*2 tomatoes, peeled and sliced*
*2 onions, sliced*
*2 tablespoons oil*
*1 cup coconut milk*
*Salt and pepper to taste*

4 servings

Simmer meat in a little water for 1 hour. After slicing plantains or bananas, keep in cold water until needed.

Sauté onion and tomato in hot oil until onions are golden. Add cooked meat, bananas, and coconut milk. If the coconut milk does not cover the meat, add some of the meat stock. Season with salt and pepper. Simmer gently until bananas are cooked and meat is tender. If using table bananas, add 15 to 20 minutes before meat is done.

Coconut is not abundant in many areas, so water becomes the liquid for stews, as in this beef dish from Uganda. In this area, too, the combination of Arabic and Indian influences contributed the curry powder to this recipe.

### BUNYORO STEW

*1 pound beef, cut in 1-inch cubes*
*Salt to taste*
*2 onions, minced*
*2 tablespoons butter or oil*
*4 tomatoes, peeled and diced*
*1 teaspoon curry powder*

4 servings

In a stewing pan, add enough water to meat to barely cover. Season with salt, bring to a boil, and simmer until tender, about 1 hour. Remove meat and drain, reserving stock.

Sauté onions in butter or oil until golden brown. Add tomatoes and continue sautéing 5 minutes. Add meat and brown. Stir in curry powder; continue cooking until flavors have blended. Add enough of reserved stock to make stew of desired consistency.

In Tanzania, too, curried dishes are a great favorite.

### THICK CURRIED MEAT

*1 pound boneless meat (lamb or beef), cut in 1½-inch cubes*
*4 or 5 small okra*

*2 large onions, sliced*
*2 tablespoons oil*
*3 tomatoes, peeled and sliced*
*Salt to taste*
*2 teaspoons flour*
*¼ cup cold water*
*2 cloves garlic, minced*
*2 teaspoons curry powder (preferably a strong one)*
*1 large potato, peeled and diced*

6 servings

Barely cover meat with water; bring to a boil and simmer until almost tender, about 45 minutes.

Wash okra and cut off ends.

In a heavy frying pan, sauté onions in oil until soft but not brown. Add tomatoes, drained meat, and salt to taste. Mix flour with ¼ cup cold water and stir into meat mixture. Add garlic, curry powder, okra, and potato. Simmer slowly, stirring occasionally, until meat and vegetables are cooked. Add meat stock as necessary to keep meat and vegetables from drying out. When done, the stew should be like a thick purée.

Broadly speaking, East Africa consists of more than the former British territories of Kenya, Uganda, and Tanzania. Farther north in Ethiopia, meat stew is usually seasoned with pepper rather than curry.

## ETHIOPIAN MEAT STEW

*4 tablespoons butter or oil*
*1 large onion, chopped*
*1 cup water*
*1 pound boneless meat (beef, lamb, or veal) in 1-inch cubes*

*½ teaspoon salt*
*¼ teaspoon each cayenne and pepper*
*½ tablespoon flour*
*2 tablespoons cold water*

4 servings

In 2 tablespoons butter or oil, sauté onions over medium heat until soft. Add remaining butter or oil and water and simmer, uncovered, about 5 minutes. Add meat, salt, cayenne, and pepper. Simmer, covered, until meat is tender, 1 to 1½ hours. Blend flour and cold water and stir into stew. Cook over medium heat, stirring constantly, until stew liquid is thickened, about 5 minutes.

These two chicken stews illustrate the differences in seasonings used in various parts of East Africa. The first, rather bland, is from Uganda; the hot version, from Tanzania.

## UGANDAN CHICKEN STEW

*1 fryer chicken, cut up*
*4 tablespoons oil*
*1 large onion, sliced*
*2 or 3 tomatoes, peeled and cut in eighths*
*2 potatoes, peeled and sliced*
*1 teaspoon salt*
*½ teaspoon pepper*

4 servings

In a heavy stewing pan, sauté chicken pieces in hot oil until nicely browned. Add onion, tomatoes, potatoes, salt, pepper, and enough water to just cover. Cover pan and simmer until chicken is cooked, 45 minutes to 1 hour.

## TANZANIAN CHICKEN STEW

*1 fryer chicken, cut up*
*2 onions*
*Salt to taste*
*3 tablespoons oil*
*3 tomatoes, peeled and sliced*
*2 cloves garlic, minced*
*1 or 2 chili peppers*
*3 whole cloves*
*2 teaspoons curry powder*
*2 green peppers, seeded and cut into strips*
*1 cup coconut milk*
*2 potatoes, peeled and sliced* 4 servings

Place chicken in a stewing pan with one of the onions (whole). Season with salt and add enough water to barely cover. Cook, uncovered, about 15 minutes at a moderately high heat so stock reduces to about 1 cup.

Meanwhile, slice remaining onion. Sauté in hot oil until yellow. Add tomatoes, garlic, chili pepper, cloves, curry powder, green peppers, and salt to taste. Sauté about 5 minutes. Drain chicken, reserving stock. Add chicken to onion mixture and fry about 5 minutes, turning chicken to brown evenly. Add 1 cup chicken stock and ½ cup coconut milk and the potatoes. Simmer, uncovered, 30 minutes, stirring occasionally. Add remaining coconut milk and continue simmering until all is tender, 10 to 20 minutes more. Remove chicken pieces to serving platter. Stir stew to break up and slightly mash the potatoes.

Serve over the chicken.

Many large lakes lie within East Africa—Victoria, Tanganyika, Rudolph, Edward, Albert—all well stocked with fish.

And there's the Nile River, too, which is abundantly endowed. (Nile trout are enormous. There's a sign in front of Chobe Lodge in Murchison Falls Park instructing fishermen to throw back any fish under 25 pounds!) In fact, my children—suspicious fish-eaters at best—heartily enjoyed *talapia,* a firm white fish that inhabits Ugandan waters in profusion.

At or near the source of supply, fresh fish provides embellishment for the stew pot. Beyond, the housewife must rely on dried fish. In this part of Africa, too, the fish supply far exceeds the demand for this high-protein potential.

In Uganda the cooking method most often used is wrapping the fish in banana leaves and dropping it into boiling water. Salt is the basic seasoning—anything else by way of flavoring depends on what's at hand. Lacking a handy supply of banana leaves, we can best ensure retention of moisture and flavor by simple steaming.

## STEAMED FISH

*1 whole, fresh fish (1½ to 2 pounds), cleaned*
*Salt to taste*
*½ cup each chopped onions and chopped tomato (optional)*

4 to 6 servings

Season fish with salt. Sprinkle with chopped onions and tomato if desired. Place fish in a steamer or on a rack in a stewing pan. Cover bottom of pan or steamer with boiling water (keep water below fish), and simmer until fish is cooked.

Steaming is employed with stewed fish, too. This recipe is from Tanzania.

## STEWED FISH

*1 whole fish (1 to 2 pounds) cleaned*
*Salt to taste*
*1 tablespoon lemon juice*
*1 onion, sliced*
*1 tomato, peeled and sliced*
*1 chili pepper, sliced*
*1 tablespoon butter*
*1 cup water*

4 to 6 servings

Mix salt to taste with lemon juice and rub over inside and skin of fish. Set aside.

Slowly sauté onion, tomato, and chili in butter until soft and just turning brown. Place fish in steamer or on a rack in stewing pan. Spread onion mixture over fish and add about 1 cup water—water should just touch bottom of the fish. Cover and simmer gently until fish is cooked, about 25 minutes. Remove cover and increase heat, evaporating enough water to make remaining liquid the consistency of a thick stew.

When dried, shark—one of the big catches in the Indian Ocean—is called *Papa*. Dried shark can be purchased in Oriental food stores.

## STEWED PAPA

*½ pound* papa *(dried shark)*
*1 onion, sliced*
*2 tomatoes, peeled and sliced*
*1 teaspoon curry powder*

*1 chili pepper*
*2 cups coconut milk*
*Salt (if necessary)*

4 servings

Cover dried shark with boiling water. Let stand 10 minutes; drain.

In a stewing pan, combine onion, tomatoes, curry powder, chili pepper, and coconut milk. Bring to a boil, then simmer gently until tomatoes and onions are cooked and liquid is beginning to thicken. Add dried shark and continue cooking 10 to 15 minutes. Taste and add salt if necessary.

Vegetables, singly or in combination, compose many East African stews.

Frequently, legumes of some sort are one of the basic ingredients—peanuts, for instance, or dried beans.

This peanut sauce is Ugandan.

## GROUNDNUT SAUCE

*1 onion, finely diced*
*2 tomatoes, peeled and finely diced*
*1 teaspoon curry powder*
*Oil*
*1 cup unsalted peanuts, finely ground*
*3 to 4 cups water*
*Salt to taste*
*1 10-ounce package frozen chopped spinach, cooked and drained*

4 servings

Combine onion and tomatoes and toss with curry powder. In a heavy stewing pan, sauté mixture in a small amount of oil until onions are yellow. Add nuts and water. Bring to a boil, then reduce to simmer, stirring constantly until simmering stage is reached. Continue cooking, uncovered, until nuts are well cooked. Season with salt to taste. At this point, if sauce is not reduced and slightly thickened, increase heat and reduce liquid until of proper consistency. Mix in cooked spinach.

A spicier spinach-peanut mixture is served in Kenya and Tanzania.

## SPINACH AND GROUNDNUT STEW

*1 onion, chopped*
*1 chili pepper, chopped*
*1 tablespoon oil*
*½ cup finely ground unsalted peanuts*
*1 cup coconut milk*
*1 10-ounce package frozen chopped spinach, thawed and drained*
*Salt to taste*

4 servings

In a heavy stewing pan, sauté onions and chili pepper in oil until onion is transparent. Add peanuts and coconut milk, slowly, stirring constantly until mixture comes to a boil. Add spinach and salt to taste. Reduce heat and simmer 15 minutes or until spinach is cooked.
VARIATION: Without the nuts and coconut milk, this becomes *Braised Spinach*. Cook and drain spinach. Sauté onion and chili in oil until onion is golden. Add cooked spinach and 1 teaspoon salt and sauté several minutes, stirring well.

The spinach-peanut combination can be made thicker.

## SPINACH AND GROUNDNUTS

*1 10-ounce package frozen spinach, thawed and drained*
*1 cup chopped onions*
*1 tablespoon oil*
*¼ cup chopped unsalted peanuts*

4 servings

Cook spinach in 1 tablespoon water until tender.

In a heavy stewing pan, fry onions in oil until golden. Add onions to spinach with peanuts and 2 tablespoons water; mix well. Bring to boiling then simmer several minutes to blend flavors.

Various other greens—pumpkin, bean, sweet potato, and cassava leaves—are prepared the same way as spinach.

Beans and peanuts are a pleasing mixture.

## BEAN AND GROUNDNUT SAUCE

*1 onion, sliced*
*1 tablespoon oil*
*1 tomato, peeled and sliced*
*½ cup unsalted peanuts, finely ground*
*1 green chili pepper, chopped*
*1 1-pound can kidney or pinto beans or black-eyed peas, drained*
*Salt to taste*
*1 cup water*

4 servings

In a heavy stewing pan, sauté onion in oil until lightly browned. Add tomato, peanuts, and chili pepper; continue sautéing about 5 minutes. Add beans, salt to taste, and water and simmer 30 minutes.

Many vegetables are stewed in coconut milk.

## BEAN SOUP

*1 1-pound can pinto or kidney beans or black-eyed peas, drained*
*1 large tomato, peeled and sliced*
*1 large onion, sliced*
*1 green pepper, seeded and sliced*
*1 cup coconut milk*
*1 teaspoon curry powder*
*Salt to taste*

4 servings

Combine drained beans, tomato, onion, and green pepper. Add coconut milk and stir in curry powder and salt to taste. Bring to a boil, then simmer 20 minutes or until mixture is thick.

## SWEET LENTIL STEW

*1 cup lentils*
*1 cup coconut milk*
*½ teaspoon cardamon*
*1 teaspoon sugar*
*Pinch salt*

4 servings

Boil lentils in water until soft, as directed on package. Drain.

Combine lentils and rest of ingredients, stir well and bring to a boil. Simmer, uncovered, until liquid thickens.

## CURRIED LENTILS

*1 onion, sliced*
*1 clove garlic, sliced*
*1 tomato, peeled and sliced*
*1 teaspoon curry powder*
*Salt to taste*
*1 tablespoon butter or oil*
*1 cup lentils, cooked and drained*
*1 cup coconut milk*

4 servings

In a heavy pan, fry onion, garlic, tomato, curry powder, and salt to taste in butter or oil until onion is golden. Add lentils and coconut milk. Bring to a boil, reduce heat, and simmer 20 minutes, uncovered, stirring occasionally. Mixture when cooked should be very thick; reduce liquid over high heat if necessary.

Sesame seeds—called *simsim* in Swahili—add an unusual nutty flavor to vegetable stews. This particular recipe is from Uganda.

## SPINACH AND SIMSIM

*½ cup sesame seeds*
*3 or 4 tablespoons water*
*1 10-ounce package frozen chopped spinach, thawed*
*1 tablespoon butter*

4 servings

In a heavy stewing pan, combine sesame seeds and water. Stir in spinach. Add more water if necessary; the amount of water used depends on how wet the spinach is. This mixture should cook in smallest amount of water possible. Bring to a boil. Simmer until seeds are cooked, 10 to 15 minutes.

Add butter just before serving, with a starch.

Many of the Indians who settled in East Africa are Ismaili Moslems, followers of the Aga Khan. This curry made of eggplant was originally one of their dishes.

## EGGPLANT CURRY

*2 onions, finely chopped*
*4 tablespoons oil*
*3 medium-sized eggplants, cubed*
*2 medium-sized potatoes, peeled and cubed*
*1 clove garlic, crushed*
*1 teaspoon curry powder*
*¼ teaspoon cayenne*
*1 teaspoon salt*
*1 tomato, peeled and chopped*
*1 teaspoon tomato paste*
*1 cup water*

4 servings

In a heavy frying pan, sauté onions in oil until golden brown. Add eggplants and potatoes and continue sautéing several minutes. Stir. Add garlic, curry powder, cayenne, and salt. Continue frying 3 or 4 minutes. Add last three ingredients and simmer until all vegetables are tender. Gravy should be thick; if it is not, reduce liquid over high heat.

*Stuffed Okra* is also of Ismaili origin.

## STUFFED OKRA

*12 medium-sized okra*
*2 teaspoons turmeric*
*2 heaping teaspoons curry powder*
*¼ to ½ teaspoon cayenne*
*1 teaspoon salt*
*2 cloves garlic, crushed*
*4 tablespoons lemon juice*
*¼ cup oil*

4 servings

Wash and dry okra. Cut off tips but leave stem end intact. Cut okra lengthwise just to but not through stem end. Combine turmeric, curry powder, cayenne, and salt. Mix lemon juice with garlic and stir into spice mixture to make a thick paste. Spread paste on cut sides of okra, then press together to close. Fry okras in oil over moderate heat until lightly browned.

Serve with *Chapatis* or rice. These would also serve as a vegetable with fried fish.

Like most Africans, those in East Africa use much okra.

## POMBO

*1 10-ounce package frozen okra, thawed and drained*
*1 small chili pepper, sliced*
*½ cup dried shrimp or crayfish*
*Salt to taste*

4 servings

Cut off ends of okra and slice into rings. Combine okra and chili pepper and boil in a small amount of salted water until okra is almost cooked. Add shrimp and continue simmering until vegetables are soft. Drain any remaining water and mash mixture well. Adjust salt.

## OKRA STEW

*1 large onion, sliced*
*1 clove garlic*
*½-inch piece ginger root*
*1 green chili pepper*
*3 tablespoons oil*
*2 10-ounce frozen packages okra, thawed and cut into ¼-inch pieces*
*1 teaspoon salt*
*1 tomato, peeled and sliced*
*½ cup water*

4 servings

In a blender, process half of the onion slices, the garlic, ginger, and green chili until ground. In hot oil in a heavy frying pan, fry remaining onion until golden. Add ground mixture and continue frying a minute or so more. Add okra and salt and sauté several minutes, stirring well. Add tomato and sauté several minutes. Add water and simmer until okra is done, about 10 minutes.

The original of this recipe for *Pumpkin Stew* called for leaves of the pumpkin plant as well as the pumpkin itself. I've substituted chopped spinach.

## PUMPKIN STEW

*1 large onion, sliced*
*1 chili pepper, sliced*

*Pinch salt*
*2 cups coconut milk*
*1 small pumpkin, peeled, seeded, and cubed*
*½ cup chopped spinach*

4 servings

In a heavy stewing pan, combine onion, chili pepper, salt, and coconut milk and bring to a boil. Add cubed pumpkin and simmer until pumpkin is almost done. Add chopped spinach and continue simmering until pumpkin is soft. Adjust salt.

## OTHER MAIN DISHES

A ground-beef dish, *Retfo,* which comes from Ethiopia, is too dry to be classified as a stew, although it is usually served with rice.

### RETFO

*1 large onion, coarsely chopped*
*1 green pepper, diced*
*3 tablespoons butter or oil*
*1½ pounds lean ground beef*
*½ to 1 tablespoon dried crushed red pepper*
*1½ teaspoons salt*
*¼ teaspoon pepper*

6 servings

In a heavy frying pan, sauté onion and pepper in butter or oil until onion is golden. Add ground beef and continue frying over moderate heat, stirring and breaking up meat, until it begins to lose its red color. Stir in crushed red pepper, salt, and pepper and continue cooking until meat is well browned. Spoon off fat.

*Pilau,* a well-known Asian rice specialty, has become a widely served dish among urban dwellers of all races.

This is one of those mixtures that vary according to how few vegetables are on hand and what sort of meat, fish, or fowl is to be cooked. The ubiquitous onion and tomato, however, are basic.

This recipe is for a simple *Pilau.* You may add any sort of vegetable you wish—cabbage, carrots, green beans, etc.

## PILAU

*2 large onions, chopped*
*2 cloves garlic, crushed*
*Butter or oil*
*1 pound lean beef, cut in 1½-inch cubes*
*2 tomatoes, peeled and sliced*
*1 cup water*
*2 cups coconut milk*
*1 cup rice*
*½ teaspoon cardamon seeds*
*1 3-inch stick cinnamon*
*2 teaspoons salt*
*½ tablespoon lemon juice*

4 to 6 servings

In a heavy stewing pan, sauté onions and garlic in 2 tablespoons butter or oil until onions are golden. Add meat cubes and tomatoes and continue sautéing until meat starts to lose its red color. Add about 1 cup water and simmer 20 to 30 minutes. Add the rest of the ingredients. The level of the liquid should be about ½ inch above the rice. Add more water if necessary. Simmer, covered, stirring occasionally with a fork, until rice is tender but firm and the mixture is still a little moist. Sprinkle 1 teaspoon oil or melted butter over the top and place, uncovered, in a moderate oven (375° F.) until all moisture is absorbed, about 20 minutes.

One fryer-chicken, cut up, may be substituted for the beef.

At many places on the continent the seasonal invasion of a kind of locust or grasshopper is welcomed enthusiastically —as long as the hordes are not of crop-destruction proportions. They provide a delicious fillip to the African's diet.

In the city or in the bush, when these insects appear, everyone mans a bucket to scoop them up by the hundreds. In a city like Kampala the streetlights draw the creatures like magnets, making the harvest easier. Each lamp base blossoms with an outcropping of children swinging at the wiggling clusters like Mexican children with a piñata. No one is surprised to see even a government official's wife order her chauffeur to stop and collect a share of the booty.

Bugandans—members of the largest single group in Uganda —call the insects *Nsenene*, but, whatever the language, they are cooked the same way wherever they are eaten. First they are steamed briefly, then drained and patted dry. After the wings and legs are peeled off, they are placed in a frying pan over a low fire and sautéed in their own fat and seasoned lightly with salt. My Ugandan friends recommend them highly.

The subject of offbeat foods brings to mind the diet of the Masai. In East Africa, the most tourist-visited area of Africa, the Masai unquestionably are the greatest tourist attraction among the various peoples of the area.

The Masai are the pastoral peoples who graze their herds

of scrawny cattle back and forth across their traditional lands, which straddle the Kenya-Tanzania border and include the Mount Kilimanjaro and Serengeti plains areas.

The tourist's shutter finger begins to itch when he sees a young Masai *moran* (warrior), tall and thin, his body and toga colored with ocher dye, his shaved head protected from the sun by an ocher-colored sheepskin wig, tending his father's herds on the thorn-tree-dotted plain. The youth will gladly turn his handsome aquiline Nilotic profile to show to best advantage his bead earrings and necklaces for a color shot—for a fee. On our first trip, that fee was a shilling (15 cents) a person for each frame exposed.

Self-sufficient, manly, unfettered, proud, and brave, the Masai are convinced their way of life is superior, that modern life has absolutely nothing to offer them. Naturally, they resist change, whether instigated in the past by colonial officials or today by independent black governments. For instance, the Tanzania government has vainly been trying to force Masai men to give up their traditional dress—a sort of mini-toga that falls from one shoulder without side seams and worn over nothing at all—and adopt pants. And since the Masai reckon their wealth in the number of cattle in their herds, they steadfastly refuse to entertain suggestions of selective breeding and herd reductions to improve the breed.

All that meat on the hoof is never slaughtered by the Masai for food—that would be as unrewarding as taking money out of the bank to eat. But the cattle do provide nourishment for the Masai. They subsist almost entirely on a kind of cheese made by mixing sour milk and blood. The blood is obtained by making a small hole in the neck vein of a cow. The hole is then plugged with a mixture of dung and mud, and the animal, temporarily a little weaker, rejoins the herd.

## STARCHES

All the starchy foods grown on the continent are also cultivated in East Africa, although the root vegetables are not as popular as corn, rice, and bananas.

The *Matoke* banana is the reigning variety of that species and gives its name to the starch staple of Uganda.

### MATOKE

12 Matoke *bananas (small green ones)*
*Salt (optional)*

4 servings

Peel bananas. Leave whole or cut up. Place in a steamer with a small amount of boiling water and steam until bananas are soft, 20 to 30 minutes, depending on size. Mash and season with a little salt if desired.

Other ingredients are added to a basic *Matoke* on occasion.

### MATOKE AND VEGETABLES

12 Matoke *bananas*
2 *tomatoes, peeled and finely diced*
2 *medium onions, minced*
1 *teaspoon salt*
1 *tablespoon butter*

4 servings

Peel bananas. In a saucepan, combine bananas, tomatoes, onions, and salt. Add only enough water so ingredients are about one-fourth covered with water. Bring to a boil, then simmer until all ingredients are soft, about 30 minutes. Drain and mash. Add butter.

## UGALI

The Swahili word for porridge. Used alone, without any adjective, the word has come to mean the cornmeal mush dish (or millet meal) known by other names elsewhere in Africa—*foofoo, nshima, putu,* etc.

Traditionally, the African cornmeal mush is extremely thick—thicker than it's ever made in this country. To give you some idea: a Tanzania *Ugali* recipe I have gives these proportions—3 cups of water for every pound of cornmeal. Of course, the cornmeal in that instance is homemade and not as fine as our commercial variety, which measures about 3 cups of meal per pound. But even so, that's a lot of meal for the water. I recommend 2 cups of water to 1 cup of cornmeal for 4 servings of *Ugali.*

Certain other vegetables cooked until very soft are made into a *Ugali.*

## PEANUT AND BEAN UGALI

*1 1-pound can kidney or pinto beans or black-eyed peas*
*1 onion, chopped*
*1 tablespoon oil*
*1 tablespoon flour*
*½ cup hot water*
*Salt to taste*
*4 tablespoons peanut butter*

4 servings

Simmer beans in their liquid until quite soft; drain.

Fry onion in oil until soft but not brown. Stir in flour and continue frying until flour is lightly browned. Slowly add water to pan, a little at a time, stirring constantly until water boils. Add salt to taste. Dilute peanut butter with several tablespoons of pan liquid and stir into pan until mixture is smooth. Mash the drained beans well and add to the pan. Stir well, then simmer about 5 minutes.

## YAM UGALI

*1 pound African yams or 1 pound white potatoes*
*Salt to taste*
*Warm milk*

4 servings

Boil yams or potatoes in water until tender. Peel and grate finely. Add salt to taste and mash with a wooden spoon until smooth, adding warm milk to make a thick, creamy porridge.

In Tanzania, yams and pumpkins are mashed together in a starch dish called *Mchanyanto.*

## MCHANYANTO

*1½ pounds African yams or white potatoes*
*2 tablespoons oil*
*1 large onion, sliced*
*2 tomatoes, peeled and sliced*
*½ cup ground unsalted peanuts*
*Salt to taste*
*1 teaspoon curry powder*
*1 cup canned mashed pumpkin*

6 servings

Peel yams or potatoes and cut in large pieces. Boil until soft. Mash coarsely.

In hot oil, sauté onion until soft. Add tomatoes, peanuts, salt, and curry powder. Cook over medium-low heat, stirring occasionally. Add yams or potatoes and pumpkin to peanut mixture and mix well. Keep over a low fire until mixture is hot and flavors blended. Consistency of this dish should be soft but thick. If needed, add water.

Note: For best results, pick a brand of canned pumpkin that is thick and not too wet.

VARIATION: A similar yam dish, called *Futari Yams,* eliminates the pumpkin.

Rice is made in the usual ways—boiled or steamed with or without seasonings—as well as in combination. When mixed with lentils, rice makes a dish called *Mseto.*

## MSETO

*1 cup lentils*
*1 cup rice*
*2 onions, sliced*
*2 tablespoons oil*
*Salt and pepper to taste*
*2 cups coconut milk (about)*

6 to 8 servings

Soak lentils overnight, then boil until almost tender. Drain.

Place rice in a saucepan and add enough water just to cover. Simmer, covered, until rice is almost tender.

Fry onions in oil until soft and just turning yellow. Season with salt and pepper. Add lentils and rice. Stir in 1 cup coconut milk and bring to a boil. Simmer gently until rice and lentils are completely cooked, adding remaining coconut milk as needed so when done, all liquid has been absorbed but mixture is not too dry.

A bread-pancake, *Chapati* in Swahili, is often served in coastal areas. It is similar to but not as rich as Cape Malay *Roti.*

### CHAPATI

*2 cups flour*
*1 teaspoon salt*
*Oil*

4 servings

Sift flour and salt into a bowl. Add enough water to make a fairly stiff dough. Knead well.

Roll out on a floured board into a fairly thick circle. Brush with oil. From the center of the circle, make a cut to one edge. Roll up dough into a cone, press both ends in and make into a ball again. Roll out, brush with oil, cut and roll into a cone and then a ball. Repeat twice more. Divide dough into four or five balls and roll each out into a thin circle.

Heat a frying pan over moderate heat and dry out each *Chapati* in the pan quickly. Brush pan with oil and fry *Chapati* slowly until golden brown on each side.

Serve hot or cold with stew or sauce.

## DESSERTS

East Africa is little different from the rest of the continent in the matter of traditional desserts—there are few examples of this luxury item and almost no baking.

Coconut and peanuts provide the makings for some desserts. Either nut may be used for *Kashata.*

## KASHATA

*⅔ cup sugar*
*¼ to ½ teaspoon cinnamon*
*2 cups grated coconut or ½ pound unsalted peanuts, finely chopped*

about 20 1-inch balls

In a heavy stewing pan or frying pan, heat sugar until it melts, stirring constantly. Add cinnamon and coconut or peanuts. Continue cooking, stirring occasionally until sugar turns light brown and reaches the soft-ball stage, about 2 minutes. Remove pan from heat and cool. When cool enough to handle but still soft, form mixture into 1-inch balls. Place on waxed paper until set.

*Maandazi* is Swahili for pastry. This is a fried cooky.

## MAANDAZI

*1 cup flour*
*1¼ teaspoons baking powder*
*2 tablespoons sugar*
*Pinch salt*
*1 egg*
*¼ cup water*
*Oil*

about 2 dozen

Sift flour and baking powder together. Add sugar and salt. Beat egg well and add water. Stir egg mixture into flour and mix until soft dough is formed. Add more water if necessary. Knead dough in the bowl until smooth but not sticky. Dough should leave the sides of the bowl cleanly. Cover with a towel and let rise in a warm place about 30 minutes. Roll out dough on a floured board until ½-inch thick. Cut into squares, strips, or triangles. Fry in deep fat until golden brown. Drain on absorbent paper.

## BEVERAGES

It was in East Africa that I first encountered *shandy*, a beer-based drink found throughout anglophonic Africa. It happened at the New Africa Hotel in Dar es Salaam, one of my very favorite spots, since I'm an antique hound and fond of old things. The building was constructed in the early 1900s for a proposed visit of Kaiser Wilhelm (Tanganyika was then a German possession). The Kaiser never came.

The building, a delightful relic of colonial architecture, evokes old movies of adventure and passion in the tropics, like *Rain* and *Trader Horn*. In fact, the New Africa looks as though Somerset Maugham had made it up. It is a two-story, thick-walled building, constructed around a small open courtyard featuring one tall coconut palm growing in the middle. The corridors ring this patio. This design makes every room an outside room, with the outermost part being a small covered porch opening off each bedroom and furnished with wicker chairs and tables. The ceilings are very high—about fifteen feet—with ceiling fans and mosquito nets that hang down like random stalactites.

The colonnaded terrace of the New Africa was the happy-hour hub of the city. Every afternoon after five, some government officials and foreigners from both East and West—tourists and expatriates—would gather at tables overlooking the old Lutheran church and the palm-fringed harbor beyond to drink and exchange gossip.

On a particularly hot and sultry day (par for this Indian Ocean port) an English woman at the next table ordered a bottle of beer and a bottle of cola. Since she had children with her, I assumed the cola was for them. But when the order came, she proceeded to pour simultaneously from each bottle into her glass. What's more, she drank the result with considerable pleasure.

I later recounted this strange occurrence to an Old African Hand friend who of course couldn't understand my amazement. That, he informed me, was a *shandy* and a very sensible drink, too, for hot, humid, tropical areas. It is more thirst-quenching than straight beer and much easier on the body functions when you drink quite a few. Cola is a fairly recent addition to a *shandy* recipe, I was told—dating from the post-World War II invasion of Coke and Pepsi into Africa. The traditional *shandy* is beer plus a carbonated lemonade or citrus-based soft drink.

## SHANDY

*1 bottle beer*
*1 bottle lemon-lime drink, or any soft drink like ginger ale, cola, bitter lemon, bitter orange, etc.*

Open bottles; mix half and half, and drink.

Centuries ago the Roman writer Pliny the Elder observed, "Always something new out of Africa." Like so many things about that ancient and fascinating continent, this is still true.

All the recipes in this book can add something new to your gustatory repertoire, and many, I know, will become firm favorites at your house, as they have at mine. Certainly you have the makings for all sorts of unusual and exotic visa stamps in your kitchen passport to foreign culinary adventures.

# GLOSSARY

ATJAR—spiced, oil-based condiment used with some Cape Malay dishes.

BEENTO—West African, particularly Nigerian, slang term for someone who has been to the United States or Great Britain.

BILTONG—Afrikaans term for salted, dried meat that is like jerky.

BLATJANG—spiced, vinegar-based condiment used with some Cape Malay dishes.

BOBOTIE—a South African curry-flavored ground-meat dish.

BOER—literally, farmer in Afrikaans; descendant of the early Dutch settlers of South Africa. As a prefix, it means country-style.

BOEREWORS—Afrikaans for country-style sausage.

BRAAI—Afrikaans term for cookout.

BREDIE—South African stew with vegetables. It's from the Malagasy word for spinach.

BSTILA (pronounced Pastilla)—Moroccan specialty of nuts, spices, eggs, and pigeon in layers and layers of flaky pastry.

CANTHARIDE—a dried beetle widely regarded as an aphrodisiac; used in some North African recipes and in spice mixtures; colloquially known as Spanish Fly.

CASSAVA—a root vegetable that is the staple in many parts of Africa. The root may be boiled or ground into flour. Leaves of the plant are also eaten. Native to South America, cassava is also known as manioc.

COUSCOUS—North African starch staple made of semolina. Also used as the name of the region's specialty of *couscous* and the stew that goes along with it.

COUSCOUSIER—pot for cooking semolina and stew. It consists of a deep stewing pot with a steaming basket that fits on top.

DIFFA—Moroccan for meal or feast.

FOOFOO—also *fuufuu, foufou, foutou;* an extremely thick porridge that is the staple in many places in West Africa; may be made of ground corn, cassava root, rice, or yams.

FOUL—a broad bean used in North Africa.

GARRI—cassava root that has been grated and roasted and then finely ground. Also refers to the stiff porridge made from the *garri.*

GROUNDNUTS—peanuts.

GUINEA CORN—sorghum.

HARIRA—a hearty North African soup, made all year but traditionally the fast-breaker during Ramadan.

JOLLOF RICE—a rice dish made with meat, poultry, or fish that is popular throughout West Africa. Name comes either from the Jollof region of Senegal or is a corruption of Wolof, the name of one of the peoples of Senegal.

KAB EL GHZAL—literally "gazelle horn" in Arabic; a crescent-shaped almond cooky.

KERRIE—Afrikaans term for curry.

Konafa—a rich dessert of nuts, spices, and butter popular in Egypt.

KONFYT—fruit preserved in heavy sugar syrup.

MANIOC—see Cassava.

MATOKE—a variety of banana grown in some parts of Central and East Africa.

MEALIE—corn.

MEDINA—old part of North African cities.

MUSSALA—also *massala;* a spice blend used in some Cape Malay dishes. It is the Indian word for spices.

NSHIMA—Zambian name for stiff mush like *foofoo.*

PAWPAW—African name for papaya.

PERI-PERI—or *Peli-peli;* South, Central, and East African name for a variety of red chili peppers.

PLANTAIN—a variety of banana that produces large, dry, starchy fruit.

PUTU—South African equivalent of *foofoo;* usually of corn-meal or sometimes sorghum; called *Pap* in Afrikaans.

RAS EL HANOUT—literally "head of the shop" in Arabic; a spice blend of 25 to 30 different spices used in Moroccan cooking.

SAFARI—Swahili for a trip or journey.

SAMBALS—fruit or vegetable side dishes served with spiced Cape Malay dishes.

SAMP—South and Central African term for dried corn.

SEMOLINA—cereal used in making *couscous;* usually made of millet crushed into granules by coarse milling.

SIMSIM—Swahili for sesame seed.

SOUK—Arabic for market.

SUNDOWNER—an English expression, still used in former British territories in East and Central Africa, meaning cocktail party.

TAJIN—North African term for stew.

TOBSIL DAIL LOUARKA—a shallow tray with a copper bottom used in Morocco for making *Bstila* dough.

TOUAJEN—plural of *Tajin.*

TUWO—Hausa name for *foofoo.*

UGALI—Swahili for porridge or mush like *foofoo.*

YAMS—a very large, dry root vegetable that is the staple in many parts of Africa; some varieties may weigh 18 to 20 pounds each; African yams look like a large, coarse potato and bear no similarity to the American variety of sweet potato.

# SUBSTITUTIONS

ABLEMANU—cornmeal lightly toasted in oven.

ALMOND PASTE—grind whole almonds until they form a paste.

ALMONDS, FINELY CHOPPED—packaged almond meal.

BOERMEAL—whole-wheat breakfast cereal like Wheatena.

CORIANDER—one bunch fresh equals one tablespoon dried or one teaspoon ground.

COUSCOUS—see Semolina.

CHILI PEPPER—one fresh equals about ⅓ tablespoon crushed red pepper or ¼ to ½ teaspoon cayenne.

CASSAVA ROOT—no substitute for the taste (or lack of it); for bulk, use a boiling potato.

CASSAVA FLOUR—all-purpose flour may be substituted for thickening and in most baked or fried items.

DISTILLED ORANGE OR ROSE WATER—no substitute available. Omitting it in recipes will alter the taste somewhat, but will have no effect on the finished product.

DRIED CRAYFISH OR SHRIMP—no substitute available; may be omitted without altering finished product.

DRIED SHARK—any dried, large, firm fish.

GARRI—Cream of Wheat.

HARISA—for canned Harisa, substitute a mixture of 1 to 2 chili peppers ground up; a pinch of saffron; ½ teaspoon each cumin, coriander and chopped parsley; 2 tablespoons olive oil; and 1 tablespoon lemon juice.

MULLET—halibut, hake or pike fillets.

MUSSALA (Massala)—use equal parts of fennel seed, cumin seed, dried coriander, and cinnamon stick, and pound or process in a blender until ground.

MEALIE MEAL—white cornmeal.

MATOKE BANANAS—under-ripe bananas; reduce cooking time.

OLIVES—in North African recipes, use Greek or Italian olives or stuffed green olives.

PRESERVED LEMONS—salt fresh lemon slices and steep briefly in boiling water.

PLANTAIN—large, under-ripe bananas; reduce cooking time.

PUMPKIN—any gourd-type squash.

PERI-PERI POWDER—ground chili peppers or cayenne.

RAS EL HANOUT—a hot curry powder plus several freshly crushed spices like allspice, cloves, black pepper, etc.

SEMOLINA—no substitute for coarse or medium semolina in couscous; in stuffings, rice may be substituted.

SEMOLINA FLOUR—all-purpose flour could be used in most recipes except baked goods; the taste would be slightly different.

SAMOSA DOUGH—frozen egg-roll dough.

SAMP—canned hominy may be used for cooked samp.

SHAD—any fatty fish like carp, lake or brook trout, catfish, tuna, or cod.

YAMS—large, dry, white potato.

# SELECTIVE LIST OF STORES CARRYING RECIPE INGREDIENTS

THIS IS A BRIEF list of stores in various parts of the country that carry some or all of the special ingredients listed in these recipes.

# Indicates stores that stock all or virtually all the specialty items.

* Signifies stores that fill mail orders. Query the store first for price lists, exact ingredients carried, and mail-order policies.

CALIFORNIA

Bezjian's Grocery, Inc. *
4725 Santa Monica Blvd.
Los Angeles, Calif. 90029

Curl's *
Farmers Market Shop 430
Third and Fairfax
Los Angeles, Calif. 90036

International Grocery *
4850 Santa Monica Blvd.
Los Angeles, Calif. 90029

Haig's Delicacies *
441 Clement St.
San Francisco, Calif. 94118

COLORADO

American Tea, Coffee, & Spice Co. *
1511 Champa St.
Denver, Colo. 80202

Pier 1 Imports *
4401 E. Evans
Denver, Colo. 80222

**ILLINOIS**

Bryn-Mawr Foods Grocerland
1124 W. Bryn Mawr
Chicago, Ill. 60626

Fujii Food Market
4654 N. Racine Ave.
Chicago, Ill. 60640

**LOUISIANA**

Central Grocery
923 Decatur
New Orleans, La. 70116

**MARYLAND**

Indian Super Bazaar *
P.O. Box 115
Mount Rainier, Md. 20822

**MASSACHUSETTS**

Cardullo's Inc. *
6 Brattle Street.
Cambridge, Mass. 02138

**MICHIGAN**

Big Ten Party Store * #
1928 Packard
Ann Arbor, Mich. 48104

Gabriel Importing Co. *
2461 Russell
Detroit, Mich. 48207

Delmar and Company
501–11 Monroe St.
Detroit, Mich. 48226

Wah Lee Co.
3409 Cass Ave.
Detroit, Mich. 48201

**MINNESOTA**

International House * #
712 Washington Ave. S.E.
Minneapolis, Minn. 55414

Lunds, Inc.
1450 West Lake St.
Minneapolis, Minn. 55408

**MISSOURI**

Quality Imported Foods
717 N. Sixth St.
St. Louis, Mo. 63101

**NEW YORK**

Delicacies Shop
Bloomingdale's
Lexington Ave. & 59th St.
New York, N.Y. 10022

K. Kalustyan #
123 Lexington Ave.
New York, N.Y. 10016

Mr. Dunderbak's *
76th St. and First Ave.
New York, N.Y. 10021

Karnig Tashjian * #
Middle East & Oriental Foods
380 Third Ave.
New York, N.Y. 10016

Trinacria Importing Co. #
415 Third Ave.
New York, N.Y. 10016

Malko Importing Corp. *
182 Atlantic Ave.
Brooklyn, N.Y. 11201

Sahadi Importing Co. *
187 Atlantic Ave.
Brooklyn, N.Y. 11201

**OHIO**

Athens Pastries Import * #
2545 Lorain Ave.
Cleveland, O. 44113

Ferrara Foods *
5750 Mayfield Rd.
Mayfield Heights, O. 44124

**OKLAHOMA**

Antone's Import Foods *
2606 S. Sheridan
Tulsa, Okla. 74129

**TEXAS**

Pier I Imports
138 Medallion Center
Dallas, Tex. 75214

Antone's Import Co. *
P.O. Box 3352
Houston, Tex. 77001

Jim Jamail & Sons Food Market
3114 Kirby Dr.
Houston, Tex. 77006

J. Weingarten, Inc.
600 Lockwood Dr.
Houston, Tex. 77001

**VIRGINIA**

Food Festival of Virginia
Tysons Corner Center
McLean, Va. 22101

**WASHINGTON**

DeLaurenti's Italian Delicatessen
Lower Pike Place Market
Seattle, Wash. 98101

**WASHINGTON, D.C.**

Acropolis Food Market *
1206 Underwood N.W.
Washington, D.C. 20012

Magruder Inc.
5626 Connecticut Ave.
Washington, D.C. 20015

Manuel Pena's Spanish Store * #
1636 17th St. N.W.
Washington, D.C. 20009

Safeway International #
1110 F St. N.W.
Washington, D.C. 20004

**WISCONSIN**

International House of Foods * #
440 W. Gorham St.
Madison, Wis. 53703

**CANADA**

The Bay *
8th Ave. & 1st St. S.W.
Calgary 2, Alberta

Food Floors *
Woodwards Department Store
Chinook Shopping Center
Calgary 9, Alberta

S. Enkin Inc. * #
1201 St. Lawrence Blvd.
Montreal 129, Quebec

The Top Banana Ltd. * #
62 William St.
Ottawa 2, Ontario

T. Eaton Co. *
190 Yonge St.
Dept. 579
Toronto, Ontario

# INDEX

# HARVA HACHTEN

Harva Hachten has traveled widely in Europe, Africa and Asia while collaborating with her husband, Professor William A. Hachten, in research and writing on international communication. She holds degrees from Stanford University and the Columbia University School of Journalism, and was for seven years the women's editor of the *Wisconsin State Journal*. She has also worked in the news media in Los Angeles, San Francisco and New York, and she taught journalism for some years at U.C.L.A. Her other publications include *The Flavor of Wisconsin* (1987) and the first edition of this book, *Kitchen Safari* (1970). She and her husband reside in Wisconsin.

They have two grown daughters and three grandsons.

***Also of interest from Hippocrene . . . .***

**Traditional South African Cookery**
***Hildegonda Duckitt***
A collection of recipes culled from two previous books by the author, this volume provides ideas for tasty, British and Dutch-inspired meals and insight into daily life in colonial Africa.
178 pages 5 x 8 ½
0-7818-0490-6 $10.95pb (352)

**Kenya and Northen Tanzania:**
**The Classic Safari Guide, 9th edition**
***Richard Cox***
Includes an illustrated supplement on Kenya's Top Lodges, Camps, Game Ranches and Safari Organizers. Crammed with up-to-date advice on health precautions, restaurants, shopping and transport help through the whole spectrum of safari planning.
300 pages 4 x 7
0-7818-0519-8 $18.95pb (659)

**Namibia: The Independent Traveler's Guide**
***Scott and Lucinda Bradshaw***
Provides information on food, lodging, and sightseeing in all four geographic regions that comprise the country: the Namib Desert, the Great Escarpment, the northern plains and the lowlands in the East, as well as the new national parks in Mudumu and Mamili.
313 pages 5 ½ x 8 ¼ 26 maps, 22 illus, index
0-7818-0254-7 W $16.95pb (109)

**Treasury of African Love Poems, Quotations & Proverbs**
***edited by Nicholas Awde***
This lovely gift edition is a bilingual selection of songs and sayings on the subject of love from numerous African languages, including Swahili, Yoruba, Amharic, and Ancient Egyptian along with side-by-side English translation. Filled with romantic imagery and philosophical musings, this charming collection provides a glimpse into each country's unique approach to affairs of the heart.
128 pages 5 x 7
0-7818-0483-3 $11.95hc (611)

## *Dictionaries and Language Guides . . .*

**Afrikaans-English/English-Afrikaans Practical Dictionary**
430 pages 4 ½ x 6 ½ 14,000 entries
0-7818-0052-8 $11.95pb (134)

**Amharic-English/English-Amharic Dictionary**
629 pages 5 ½ x 9 over 20,000 entries
0-7818-0115-X $40.00hc (75)

**The Handbook of Egyptian Hieroglyphs**
175 pages 5 ½ x 8 ½
0-87052-102-0 $16.95pb (384)

**Fulani-English Practical Dictionary (Western Africa)**
264 pages 5 x 7 ¼
0-7818-0404-3 $14.95pb (38)

## Dictionaries and Language Guides . . .

**Afrikaans-English/English-Afrikaans Practical Dictionary**
430 pages • 4 ½ x 6 ½ • 14,000 entries
0-7818-0052-8 • $11.95pb • (134)

**Amharic-English/English-Amharic Dictionary**
629 pages • 5 ½ x 9 • over 20,000 entries
0-7818-0115-X • $40.00hc • (75)

**The Handbook of Egyptian Hieroglyphs**
175 pages • 5 ½ x 8 ½
0-87052-102-0 • $16.95pb • (384)

**Fulani-English Practical Dictionary (Western Africa)**
264 pages • 5 x 7 ¼
0-7818-0404-3 • $14.95pb • (38)

**Hausa-English/English-Hausa Practical Dictionary**
431 pages • 5 x 7 • 18,000 entries
0-7818-0426-4 • $16.95pb • (499)

**Lingala-English/English-Lingala Dictionary and Phrasebook**
120 pages • 3 • x 7
0-7818-0456-6 • $11.95pb • (296)

**Understanding Everyday Sesotho**
94 pages • 5 ¼ x 8 ½
0-7818-0305-5 • $16.95pb • (333)

**Popular Northern Sotho Dictionary: Sotho-English/English-Sotho**
335 pages • 4 • x 5 • 25,000 entries
0-7818-0392-6 • $14.95pb • (64)

**Swahili Phrasebook**
184 pages • 4 x 5
0-87052-970-6 • $8.95pb • (73)

**Beginner's Swahili**
200 pages • 5 ½ x 8 ½
0-7818-0335-7 • $9.95pb • (52)
2 Cassettes: 0-7818-0336-5 • $12.95 • (55)

**Twi Basic Course**
225 pages • 6 ½ x 8 ½
0-7818-0394-2 • $16.95pb • (65)

**Venda Dictionary: Venda-English**
490 pages • 6 x 8 ½ • 20,000 entries
0-6270-1625-1 • $39.95hc • (62)

**Yoruba-English/English-Yoruba Concise Dictionary**
257 pages • 4 x 6
0-7818-0263-6 • $14.95pb • (275)

**English-Zulu/Zulu-English Dictionary**
519 pages • 4 • x 7 ¼ • 30,000 entries
0-7818-0255-5 • $29.50pb • (203)

**All prices subject to change. TO PURCHASE HIPPOCRENE BOOKS contact your local bookstore, call (718) 454-2366, or write to: HIPPOCRENE BOOKS, 171 Madison Avenue, New York, NY 10016. Please enclose check or money order, adding $5.00 shipping (UPS) for the first book and $.50 for each additional book**